Merchant Crusaders in the Aegean
1291–1352

T0385886

WARFARE IN HISTORY

ISSN 1358–779X

Series editors
Matthew Bennett, Royal Military Academy, Sandhurst, UK
Anne Curry, University of Southampton, UK
Stephen Morillo, Wabash College, Crawfordsville, USA

This series aims to provide a wide-ranging and scholarly approach to military history, offering both individual studies of topics or wars, and volumes giving a selection of contemporary and later accounts of particular battles; its scope ranges from the early medieval to the early modern period.

New proposals for the series are welcomed; they should be sent to the publisher at the address below.

Boydell and Brewer Limited, PO Box 9, Woodbridge, Suffolk, IP12 3DF

Previously published titles in this series are listed at the back of this volume

Merchant Crusaders in the Aegean 1291–1352

Mike Carr

THE BOYDELL PRESS

First published 2015
The Boydell Press, Woodbridge
Paperback edition 2019

ISBN 978–1–84383–990–3 hardback
ISBN 978–1–78327–405–5 paperback

The Boydell Press is an imprint of Boydell & Brewer Ltd
PO Box 9, Woodbridge, Suffolk IP12 3DF, UK
and of Boydell & Brewer Inc.
668 Mt Hope Avenue, Rochester, NY 14620–2731, USA
website: www.boydellandbrewer.com

A CIP catalogue record for this book is available
from the British Library

The publisher has no responsibility for the continued existence or accuracy of
URLs for external or third-party internet websites referred to in this book,
and does not guarantee that any content on such websites is,
or will remain, accurate or appropriate

This publication is printed on acid-free paper

Contents

Illustrations

Maps

Figures

This book is produced with the generous assistance of a grant
from Isobel Thornley's Bequest to the University of London

Preface

The role of merchants in the crusades has fascinated me for a while now, especially the careful balancing act they had to play between defending the faith and trading with the perceived enemies of Latin Christendom. I initially came across the topic when studying for my PhD at the University of London, where my supervisor Professor Jonathan Harris pointed me towards the fourteenth-century Aegean as a fruitful area of research. Here the Latin response to the collapse of Byzantium and the rise of the Anatolian Turks added another layer to the practices of trade and crusade. I explored these areas further during my time as an Alan Pearsall Fellow in Naval and Maritime History at the Institute of Historical Research (IHR) and as a Rome Fellow at the British School at Rome (BSR). This book is therefore a combination of my PhD thesis and my postdoctoral research.

I owe a great debt of thanks to the many people who have provided me with invaluable assistance on an academic and personal level over the years spent researching and writing this book. First and foremost is Jonathan Harris whose careful guidance during my PhD, as well as kind support and advice in subsequent years, has helped to shape my research, teaching and approach to history in general. I would also like to express my sincerest gratitude to Bernard Hamilton and Tony Luttrell for kindly reading draft manuscripts of this book and providing encouraging and helpful corrections and comments. Likewise, I am grateful to Georg Christ and Cristian Caselli for commenting on provisional chapters, Renee Shenton and Hannes Kleineke for help with Latin and palaeography, Brian Mclaughlin for help with Greek, Petros Mechtidis for providing me with the image of Smyrna, and Caroline Palmer for assistance during the editing process. I am also indebted to the staff of the libraries and archives I have used, especially those of the IHR, BSR and the Archivio segreto Vaticano. Finally, I am thankful to those who assisted me with my original PhD, of whom there are too many to mention, as well as my thesis examiners Norman Housley and Brenda Bolton. Any mistakes in this book are purely my own.

I am fortunate to have been able to discuss my ideas and write portions of this book in the thriving academic environments of the Universities of London and Edinburgh, as well as at the IHR and the BSR. These places provided me with ideal intellectual surroundings for such an undertaking and I would like to thank my friends and colleagues from the various seminars, workshops and social gatherings of these institutions, along with

Jonathan Phillips at Royal Holloway, Miles Taylor at the IHR and Christopher Smith at the BSR, for their help and support during this time.

This work was made possible by generous financial support from the above institutions as well as research grants from the Department of History and the Hellenic Institute at Royal Holloway, the Scouloudi Foundation, the Central University Research Fund (University of London), the British Institute at Ankara, the Royal Historical Society and the Deutscher Akademischer Austausch Dienst. This book is produced with the generous assistance of a grant from Isobel Thornley's Bequest to the University of London.

Finally, I would have been unable to write this book without the unwavering support of my friends and family, especially my parents who have always been exceptionally supportive of my interest in history. But I reserve my greatest thanks to my wife Phoebe, who has had to endure my ramblings about the Latins in the Aegean for many years now. Her enthusiasm for my research and patience for my lifestyle as an itinerant academic continually amaze me. I am proud to dedicate this book to her.

Mike Carr

Abbreviations

AE	*Annales Ecclesiastici*, ed. C. Baronio, O. Raynaldi and J. Laderchi, 37 vols (Paris, 1608–1883).
ASVat	Archivio Segreto Vaticano
ASVen	Archivio di Stato di Venezia
BEFAR	*Bibliothèque des Écoles françaises d'Athènes et de Rome*
Benedict XII, *Lettres à la France*	*Benoît XII (1334–1342): Lettres closes, patents et curiales se rapportant à la France*, ed. G. Daumet, *BEFAR* (Paris, 1920).
Benedict XII, *Lettres autres que la France*	*Benoît XII (1334–1342): Lettres closes et patentes intéressant les pays autres que la France*, ed. G. Mollat and J.-M. Vidal, *BEFAR* (Paris, 1913–50).
Benedict XII, *Lettres communes*	*Les registres du Benoît XII, lettres communes*, ed. J.M. Vidal, *BEFAR*, 3 vols (Paris, 1903–11).
Clement V, *Regestum*	*Regestum Clementis Papae V, editum cura et studio monachorum Ordinis S. Benedicti*, 10 vols (Rome, 1885–92).
Clement VI, *Lettres à la France*	*Lettres closes, patentes et curiales du pape Clément VI se rapportant à la France*, ed. E. Depréz *et al.*, *BEFAR*, 3 vols (Paris, 1901–61).
Clement VI, *Lettres autres que la France*	*Lettres closes, patentes et curiales du pape Clément VI intéressant les pays autres que la France*, ed. E. Depréz and G. Mollat, *BEFAR* (Paris, 1960–1).
DOC	*Diplomatari de l'Orient català, 1301–1409: colleció de documents per a la història de l'expedició catalana a Orient i dels ducats d'Atenes i Neopàtria*, ed. A. Rubió i Lluch (Barcelona, 1947).
DVL	*Diplomatarium Veneto-Levantinum: sive Acta et Diplomata res Venetas Graecas atque Levantis Illustrantia a. 1300–1454*, ed. G.M. Thomas, 2 vols (Venice, 1880–99).
John XXII, *Lettres communes*	*Lettres communes de Jean XXII (1316–1334): analyses d'après les registres dits d'Avignon et du Vatican*, ed. G. Mollat, *BEFAR*, 16 vols (Paris, 1904–47).
John XXII, *Lettres secrètes*	*Lettres secrètes et curiales du pape Jean XXII (1316–1334), relatives à la France*, ed. A. Coulon and S. Clémencet, *BEFAR*, 4 vols (Paris, 1900–72).
Le deliberazioni (Senato)	*Le deliberazioni (Senato): Serie 'mixtorum'*, ed. R. Cessi and P. Sambin, 2 vols (Venice, 1960).

MGHSS	Monumenta Germaniae Historica: Scriptores
RA	*Registra Avenionensia*
RIS	*Rerum Italicarum Scriptores*, ed. L.A. Muratori *et al.*, 25 vols (Milan, 1723–51).
RISNS	*Rerum Italicarum Scriptores*, nuova serie, ed. G. Carducci *et al.*, 34 vols (Bologna, etc., 1904–75).
RS	*Registra Supplicationum*
RV	*Registra Vaticana*
Theotokes, Thespismata	'Thespismata tês Benetikês gerousias: 1281–1385', in *Istorika krêtika eggrafa ekdidomena ek tou arheiou tês Benetias*, ed. S.M. Theotokes, 2 vols (Athens, 1933–7).
Thiriet, *Assemblées*	*Délibérations des assemblées Vénitiennes concernant la Romanie: 1160–1463*, ed. F. Thiriet, 2 vols (Paris, 1966–71).
Thiriet, *Sénat*	*Régestes des délibérations du sénat de Venise concernant la Romanie: 1329–1463*, ed. F. Thiriet, 3 vols (Paris, 1958–61).

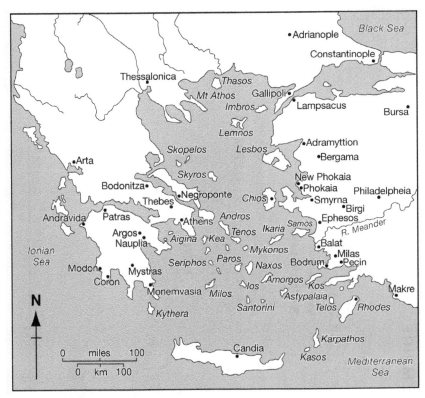

Map 1. The Aegean.

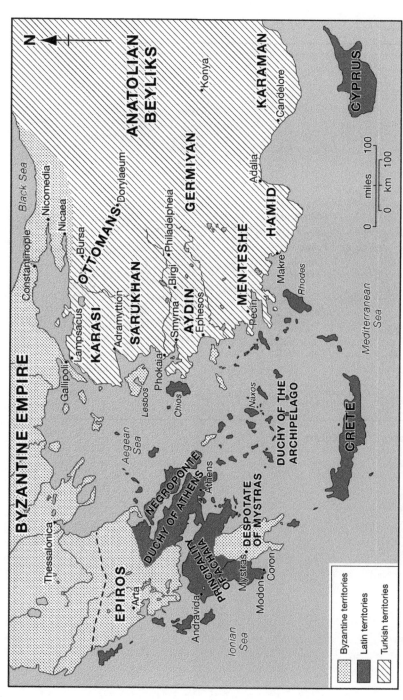

Map 2. The Aegean and Asia Minor c.1328.

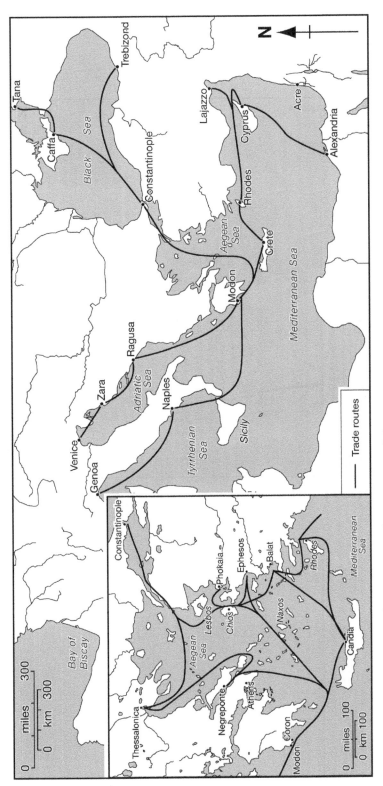

Map 3. Shipping routes in the eastern Mediterranean and Aegean.

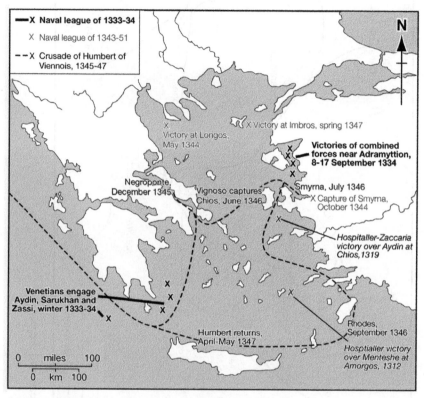

Map 4. Selected naval actions, 1300–1350.

Introduction

The eastern Mediterranean during the period 1291–1352 underwent a series of dramatic transformations which would alter its religious and political makeup for centuries to come. In some senses the period can be considered as one in which the eastern frontiers of Christendom were eroded in the face of unrelenting Islamic expansion. That was certainly the case in the south-eastern Mediterranean, where the last of the crusader outposts on the Syrian coast were expunged by the Mamluks of Egypt, who gradually extended their empire across the coast of north Africa and through Syria up to the borders of Asia Minor and Cilician Armenia. This was also the case further north where the Turks quickly overran the Byzantine territories in western Anatolia and began to extend their influence into the Aegean and Greece. By the end of the period the Ottomans were poised to cross into Europe, leading to the Turkish domination of the Balkans and eastern Europe in the later fourteenth and fifteenth centuries.

Crusading at this time changed in response to the expansion of these Muslim groups. Initially plans were made to recover the Holy Land from the Mamluks and as the fourteenth century progressed attention was increasingly turned to halting the advances of the Turks in the Aegean. However, while the expansion of the Mamluks and Turks at the expense of the Byzantines and Latins cannot be disputed, the period should not be simply viewed as one of Islamic expansion and crusade. Italian commercial contacts with the Levant continued despite the loss of the crusader states and the volume of merchant traffic visiting Mamluk ports, as well as the size and importance of Latin merchant colonies, increased throughout the period. In the Aegean especially, things were even more complicated and the policies of the different groups in the region were not always aligned to simplistic religious affiliations: the Turkish principalities were often in conflict with one other, as were the Latin and Byzantine states. In fact most of the Aegean powers fought amongst themselves and made informal alliances and traded with those of different cultural and religious backgrounds when it suited them.

This book examines crusading in the Aegean region during this convoluted and transformative period from the perspective of the Latin merchants who operated there, men like the Genoese Zaccaria lords of Chios or the Venetians who participated in the naval leagues against the Turks. These "merchant crusaders" as I have called them came to be considered as the most suitable defenders of Latin Christendom in the region, rather than the monarchs and nobles of Western Europe who formed the backbone of crusading in earlier years. The term "merchant crusaders" is, however, a loose one into which many people could fit in one way or another; most of the Latin polities in the area were involved in crusading in some way and all were engaged in trade, often with neighbouring Greeks and Turks who were themselves targets of crusades. Because of this, merchant crusaders cannot be studied in isolation and other groups connected to crusading in the region also have to be considered. This book therefore analyses crusading against the wider backdrop of trade and conflict in the Aegean where actions were driven by a host of conflicting factors, ranging from papal policy to commercial necessity. But at all times the defence of the faith had to be carefully balanced with the competing priorities of secure trade and predominance over commercial rivals. It is the attempts of the Latin powers to overcome these apparent contradictions that this book aims to address.

Trade and Crusade

Studies on the crusades traditionally treated the period as ending in 1291; but with the acceptance of the pluralist definition the subject has gradually broadened. Now crusading in the centuries after the fall of Acre has become an area of considerable vitality in its own right, even if it does not receive the same level of attention as that given to the earlier period.[1] Joseph Delaville le Roulx and Nicolai Jorga pioneered the study of the later crusades and were followed by Aziz Atiya, who published his now rather dated, but nevertheless landmark, monograph, *The Crusade in the Later Middle Ages*, in 1938.[2] This was surpassed forty years later by Kenneth Setton in his monumental multi-volume work *The Papacy and the Levant*, which covered over 350 years of history, from 1204–1571.[3] Setton received much criticism for the narrative focus of his study, although it still impresses with its vast scope and level of detail. Within the period of the later crusades, the fourteenth century in particular enjoyed considerable attention during the 1980s and 1990s when Norman Housley, Christopher Tyerman and Silvia Schein, amongst others, all contributed significant studies which demonstrated the vigour and popularity of the crusading movement at this time, despite the ultimate failure

---

[1]   For an overview, see N. Housley, *Contesting the Crusades* (Oxford, 2006), pp. 122–43.

[2]   J. Delaville le Roulx, *La France en Orient au XIVe siècle*, 2 vols (Paris, 1886); Idem, *Les Hospitaliers en Terre Sainte et à Chypre: 1100–1310* (Paris, 1904); Idem, *Les Hospitaliers à Rhodes, 1310–1421* (Paris, 1913; repr. London, 1974); N. Jorga, *Philippe de Mézières, 1327–1405, et la croisade au XIVe siècle* (Paris, 1896); A.S. Atiya, *The Crusade in the Later Middle Ages* (London, 1938).

[3]   K.M. Setton, *The Papacy and the Levant: 1204–1571*, 4 vols (Philadelphia, 1976–84).

to recover the Holy Land.[4] Since then a number of scholars have focussed on particular themes within this time-frame, including the naval leagues and the works of the crusade theorists.[5] Understandably, studies into the crusades have focussed mainly on cultural and military opposition between Latins, Greeks and Muslims in the period, with a heavy reliance on sources from the papacy, as well as the churchmen, monarchs and advisors who discussed crusade planning in the courts of western Europe. As a result the priorities and commercial concerns of the local powers in the Aegean, which are the focus of this book, have sometimes been overshadowed.

In more recent years, studies of the crusades in the fourteenth century have largely given way to those focussing on crusading and the relations between the western powers and the Ottoman empire in the fifteenth century and beyond. One approach has been to explore the image of the Turks from the European perspective, especially within the context of the literature produced by the Renaissance humanists, an area which is touched on in this book.[6] These studies have helped to re-balance western perceptions of Islam during the later Middle Ages and the Renaissance, with this

---

[4]   See, in particular N. Housley, *The Avignon Papacy and the Crusades, 1305–1378* (Oxford, 1986); Idem, *The Later Crusades, 1274–1580. From Lyons to Alcazar* (Oxford, 1992) and the collection of articles in Idem, *Crusading and Warfare in Medieval and Renaissance Europe*, Variorum Reprints (Aldershot, 2001); C.J. Tyerman, 'Marino Sanudo Torsello and the lost crusade: lobbying in the fourteenth century: the Alexander Prize essay', *Transactions of the Royal Historical Society* 32 (1982), 57–73; Idem, 'Sed nihil fecit? The last Capetians and the recovery of the Holy Land', in *War and Government in the Middle Ages*, ed. J. Gillingham and J.C. Holt (Woodbridge, 1984), pp. 170–81; Idem, 'Philip VI and the recovery of the Holy Land', *English Historical Review* 100 (1985), 25–52 (Tyerman's articles are reprinted in Idem, *The Practices of Crusading: Image and Action from the Eleventh to the Sixteenth Centuries*, Variorum Reprints (Farnham, 2013), I, III, V); S. Schein, *Fideles Crucis: The Papacy, the West, and the Recovery of the Holy Land 1274–1314* (Oxford, 1991).

[5]   Of particular relevance are T. Guard, *Chivalry, Kingship and Crusade: The English Experience in the Fourteenth Century* (Woodbridge, 2013); A. Leopold, *How To Recover the Holy Land: The Crusade Proposals of the Late Thirteenth and Early Fourteenth Centuries* (Aldershot, 2000); A. Demurger, 'Le pape Clément VI et l'Orient: ligue ou croisade?', in *Guerre, pouvoir et noblesse au Moyen Âge, Mélanges en l'honneur de Philippe Contamine*, ed. J. Paviot and J. Verger (Paris, 2000), pp. 207–14; V. Ivanov, '*Sancta Unio* or the Holy League 1332–36/7 as a political factor in the eastern Mediterranean and the Aegean', *Études Balkaniques* 48 (2012), 142–76; C.J. Tyerman, 'New wine in old skins? The crusade and the eastern Mediterranean in the later Middle Ages', in *Byzantines, Latins and Turks in the Eastern Mediterranean World after 1150*, ed. C. Holmes and J. Harris (Oxford, 2012), pp. 265–89. See also the contributions by Ryder, Lock, Carr and Binbaş in *Contact and Conflict in Frankish Greece and the Aegean,1204–1453*, ed. M. Carr and N.G. Chrissis (Farnham, 2014), pp. 97–112, 115–34, 135–49, 153–75.

[6]   See notably R. Schwoebel, *The Shadow of the Crescent: The Renaissance Image of the Turk (1453–1517)* (Nieuwkoop, 1967); M.J. Heath, 'Renaissance scholars and the origins of the Turks', *Bibliothèque d'Humanisme et Renaissance* 41 (1979), 453–471; J. Hankins, 'Renaissance crusaders: humanist crusade literature in the age of Mehmed II', *Dumbarton Oaks Papers* 49 (1995), 111–207; N. Bisaha, *Creating East and West: Renaissance Humanists and the Ottoman Turks* (Philadelphia, 2004); M. Meserve, *Empires of Islam in Renaissance Historical Thought*

sub-genre now enjoying a popularity comparable to the study of Christian–Muslim relations during the period of the traditional crusades to the
Holy Land from 1095 to 1291. However, many of these studies do not give
significant attention to the earlier fourteenth century – possibly because this
period is regarded as preceding the traditional era of Renaissance humanism,
but also because scholars studying the Turks have tended to overlook the
period of the beyliks in favour of the Ottoman empire.[7] This is surprising
given that the images and rhetoric born in the early fourteenth century had
a direct influence on the nature of Latin–Turkish perceptions formulated in
later years, as is explained in Chapter 2 of this book.

   Research into Latin–Turkish interaction has benefited from its relevance
to the growing field of Mediterranean Studies, which places much importance on cross-cultural contacts, as well as the debates over notions of East
and West and otherness, especially in the early modern period.[8] The crusades,
although traditionally regarded as representing an earlier age, are nevertheless inherently connected to these themes. So too are studies relating to
Levantine commerce which have been viewed as providing the other side of
the story, i.e. that of trade and exchange rather than conflict. Early examples
of these studies include the monumental multi-volume works of Depping,
Hopf and Heyd, who helped to demonstrate the connectivity of the Mediterranean during the Middle Ages and the complexities of exchange between
its many peoples and regions.[9] Later Shelomo Goitein and Eliyahu Ashtor
did much to expand knowledge of trade in the Islamic world, through their
use of commercial documents from the Cairo Geniza and Arabic archives.[10]
To add to this, Freddy Thiriet and Michel Balard produced extensive studies

(Cambridge, MA, 2008), p. 150; N. Housley, *Crusading and the Ottoman Threat: 1453–1505*
(Oxford, 2012), with an overview of the historiography on pp. 1–6.
[7]   See C. Hillenbrand, *Turkish Myth and Muslim Symbol: The Battle of Manzikert* (Edinburgh,
2007), pp. 3–4.
[8]   This has been the focus of a series of review articles, for example, S. Kinoshita, 'Re-viewing
the eastern Mediterranean', *Postmedieval: A Journal of Medieval Cultural Studies* 2 (2011),
369–85; E.R. Dursteler, 'On bazaars and battlefields: Recent scholarship on Mediterranean
cultural contacts', *Journal of Early Modern History* 15 (2011), 413–34, esp. 419–22; F. Trivellato,
'Renaissance Italy and the Muslim Mediterranean in recent historical works', *Journal of
Modern History* 82 (2010), 127–55, esp. 140–4; M. O'Connell, 'The Italian Renaissance in the
Mediterranean, or, between East and West: A review article', *California Italian Studies Journal*
1 (2010), 1–30, esp. 17–21. For an international perspective of cross-cultural trade, see P.D.
Curtin, *Cross-Cultural Trade in World History* (Cambridge, 1984), esp. pp. 1–14, 109–35.
[9]   G.-B. Depping, *Histoire du commerce entre le Levant et l'Europe depuis les croisades jusqu'à
la fondation des colonies en Amérique*, 2 vols (Paris, 1830); K. Hopf, *Geschichte Griechenlands
vom Beginn des Mittelalters bis auf unsere Zeit*, 2 vols (Leipzig, 1867–8); W. Heyd, *Histoire
du commerce du Levant au moyen-âge*, 2 vols (Leipzig, 1885–6). For a discussion of these
works, see G. Christ, 'Materials, products and services of exchange 300–1550', in *Mapping
the Medieval Mediterranean, c. 300–1550*, ed. A. Nichols Law (Leiden, 2015), forthcoming.
[10]   S.D. Goitein, *A Mediterranean Society: The Jewish Communities of the Arab World as*

into the Venetians and Genoese in the north-eastern Mediterranean and Black Sea from the twelfth to the fifteenth centuries.[11] Since then there has been a growing interest in the relationships between merchant communities and their host societies.[12] Within this hybrid field of economic and cultural history, the Aegean has received particular attention, precisely because of its highly fragmented and complex nature.[13] However, it is not the primary purpose of these studies to engage with the influence of the Latin Church on trade, or of the spiritual concerns of merchants, both of which heavily influenced the activities and policies of the resident powers in the Aegean theatre and are discussed in this book.

Studies into the interplay between the great themes of crusade, commerce and cross-cultural contact are therefore relatively thin on the ground when compared with those which focus on either the economic history of the eastern Mediterranean or the later crusades. In fact, in the past historians have often misinterpreted the role of the merchant republics in the crusades as one primarily motivated by greed and a desire to manipulate 'religious' zeal in an attempt to further commercial ends.[14] However, in more recent years this view has been modified, as a more balanced appreciation of the complex interplay between holy war and commercial exchange has been adopted. This has been helped by recent research into the mechanisms used to facilitate and obstruct commercial exchange across cultural boundaries, notably those dedicated to illicit trade in the Mediterranean and in particular

---

Portrayed in the Documents of the Cairo Geniza, 6 vols (Berkeley, 1967–93); E. Ashtor, *Levant Trade in the Later Middle Ages* (Princeton, 1983).

[11] F. Thiriet, *La Romanie vénitienne au moyen âge: le développement et l'exploitation du domaine colonial vénitien, XIIe–XVe siècles* (Paris, 1959); M. Balard, *La Romanie génoise, XIIe – début du XVe siècle*, 2 vols (Rome, 1978).

[12] See, for example G. Christ, *Trading Conflicts: Venetian Merchants and Mamluk Officials in Late Medieval Alexandria* (Leiden, 2012), esp. pp. 113–19; F. Trivellato, *The Familiarity of Strangers: The Sephardic Diaspora, Livorno, and Cross–Cultural Trade in the Early Modern Period* (New Haven, 2009); P. Skinner, *Medieval Amalfi and its Diaspora, 800–1250* (Oxford, 2013). Many other relevant works are discussed in the review articles noted in n. 8 above.

[13] Of particular interest is Epstein, *Purity Lost*, esp. pp. 52–136. See also the recent collections of essays and their bibliographies in *Contact and Conflict in Frankish Greece and the Aegean, 1204–1453*, ed. M. Carr and N.G. Chrissis (Farnham, 2014); *A Companion to Medieval Greece*, ed. N.I. Tsougarakis and P. Lock (Leiden, 2014); *Byzantines, Latins, and Turks in the Eastern Mediterranean World after 1150*, ed. C. Holmes, J. Harris and E. Russell (Oxford, 2012); *Identities and Allegiances in the Eastern Mediterranean after 1204*, ed. J. Herrin and G. Saint-Guillan (Farnham, 2011).

[14] These views are especially prevalent for literature concerning the First Crusade, see the citations in M. Carr, 'Between Byzantium, Egypt and the Holy Land: The Italian maritime republics and the First Crusade', in *Jerusalem the Golden: The Origins and Impact of the First Crusade*, ed. S.B. Edgington and L. García–Guijarro (Turnhout, 2014), pp. 75–87, at 81–3 and also Carr, 'Trade or crusade?', pp. 115–16.

the papal trade embargo.[15] The numerous works of David Jacoby should be mentioned here as being of particular importance in this regard.[16] In many ways Elizabeth Zachariadou has come closest to striking a balance between the analysis of commerce and crusade with her landmark work published in 1983 on the commercial relations between Venetian Crete and the beyliks of Aydin and Menteshe.[17] Zachariadou analyses in detail the surviving treaties made with the Turks, publishing many of them for the first time. Unfortunately papal policy is not studied in enough depth for a detailed discussion of crusading ideology, but her work nevertheless remains essential for information on commercial contacts between Crete and the emirates, as well as the Venetian contribution to the crusading ventures of the period.

This book aims to cut across the sub-genres of economic and crusading history. It has three main objectives: first, to look at the changing Latin perceptions of the Turks in this period, as they came to dominate crusade thinking and supplant the Byzantines and Mamluks as a target for western military aggression; second, to study the nature of the Latin military response to the Turks, which became dominated by the maritime crusaders in the Aegean; and third, to analyse the relationship between the papacy and the merchant republics in the context of an Aegean crusade, or in other words, to explore the interplay between mercantile objectives and the crusading ideals of the popes.

With this in mind, Chapters 1 and 2 address the first objective of this book. Chapter 1 sets the scene in the Aegean by analysing the fragmentation of the Byzantine empire after 1204 and the evolution of crusading against

[15] The best treatment of the embargo is given by S. Stantchev, *Spiritual Rationality: Papal Embargo as Cultural Practice* (Oxford, 2014); Idem, 'The medieval origins of embargo as a policy tool', *History of Political Thought* 33.3 (2012), 373–99, and also G. Christ, 'Kreuzzug und Seeherrschaft. Clemens V., Venedig und das Handelsembargo von 1308', in *Maritimes Mittelalter*, ed. N. Jaspert and M. Borgolte (Ostfildern, 2015), pp. 261–82; A. Esch, 'Der Handel zwischen Christen und Muslimen im Mittelmeer-Raum. Verstöße gegen das päpstliche Embargo geschildert in den Gesuchen an die Apostolische Pönitentiarie (1439–1483)', *Quellen und Forschungen aus italienischen Archiven und Bibliotheken* 92 (2012), 85–140. On slavery, see H. Barker, 'Egyptian and Italian Merchants in the Black Sea Slave Trade, 1260–1500' (Unpublished PhD thesis, Columbia University, 2014).

[16] See, for example, the following Variorum Reprints: D. Jacoby, *Société et démographie à Byzance et en Romanie latine* (London, 1975); Idem, *Recherches sur la Méditerranée orientale du XIIe au XVe siècle: peuples, sociétés, économies* (London, 1979); Idem, *Studies on the Crusader States and on Venetian Expansion* (Northampton, 1989); Idem, *Trade, Commodities and Shipping in the Medieval Mediterranean* (Aldershot, 1997); Idem, *Byzantium, Latin Romania and the Mediterranean* (Aldershot, 2001); Idem, *Commercial Exchange across the Mediterranean: Byzantium, the Crusader Levant, Egypt and Italy* (Aldershot, 2005); Idem, *Latins, Greeks and Muslims: Encounters in the Eastern Mediterranean, Tenth–Fifteenth Centuries* (Farnham, 2009).

[17] Zachariadou, *Trade and Crusade*, the treaties are published on pp. 187–239. See also the collections in Idem, *Romania and the Turks, c.1300–1500* (London, 1985); Idem, *Studies in pre-Ottoman Turkey and the Ottomans* (Aldershot, 2007).

the Greeks until the third decade of the fourteenth century. This is followed in Chapter 2 by an overview of the emergence of the Turkish beyliks in the consciousness of western Europe during the first half of the fourteenth century. Particular attention is given to chronicles and documentary sources depicting the Turks. These elucidate the transitional period when perceptions of the Turks shifted from one of amity to one of aggression, as they came to be considered as posing the greatest danger to Christians in the East, eventually supplanting the Mamluks of Egypt and the Holy Land. This change in perception manifested itself in the person of Umur Pasha, the Turkish lord of Smyrna, who became portrayed as the scourge of Latin interests in the region. Umur was depicted in several Italian sources of the mid-fourteenth century, where his persona was adapted to suit various situations. His actions were used to justify crusades against him, but also as a means to critique political strife within the Italian peninsula; a motif which was commonly used when portraying Ottoman sultans in the fifteenth century.

Chapters 3 and 4 focus on the nature of the Latin military response to the rising power of the Turks. This took the form of a naval league, a new military strategy which took advantage of the maritime capabilities of the merchant crusaders who organized and participated in the campaigns. In Chapter 3, the evolution of the concept of a league is mapped out, from its origins in the papal economic embargo and plans to patrol the eastern Mediterranean, to the pragmatic alliances formed by the eastern Aegean states in the early fourteenth century. It finishes with a detailed analysis of the campaigns of the naval leagues of 1333–34 and 1343–52. Chapter 4 discusses the logistics and strategies used by the Latin captains against the Turks. The military campaigns in the Aegean were not recorded in detail by many chroniclers, but the wealth of archival evidence relating to the planning of the leagues as well as surviving reports of the battles allows for a reconstruction of the tactics employed and of the numbers involved. The leagues attracted significant participation and the Latins relied upon a sophisticated network of communication to ensure superiority on the sea.

Chapters 5 and 6 address the the interplay between papal crusade policy and the commercial concerns of the merchant republics in the East. These two chapters blend together two facets of research which have usually been the preserve of either economic or crusade historians and have consequently often been studied in isolation. Chapter 5 assesses the leagues specifically within the context of wider papal crusading strategy in the fourteenth century. As will be shown, papal commitment to the Aegean ventures was by no means whole hearted. In many instances other matters, such as conflicts within Europe and the influence of Franco-Angevin initiatives, took precedence over military campaigns against the Turks. An important part of this discussion is the implementation of crusade mechanisms in the Aegean theatre. Indulgences, in particular, can be very illustrative in determining papal commitment to a venture and the motivations of partici-pants. The chapter therefore ends with a detailed discussion of the spiritual privileges issued to those fighting in the Aegean. These ranged from lesser indulgences, granted *in articulo mortis*, in the earlier decades of the century, when the Turks had yet to evolve into the main target of crusading, to the full crusade indulgence, accompanied by all the usual mechanisms associ-ated with a crusade to the Holy Land issued for the Crusade of Smyrna.

Chapter 6 explores the other side of Latin-Turkish relations during the period, that of commercial contact in contested border zones and the prob-lems this caused for crusading. As the merchant republics became increas-ingly central to the upholding of Latin territories in the Aegean, the Church became aware of the need to adopt new methods which would encourage the defence of faith but also facilitate limited trade with the infidel. Strong commercial contacts were essential to the survival of the Latin colonies in the eastern Mediterranean, but were hampered by crusading campaigns. The need for a solution to this conundrum triggered a change of thinking which resulted in the issuing of numerous trading exemptions, many of which specifically permitted trade with Mamluk Egypt in order to facilitate crusades against the Turks in the Aegean. As will be shown, this policy consequently balanced the crusading objectives of the papacy with the commercial concerns of the merchant republics.

Sources for the Aegean Crusades

The wealth of archival sources from the Vatican and the Italian republics in the fourteenth century means that they represent the core source-base for this area. Chronicles, which usually form the backbone of crusading history, unfortunately provide far less information on crusading in the Aegean than they do for the earlier crusades to the Holy Land, or even for those launched against the Ottomans in the later fourteenth and fifteenth centuries.[18] As a result, vivid descriptions of the campaigns in the Aegean and the accounts of those who participated are hard to come by, making assessments of the professed motivations of crusaders sometimes difficult to determine. However, the rich documentary evidence does compensate for this in many ways. It provides a level of detail in regard to economics, logistics and spiritual provisions that is not always presented in narrative sources, and sometimes – especially when petitions can be consulted – it provides a new insight into the priorities and concerns of those involved. It is the combination of documentary sources relating to trade and crusade,

---

[18] There are of course some chronicles which provide useful information on the Aegean crusades. These are discussed below at pp. 12–15.

augmented by the narrative sources, that provides the most cohesive picture of crusading in the Aegean.

The Vatican *Archivio segreto* contains many documents integral for the understanding of papal crusade policy which will be used throughout this study. Of especial importance to this book are the drafts of the papal letters held in the *Registra Avenionensia* series, many of which were later duplicated in the parchment series of the *Registra Vaticana*.[19] The majority of the letters in these registers are the so-called 'common' letters – those issued in response to written petitions submitted to and approved by the Roman Curia. They consist usually of favours of some kind bestowed upon individuals or institutions. Other notable letters found in these registers are the so-called 'secret' letters. These usually contain political correspondence and were not issued as a result of a petition, but from curial initiative.[20]

Most of the registers of the popes relevant to this study have been published, or partly published, in the great editions of the *Bibliothèque des Écoles françaises d'Athènes et de Rome*.[21] It should be noted, however, that these editions do not include the full text of every document. This is illustrated most pertinently by the common letters of John XXII which are only published in calendar form, with the result that many important documents, such as the granting of indulgences to those fighting in the Aegean, are not printed in full. When this is the case, the original manuscripts have been consulted.[22] The registers of Clement VI also contain some very inadequate summaries of important letters. Take for example the bull *Insurgentibus contra fidem* proclaiming the Crusade of Smyrna. This is only given a nineteen-word summary by the editors, despite the full document spanning five pages of printed text and containing arguably the most important

---

[19] The *Registra Vaticana* are at least two removes from the original letters, which were first drafted or registered in the *Registra Avenionensia*. Where possible I have referenced both the *Registra Avenionensia* and the *Registra Vaticana*, but the former are sometimes extremely damaged and hard to read. A detailed discussion of these series is given by L.E. Boyle, *A Survey of the Vatican Archives and of its Medieval Holdings* (Toronto, 1972), pp. 103–31.

[20] See P.N.R. Zutshi, 'The letters of the Avignon popes (1305–1378): A source for the study of Anglo-Papal relations and of English ecclesiastical history', in *England and Her Neighbours, 1066–1453: Essays in Honour of Pierre Chaplais*, ed. M. Jones and M. Vale (London 1989), pp. 259–75, at p. 261; Idem, 'The personal role of the pope in the production of papal letters in the thirteenth and fourteenth centuries', in *Vom Nutzen des Schreibens: soziales Gedächtnis, Herrschaft und Besitz im Mittelalter*, ed. W. Pohl and P. Herold (Vienna, 2002), pp. 225–36, at pp. 225–6.

[21] For example, John XXII, *Lettres communes*; John XXII, *Lettres secretes*; Benedict XII, *Lettres à la France*; Benedict XII, *Lettres autres que la France*; Benedict XII, *Lettres communes*; Clement VI, *Lettres à la France*; Clement VI, *Lettres autres que la France* and also Clement V, *Regestum*, which are not edited by the *Écoles françaises*. Some papal documents are also published in the *Annales Ecclesiastici*, ed. C. Baronio, O. Raynaldi and J. Laderchi, 37 vols (Paris, 1608–1883).

[22] See, for example, the grant of indulgences published in Appendix 4, doc. 2, pp. 158–9.

information for crusading against the Turks in the period.[23] The document is of such significance that a full translation has been published by Norman Housley.[24] Overall, the papal registers are extremely useful for portraying the papal reaction to events in the Aegean and of European crusading trends in general. They are also the sources which, unsurprisingly, provide the most detail about the spiritual privileges which were granted to crusaders. As will be shown in Chapter 5, a close analysis of crusading indulgences implemented in the Aegean demonstrates the evolving papal attitude towards a crusade against the Turks and also reflects the spiritual concerns of the participants. When used in conjunction with other sources, papal sources can also help to clarify specific details of a crusade, such as dates, finance, numbers of men involved, galleys contributed, and so forth.

Throughout this study, emphasis has been placed on the problem of using common letters as an indicator of papal policy. The initiative in issuing them did not lie with the pope, so they are in many senses more informative about the motivations of those making the petitions than about those of the papacy.[25] Where possible the petitions copied into the Vatican registers of supplications (*Registra Supplicationum*) have also been consulted. These are important because in many instances no outgoing letter was issued in response to them, even when the petition was successful. Furthermore, they provide an unparalleled glimpse of the concerns of those who made the supplication, how they voiced these to the pope, and of the papal response. The petitions for trade licences, in particular, are vital for assessing the contrasting spiritual and economic motives of merchant crusaders and have been studied extensively in Chapter 6.[26] Unfortunately, however, the registers of supplications were only begun at the start of Clement VI's pontificate in 1342, which means that petitions do not survive for previous popes.[27] This is a great shame as earlier supplications, particularly those made to John XXII, might be extremely informative. Fortunately, in many outgoing papal letters some details of the original petition are included, which can be analysed in the same manner. This information is of course inferior in

---

[23] Summary in Clement VI, *Lettres à la France*, vol. 1, doc. 433; full text in *Acta Pontificum Suecica*, ed. L.M. Baath, 2 vols (Stockholm, 1936–57), vol. 1, pp. 369–71, doc. 337.

[24] *Documents on the Later Crusades, 1274–1580*, ed. and trans. N. Housley (London, 1996), pp. 78–80, doc. 22.

[25] Zutshi, 'The letters of the Avignon popes', 266–7.

[26] For more on the process of petitioning and the value of the *Registra Supplicationum*, see M. Carr, 'Crossing boundaries in the Mediterranean: Papal trade licences from the *Registra Supplicationum* of Pope Clement VI (1342–1352)', *Journal of Medieval History* 41 (2015), 107–29, esp. 110–15.

[27] On this, see P.N.R. Zutshi, 'The origins of the registration of petitions in the Papal Chancery in the first half of the fourteenth century', in *Suppliques et requêtes: Le gouvernement par la grâce en Occident (XIIe–XVe siècle)*, ed. Hélène Millet (Paris, 2003), pp. 177–91, esp. pp. 178–80.

detail to the original petitions as entered in the *Registra Supplicationum*, but it at least partly compensates for the absence of the registers of supplications prior to 1342.

The motives and priorities of crusaders in the Aegean can only be sufficiently analysed when set against the backdrop of trade in the eastern Mediterranean. As a consequence, the other core body of archival material for this study is that from the Italian merchant republics. In the case of Venice, the most relevant are the deliberations of the Great Council (*Deliberazioni del Maggior Consiglio*) and of the Senate (*Deliberazioni Misti del Senato*), as well as the acts of notaries overseas, such as on Crete. Although many of these records have now been summarized or even published in full, it still been necessary to consult some of the original manuscripts.[28] The Venetian archival material often includes the decisions of the various administrative bodies situated either in Venice or on Crete in regard to the Turks, Byzantines, and the other Latin powers in the Aegean. It thus provides an insight into the state policy of the Republic, as well as a valuable account of Venetian attitudes towards these different groups in the context of crusading and commercial exchange. Like the papal documents, the Venetian archives also provide specific details and dates for the intricate preparations precluding a crusade.[29]

The Venetian archives, however, do not give the full picture of Latin involvement in the Aegean. They are not concerned with the activities of the Genoese, the details of which are partially held in the various archives of that city. These contain information on the involvement of the Commune and its citizens in eastern Mediterranean trade, but unfortunately for the early fourteenth century many of the records are notoriously fragmented; civil war wracked the city for most of this period causing extreme instability, whilst the archives of the most important Genoese overseas colony for this study – that of the Zaccaria of Chios and Phokaia – do not survive.[30] Nevertheless, some Genoese material for this period is of considerable value, especially notarial records which record the shipments of goods from the

---

[28] See notably, the recent transcriptions of the *Misti del Senato* in *Venezia-senato: deliberazioni miste*, ed. F.-X. Leduc *et al.*, 20 vols (Venice, 2004–, ongoing) and also Theotokes, *Thespismata*; Thiriet, *Assemblées*; Thiriet, *Sénat*.

[29] A detailed discussion of the relevant Venetian archival sources can be found in D. Jacoby, 'Social evolution in Latin Greece', *A History of the Crusades*, ed. K.M. Setton, 6 vols (Madison, 1969–1989), vol. 6, pp. 175–221, at pp. 175–80, n. 1; Thiriet, *La Romanie vénitienne*, pp. 9–15.

[30] On the Genoese archival material, see the collections of notarial acts from the Genoese overseas, published by the Collana storica di Fonti e Studi in seven volumes, the latest at the time of writing being: *Gênes et l'outre-mer: Actes notaries de Famagouste et d'autres localités du Proche-Orient (XIVe-Xve s.)*, ed. M. Balard, L. Balletto and C. Schabel (Nicosia, 2013) and also C.F. Wright, *The Gattilusio Lordships and the Aegean World, 1355–1462* (Leiden, 2014), pp. 10–11; K. Fleet, *European and Islamic Trade in the Early Ottoman State: The Merchants of Genoa and Turkey* (Cambridge, 1999), pp. 1–2.

Genoese colonies in the eastern Mediterranean to western Europe, and those which provide evidence of Genoese trade with the Turks in the late thirteenth and early fourteenth centuries.[31] In addition to Venice and Genoa, archival material relating to the Hospitallers of Rhodes and the Catalans in the Aegean has been consulted.[32] The reconstruction of commercial activities in the Aegean can be aided further by sources relating to specific merchants, such as the trading handbook of Francesco Balducci Pegolotti and the collection of letters written to Pignol Zucchello.[33] To add to this, archaeological and numismatic evidence can help to fill the gaps in the documentary material, this is especially the case in regard to the Zaccaria, who minted coins during their rulership of Chios which survive.[34]

The substantial archival evidence has been supplemented by chronicles, histories and treatises, which although common for the period, are sporadic in their coverage of crusading or of events in the Aegean. Nevertheless, there are some which provide valuable information on these matters, such as the chronicle of Ramon Muntaner, for the early fourteenth century. Muntaner was a member of the Catalan Company in Anatolia and Greece from 1302 to 1307 and provides a detailed account of the expansion of the Turkish beyliks and the Catalan involvement in the crusade plans of the early fourteenth century.[35] The work of the Venetian crusade theorist Marino Sanudo Torsello is also of the utmost importance. Like Muntaner, he was familiar

---

[31] For example *Les relations commerciales entre Gênes, la Belgique et l'Outremont d'après les archives notariales génoises aux XIII et XIV siècles*, ed. R. Doehaerd, 3 vols (Brussels, 1941), vol. 3, docs 1356, 1357, 1530, 1667, 1675, 1723.

[32] Sources from these archives have, however, been limited to printed material, for example *DOC; Cartulaire général des hospitaliers de S. Jean de Jérusalem, 1100–1310*, ed. J. Delaville le Roulx, 4 vols (Paris, 1894–1905). On the Hospitaller sources, see A.T. Luttrell, *The Town of Rhodes: 1306–1356* (Rhodes, 2003), pp. 1–11.

[33] Francesco Balducci Pegolotti, *La Pratica Della Mercatura*, ed. A. Evans (New York, 1936); *Lettere di Mercanti a Pignol Zucchello (1336–1350)*, ed. R. Morozzo della Rocca (Venice, 1957).

[34] For an overview of the archaeology of the Aegean region, see A.K. Vionis, *A Crusader, Ottoman and Early Modern Aegean Archaeology: Built Environment and Domestic Material Culture in the Medieval and Post-Medieval Cyclades, Greece (13th–20th Centuries AD)* (Leiden, 2014), esp. pp. 27–45; J.L. Bintliff, *The Complete Archaeology of Greece: From Hunter-Gatherers to the 20th Century AD* (Chichester, 2012), pp. 416–35; P. Lock and G.D.R. Sanders, *The Archaeology of Medieval Greece* (Oxford, 1996). On numismatic evidence, see G. Schlumberger, *Numismatique de l'orient Latin*, 2 vols (Paris, 1878); D. Promis, *La Zecca di Scio durante il dominio dei Genovesi* (Turin, 1865); D.M. Metcalf, *Coinage of the Crusades and the Latin East in the Ashmolean Museum, Oxford*, 2nd edition (London, 1995); A. Mazarakis, 'The Chios mint during the rule of the Zaccaria family (1304–1329)', *Nomismatika Chronika*, 2 (1992), 43–52; Idem, 'A martinello of Manuele and Paleologo Zaccaria (1307–1310)', trans. M.J. Tzamali, *Nomismatika Chronika* 18 (1999), 111–18.

[35] Ramon Muntaner, *The Catalan Expedition to the East: from the Chronicle of Ramon Muntaner*, trans. R. Hughes (Barcelona, 2006). For more on Muntaner's chronicle, see R.G. Keightley, 'Muntaner and the Catalan Grand Company', *Revista Canadiense de Estudios Hispánicos* 4 (1979), 37–58.

with the eastern Mediterranean, having travelled there extensively since the 1280s. During his life Sanudo wrote two major works, 'Liber Secretorum Fidelium Crucis' (1307–21) and *Istoria del regno di Romania* (c.1326–33), as well as numerous letters between 1323 and 1337 to important dignitaries concerning the crusade, of which forty-two now survive.[36] Sanudo sheds much light on the logistics of crusade planning as well as providing an invaluable insight into the changing Latin perceptions of the Turks, especially in his letters. The other crusade theorists are also helpful in this regard, in particular the Dominican William of Adam who travelled to the East in the first decades of the fourteenth century.[37] William spent time in the Aegean and most probably visited Chios, as he regularly praises the activities of the Zaccaria family in their military endeavours against the Turks.[38] Also worth mentioning here is the work of the French knight and crusader Philippe de Mézières. He wrote mostly towards the end of the fourteenth century, but was present at the Crusade of Smyrna as a young man. Philippe's views of the Turks mostly concern the Ottomans, but at times he does shed light on the maritime beyliks in the early period.[39]

In addition to this, some chroniclers based in Italy commented on events in the Aegean, possibly because of their close link to trade in the eastern Mediterranean. The Florentine Giovanni Villani, for example, remarked on maritime encounters against the Turks, whilst many of the characters of Boccaccio's *Decameron*, written in c.1351, were inspired by real individuals, some of whom can be connected to the Aegean region.[40] In addition to

[36] Marino Sanudo Torsello, 'Liber Secretorum Fidelium Crucis' in *Gesta Dei per Francos*, ed. J. Bongars, 2 vols (Hannover, 1611; repr. Jerusalem, 1972), vol. 2, pp. 1–287; *Istoria di Romania*, ed. and Greek trans. E. Papadopoulou (Athens, 2000). For more on Sanudo, see Marino Sanudo Torsello, *Book of the Secrets of the Faithful of the Cross*, trans. P. Lock (Farnham, 2011), pp. 1–20. Sanudo's letters are published in various works listed in the bibliography, and translated in S. Roddy, 'The Correspondence of Marino Sanudo Torsello' (unpublished doctoral thesis, University of Pennsylvania, 1971). On Venetian chronicles from the period, see F. Thiriet, 'Les chroniques vénitiennes de la Marcienne et leur importance pour l'histoire de la Romanie Gréco-vénitienne', *Mélanges d'archéologie et d'histoire* 66 (1954), 241–92.

[37] William of Adam, *How To Defeat the Saracens*, ed. and trans. G. Constable (Washington, 2012).

[38] The anonymous author of the *Directorium ad Passagium Faciendum*, writing in c.1332, also claimed to have spent time with the Zaccaria overseas: 'Directorium ad Passagium Faciendum', in *Recueil des historiens des croisades: documents arméniens*, 2 vols (Paris, 1869–1906), vol. 2, pp. 367–517. For the connection between the two authors, see William Adam, *How To Defeat the Saracens*, pp. 5–8.

[39] See, for example, Philippe de Mézières, *Une epistre lamentable et consolatoire, adressée en 1397 à Philippe le Hardi, duc de Bourgogne, sur la défaite de Nicopolis, 1396*, ed. P. Contamine and J. Paviot (Paris, 2008), pp. 212–15. For an overview of Philippe and his many works, see the introduction to *Philippe de Mézières and His Age: Piety and Politics in the Fourteenth Century*, ed. R. Blumenfeld-Kosinski and K. Petkov (Leiden, 2011), pp. 1–16.

[40] See, for example Giovanni Villani, *Nuova cronica*, ed. G. Porta, 3 vols (Parma, 1990–1),

this, the chronicle of the Anonimo Romano, written c.1357–60, provides a detailed description of the Crusade of Smyrna, embellished with fantastic details and apocryphal tales.[41] Possibly connected to the Anonimo Romano is the anonymous apocryphal letter known as the *Epistola Morbasiani*, supposedly written by Umur Pasha to Pope Clement VI.[42] This fascinating source, along with the Anonimo Romano, is highly critical of the policy of the Venetians in the Aegean, and although it should not be taken at face value, it is illustrative of contemporary feeling on the Italian peninsula, as well as of popular perceptions of the Turks outside of the eastern Mediterranean. These sources are explored in detail in Chapter 2.

Other authors closer to events than the Italians were the Byzantines. Of them, George Pachymeres gives a vivid account of the Turkish advances in the early fourteenth century, although his attention was mostly focussed on political events within the empire itself.[43] John Kantakouzenos, who later became emperor, and Nikephoros Gregoras are more useful for Byzantine relations with the Latins during crusade negotiations of the 1320s onwards and also for Greek relations with the Turks.[44] Kantakouzenos, for instance, was an eye-witness to the capture of Chios from Martino Zaccaria by Andronikos III and he also later formed an alliance with Umur of Aydin during the Byzantine civil wars.[45] However, the accounts of these authors tend to contradict one another and can be confusing when attempting to re-construct certain episodes: Kantakouzenos does not write within a strict chronological framework, whilst Gregoras has a tendency to telescope events. Like Pachymeres, both should be considered first and foremost as concerned with the situation within the Byzantine empire itself, rather than relied on for information regarding the Latins or political developments in the Aegean.[46]

vol. 2, bk. 9, ch, 106, pp. 198–9, bk. 10, ch. 120, p. 323, vol. 3, bk. 12, ch. 18, p. 58, bk. 13, ch. 49, pp. 388–91; Giovanni Boccaccio, *The Decameron*, pp. 83–7 (II:4), pp. 124–5 (II.7).

[41] Anonimo Romano, *Cronica*, ed. G. Porta, 2nd edition (Milan, 1981), esp. pp. 100–17. For information on the author and the writing of the chronicle, see G. Seibt, *Anonimo romano: scrivere la storia alle soglie del Rinascimento* (Rome, 2000), pp. 1–107; M. Carr, 'Humbert of Viennois and the Crusade of Smyrna: A reconsideration', *Crusades* 13 (2014), 237–51, at 250.

[42] There are over eighty manuscript variants of the *Epistola Morbasiani*. For a discussion, see Chapter 2, pp. 53–5.

[43] See, for example, George Pachymeres, *Relations historiques*, vol. 4, bk. 10, ch. 19–22, pp. 346–52, ch. 25, pp. 358–67, ch. 29, pp. 376–7.

[44] For example, Nikephoros Gregoras, *Byzantina Historia*, ed. L. Schopen and I. Bekker, 3 vols (Bonn, 1829–55), vol. 1, bk. 11, ch. 1, pp. 523–5, vol. 2, bk. 13, ch. 13, p. 689, bk. 16, ch. 7, pp. 834–5.

[45] For his account of the Zaccaria, see John Kantakouzenos, *Ioannis Cantacuzeni eximperatoris Historiarum libri IV*, ed. L. Schopen and B.G. Niebuhr, 3 vols (Bonn, 1828–32), vol. 1, bk. 2, ch. 10–12, pp. 370–88.

[46] For a discussion of the Byzantine sources, see in particular A.E. Laiou, 'Italy and the

The Turks for their part did not produce a great deal of historical writing
in the pre-Ottoman period and even Persian and Arabic accounts of the
beyliks are rare for the fourteenth century.[47] Only the *Düstürnāme*, an epic
poem by the poet-chronicler Enveri, contains any significant information on
relations with the Latins. This source, written in c.1465, although possibly
based on a lost contemporary account, contains a whole section (Book 18)
devoted to the heroic exploits of Umur of Aydin. These include details of his
raids against the Latins in the run up to the first naval league, his alliances
with the Byzantines, and the Crusade of Smyrna.[48] It is worth noting that
many Greeks served in the fledgling administrations of the beyliks and the
international diplomatic language they used was Greek, as was that of the
Seljuks before them and even the Ottomans until the end of the fifteenth
century.[49]

The Greek and Turkish sources are therefore used to complement the
western material, which provides the greatest amount of information for the
Aegean crusades. Crucially it is the combination of one corpus of material,
relevant to the papacy and crusading, with another, relating to the merchant
republics and trade, that allows for the most nuanced analysis of the organization and prosecution of crusading in the Aegean during this period.

Italians in the political geography of the Byzantines (14th century)', *Dumbarton Oaks Papers*
49 (1995), 73–98 and also G. Page, *Being Byzantine: Greek Identity Before the Ottomans*
(Cambridge, 2008), esp. pp. 141–6; *Sources for Turkish History in the Hospitallers' Rhodian
Archive: 1389–1422*, ed. A.T. Luttrell and E.A. Zachariadou (Athens, 2008), pp. 23–4.

[47] On the dearth of historical sources regarding the Turks for this period, see Kafadar,
Between the Two Worlds, pp. 93–4.

[48] Enveri, *Le destān d'Umūr Pacha (Düstürnāme-i Enverī)*, trans. I. Mélikoff-Sayar (Paris,
1954). The work is discussed in more detail in Chapter 2, pp. 51–2, and also in P. Lemerle,
L'émirat d'Aydin, Byzance et l'occident: Recherches sur 'La geste d'Umur pacha' (Paris, 1957),
passim.

[49] On the language used by the beyliks, see Zachariadou, *Trade and Crusade*, pp. 185–6. For
more on Turkish sources during this period, see Kafadar, *Between the Two Worlds*, pp. 60–117;
Sources for Turkish History in the Hospitallers' Rhodian Archive, pp. 21–3.

1

The Splintered Aegean World

> In this calling [as a pirate], [Landolfo] fared considerably better than he had done as a trader: within a year he had taken and stripped so many Turkish ships that he had not merely recovered all he had lost in trade, but he had more than doubled his assets.
>
> Giovanni Boccaccio, *The Decameron*, II:4, written c.1351.[1]

In the passage above Giovanni Boccaccio tells the tale of the Amalfitan merchant Landolfo Rufolo, a story which encapsulates the splintered Aegean world of the fourteenth century. Landolfo, like many Italian merchants, had amassed great riches from trading in the eastern Mediterranean, but after losing his fortune he turned to piracy and redoubled his wealth by preying on Turkish vessels. Landolfo's luck, however, soon ran out when he fell victim to the hazards of the Aegean Sea: first he was forced to take shelter on a small island after a sirocco blew up, and then his vessel was seized by two Genoese merchant ships who had also sought shelter on the same island. As Boccaccio writes, 'Landolfo was taken on board one of the two stout merchantmen, while his vessel was stripped bare then scuttled, leaving the prisoner in nothing but his shirt'.

The story of Landolfo aptly demonstrates the insecurity of the Aegean, where the high concentration of islands and a mixture of competing peoples and states made the region notoriously difficult to police. Ships were vulnerable to attack and piratical raids were a constant threat to those living near the shore. The situation was compounded by the lack of a dominant power in the region, where Latins, Greeks and Turks all vied for control, but rarely enjoyed supremacy.[2] As Steven Epstein has commented, 'No other region of

---

[1] Giovanni Boccaccio, *The Decameron*, trans. G. Waldman, ed. J. Usher (Oxford, 1993), pp. 83–4 (II:4).

[2] On piracy in the Aegean, see M. Angold, 'Michael VIII Palaiologos and the Aegean', in *Liquid and Multiple: Individuals and Identities in the Thirteenth-Century Aegean*, ed. G. Saint-Guillain and D. Stathakopoulos (Paris, 2012), pp. 27–44; P. Charanis, 'Piracy in the Aegean during the reign of Michael VIII Palaeologus', *Annuaire de l'Institut de Philologie et d'Histoire Orientales et Slaves* 10 (1950), 127–36; G. Airaldi, 'Roger of Lauria's expedition to the Peloponnese', *Mediterranean Historical Review* 10 (1995), 14–23. In a wider Mediterranean context: C.R. Backman, 'Piracy', in *A Companion to Mediterranean History*, ed. P. Horden and S. Kinoshita (Chichester, 2014), pp. 172–83.

Europe or the Mediterranean became a cynosure of so many ethnicities in such a small place'.[3] It is within this land of maximum fragmentation, at a time when the tales of knights and hermits had been replaced by those of merchants and pirates, that the Latin powers would trade and ally with, but also struggle against, the Turkish and Greek peoples of the region.[4]

The Aegean Sea was politically and geographically fragmented, but also of enormous strategic importance. It is this combination that made control of the region such a great aspiration, but also so difficult to achieve. Without control of the Aegean, no state could establish itself as the supreme power in the north-eastern Mediterranean, as the Byzantines had done before 1204 and the Ottomans were to do after 1453.[5] It lay at the heart of the great trade routes extending from Egypt and Syria in the south, and from the king-doms of Europe in the west. Ships travelling to the eastern Mediterranean sailed the main artery that ran along the southern coast of the Peloponnese, from where they took several routes through Aegean waters. Two of these proceeded to Constantinople and the lucrative markets of the Black Sea beyond; one along the northern shore via Negroponte and Thessalonica and another via Chios. Further routes ran via Crete and the southern Aegean to Asia Minor, while vessels making their way to Egypt commonly sailed from Crete to Cyprus and further east, or made their way across the Aegean to Rhodes and proceeded from there across the open sea, or along the southern shore of Asia Minor, to the Levant (see Map 3).[6]

The many islands in the Aegean also provided sailors with numerous

[3] S.A. Epstein, *Purity Lost: Transgressing Boundaries in the Eastern Mediterranean, 1000–1400* (Baltimore, 2007), p. 110. See also the discussion of shifting identities and boundaries in J. Preiser-Kapeller, 'Liquid frontiers: A relational analysis of maritime Asia Minor as a religious contact zone in the thirteenth–fifteenth centuries', in *Islam and Christianity in Mediaeval Anatolia*, ed. A.C.S. Peacock, B. de Nicola and S.N. Yıldız (Ashgate, 2015), pp. 117–45.

[4] See the comments on Mediterranean literature by S. Kinoshita, 'Locating the eastern Mediterranean', in *Locating the Middle Ages: The Spaces and Places of Medieval Culture*, ed. J. Weiss and S. Salih (London, 2012), pp. 39–52, at p. 45.

[5] A useful introduction to the medieval Aegean is given by P. Lock, *The Franks in the Aegean, 1204–1500* (London, 1995); and also Epstein, *Purity Lost*, pp. 52–95, 110–15.

[6] For a discussion of Aegean trade within a wider Mediterranean context, see D. Jacoby, 'The economy of Latin Greece', in *A Companion to Latin Greece*, ed. N.I. Tsougarakis and P. Lock (Leiden, 2014), pp. 185–216, esp. 211–15. In regard to navigation, it should be noted that the main trunk routes were not the only ones used by sailors, especially those of smaller craft. For a recent study, see R. Gluzman, 'Between Venice and the Levant: Re-evaluating maritime routes from the fourteenth to the sixteenth century', *The Mariner's Mirror* 96 (2010), 264–94. This is a reappraisal of the traditional interpretation given by J.H. Pryor, *Geography, Technology and War: Studies in the Maritime History of the Mediterranean, 649–1571* (Cambridge, 1988), pp. 12–24, 87–101 (see 97–99 for the Aegean); idem, 'The geographical conditions of galley navigation in the Mediterranean', in *The Age of the Galley: Mediterranean Oared Vessels Since Pre-Classical Times*, ed. R. Gardiner (London, 1995), pp. 206–16.

Figure 1. The coast of Asia Minor from Rhodes Town

ports of call and allowed for relatively easy navigation. In addition, the location of important harbour-cities along its shores, especially in Greece and Asia Minor, allowed access to the interiors of those lands and beyond.[7] To add to this, Asia Minor and the Aegean islands were sources of much natural wealth, such as alum from the Phokaia mines and mastic from Chios: goods which were exported to far-away markets in the east and west. The region was thus a hub of thriving local industry and an important economic centre in its own right.[8] The Aegean islands also gained heightened significance because of their proximity to one another and their strategic location. Rhodes and Chios, for example, were within eyesight of the Turkish coast. This allowed them to influence the passage of ships sailing to and from the nearby Anatolian ports, as well as command the trade routes running from Famagusta and Alexandria in the south to Constantinople and the Black Sea in the north (see Fig. 1).

[7] To give some context, medieval sources list almost 100 ports and landing places along the southern coast of Asia Minor alone: Preiser-Kapeller, 'Liquid frontiers', p. 117; H. Hellenkemper and F. Hild, *Lykien und Pamphylien* (Vienna, 2004), pp. 288–93.
[8] For more on inter-Aegean trade and commodities, see D. Jacoby, 'The eastern Mediterranean in the later Middle Ages: An island world?', in *Byzantines, Latins, and Turks in the Eastern Mediterranean World after 1150*, ed. C Holmes, J. Harris and E. Russell (Oxford, 2012), pp. 93–117.

Byzantium and its Rivals after 1204

In the aftermath of the Fourth Crusade, the Frankish principalities founded in the regions of Romania (Ρωμανία), that is the lands of the Byzantine empire before 1204, included the Latin empire of Constantinople, the kingdom of Thessalonica, the principality of Achaia, the duchy of Athens and Thebes, the duchy of the Archipelago (also called the duchy of Naxos), and several Venetian lordships in the Aegean.[9] The remaining Byzantine factions also formed their own successor states on the fringes of the empire, at Nicaea and Trebizond in Asia Minor, and at Epiros in north-eastern Greece. The Fourth Crusade therefore shattered the Byzantine empire, not just into fragments ruled by the victorious Latin powers, but also into parts governed by rival Greek claimants to the imperial throne. Even after the recovery of Constantinople by the emperor of Nicaea, Michael VIII Palaiologos, in 1261, the Byzantine emperors would never enjoy the benefits of a united empire as their predecessors had done. In fact, the restored empire became the vacuum in the Aegean world, which sucked in various outside powers who sought to establish, maintain or expand their influence in the region.

At the death of Michael VIII in 1282, the empire inherited by his son, Andronikos II Palaiologos, consisted of the western portion of Asia Minor, the southern areas of Thrace and Macedonia, a smattering of the Aegean islands, including Lesbos, Rhodes and Chios, and several important cities, including Thessalonica and the capital, Constantinople. Michael VIII had been able to recover part of the Peloponnese from the Latins and some territories from a weakened Bulgaria, but the majority of Greece was still under Frankish control and the northern borders were under threat from the rising power of Serbia. Moreover, Thessaly and Epiros were in the hands of the rival Angeli dynasty and the northern half of the Balkan peninsula remained under the control of the Serbs. Apart from a brief interlude in the early 1290s, Andronikos II was never able to assert control over the Balkans and as his reign progressed, he struggled to maintain his northern and western frontiers. The Serbs in particular were to become the dominant power in these regions and were soon able to penetrate more deeply into the old Byzantine territories. The weakness of the empire was further compounded by internal instability. Michael VIII had angered large portions of the populace by agreeing to the union of the Greek and Latin Churches at the Second Council of Lyons in 1274 and although Andronikos II had

---

[9]   For the Fourth Crusade, see D.E. Queller and T.F. Madden, *The Fourth Crusade: The Conquest of Constantinople*, 2nd edition (Philadelphia, 1997); M. Angold, *The Fourth Crusade: Event and Context* (Harlow, 2003). For the Latin states in Romania, see R.L. Wolff, *Studies in the Latin Empire of Constantinople*, Variorum Reprints (London, 1976); Lock, *Franks in the Aegean*.

been careful to repudiate the union on his accession, many who opposed his father also opposed him. As the empire became increasingly enfeebled factions inevitably emerged which looked to other members of the Byzantine ruling elite, such as the emperor's grandson, the future Andronikos III, or even to outside rulers to protect their interests. Political and religious strife combined with economic and military weakness became a toxic formula which the restored empire was never able to sufficiently deal with.[10]

The situation was, however, even more dire on the empire's eastern frontier, where great swathes of territory were being lost to the Turks. The origins of the Turks will be dealt with in the next chapter, but for now it is worth recounting the vivid testimony that Byzantine sources give to the threat which they posed to the empire at this time. In a letter written at the turn of the fourteenth century, the patriarch of Constantinople urged Andronikos II to return to Constantinople from Thessalonica as soon as possible because of the impending threat from the Turks – 'the murderous Ishmaelites' – who he wrote were 'devouring the patrimony of Christ'.[11] By this time the first references to Turkish raids on Greek islands in the Aegean also appear. A striking account is given by the Greek historian George Pachymeres, who reported that many Turks had advanced from the interior of Asia Minor to the coastal regions, where they had forced the native inhabitants to flee. They then constructed vessels, with which they plundered the Cyclades and a number of other Aegean islands, including Chios, Samos, Karpathos and Rhodes. These assaults were so severe, lamented the author, that they deprived the islands of almost all their inhabitants and caused great suffering to those who remained on them and on the mainland. Even the regions of the interior were being devoured by the Turks like wildfire and every day new disasters were being announced to the emperor, who was unable to deal with one tragedy after another.[12] This bleak picture was corroborated by the Catalan chronicler Ramon Muntaner, who commented that in the winter of 1302/3 the Turks were launching regular raids against Chios

[10] For a background to the Byzantine successor states, the restored empire and its northern neighbours in this period, see M. Angold, *A Byzantine Government in Exile: Government and Society under the Laskarids of Nicaea, 1204–1261* (London, 1974); A.A.M. Bryer, *The Empire of Trebizond and the Pontos* (London, 1980); A.E. Laiou, *Constantinople and the Latins: The Foreign Policy of Andronicus II, 1282–1328* (Cambridge, MA, 1972); D.M. Nicol, *The Despotate of Epiros 1267–1479: A Contribution to the History of Greece in the Middle Ages* (Cambridge, 1984); Idem, *The Last Centuries of Byzantium, 1261–1453*, 2nd edition (Cambridge, 1993), pp. 114–56; G. Ostrogorsky, *History of the Byzantine State*, trans. J. Hussey, 2nd edition (London, 1968), pp. 478–98.

[11] Athanasios I, *The Correspondence of Athanasius I Patriarch of Constantinople: Letters to the Emperor Andronicus II, Members of the Imperial Family and Officials*, ed. and trans. A.-M.M. Talbot (Washington, 1975), pp. 2–5, doc. 1 (April 1299–October 1300).

[12] George Pachymeres, *Relations historiques*, ed. A. Failler, trans. V. Laurent, 5 vols (Paris, 1984–1999), vol. 4, bk. 10, ch. 29, pp. 376–7.

and the neighbouring Greek islands.[13] The contemporary Venetian writer
Marino Sanudo Torsello also grieved at the 'cruellest destruction' inflicted
by the Turks on the eastern Aegean islands, which by this time were in a
state of total devastation.[14] The Turkish advance was so swift that by c.1305
the important Byzantine city of Ephesos on the Aegean coast had fallen.[15]

The weakening of Byzantium up to this point, coupled with the events
of 1204, led to the consolidation of various Latin states in the Aegean and
Greece. The first to be discussed are those established by the Italian merchant
republics. The Italians were a dominant force in the Aegean before the Fourth
Crusade, but became even more influential afterwards as the expansion of
commercial networks stimulated new levels of international trade and led to
the settlement of Italian craftsmen in major centres throughout Romania.[16]
The Genoese, as fierce rivals of the Venetians, had been traditional allies of
the exiled Byzantine emperors, especially Michael VIII, whom they assisted
in his struggle against the Latin empire. After the recovery of Constantinople, Michael rewarded the Genoese for their support by granting them
permission to trade in the Black Sea, a measure which he also extended to
the Venetians in the following years. This allowed Italian merchants direct
access to the Mongol ports of the Golden Horde and the markets of Central
Asia, the importance of which increased even more after the fall of Acre
and the last Latin outposts on the Syrian coast to the Mamluks in 1291.
The surrendering of Byzantine commercial independence to the Genoese
and Venetians was a result of the fragile condition of the empire and meant
that the long-term commercial ambitions of both maritime republics now
centred on maintaining control of their Aegean outposts.[17] The two Italian
powers began to consolidate their dominance over specific waterways and
maritime spaces, and by the turn of the fourteenth century the Aegean had
become divided along political lines which reflected the fierce rivalry of

[13] Ramon Muntaner, *The Catalan Expedition to the East: from the Chronicle of Ramon
Muntaner*, trans. R. Hughes (Barcelona, 2006), p. 52.
[14] Marino Sanudo, 'Liber Secretorum', p. 29; English translation: *Book of the Secrets of the
Faithful of the Cross*, trans. P. Lock (Farnham, 2011), p. 59. These comments are further
backed up by archaeological evidence that attests to the widespread depopulation of the
region at this time: Bintliff, *The Complete Archaeology of Greece*, pp. 429–31.
[15] There is some debate as to whether the city fell in 1304 or 1305 see A. Failler, 'Éphèse
fut-elle prise en 1304 par les Turcs de Sasan?', *Revue des études byzantines* 54 (1996), 245–8.
For more on Sasa, see Lemerle, *L'émirat d'Aydin*, pp. 19–24.
[16] See, for example, Bintliff, *The Complete Archaeology of Greece*, p. 419.
[17] M. Balard, 'Latins in the Aegean and the Balkans in the fourteenth century', *The New
Cambridge Medieval History*, ed. M. Jones, 7 vols (Cambridge, 1995–2005), vol. 6, pp. 825–38,
at pp. 825–6.

the republics, with the Venetians controlling regions in the west and the Genoese and their allies in the east of the sea.[18]

Venetian possessions included the large island of Crete on the southern border of the Aegean, parts of Euboea (Negroponte) off the eastern coast of Greece and the districts of Modon and Coron on the south-eastern tip of the Morea (the Peloponnese peninsula), as well as a scattering of other smaller islands and districts.[19] In addition, the Venetian Sanudo family ruled the duchy of the Archipelago, incorporating most of the Cyclades, although strictly speaking they were not vassals of Venice but of the Latin emperor.[20] These regions were extremely important for the defence and expansion of Venetian trade in the eastern Mediterranean, primarily because they offered protection and acted as staging posts for the merchant vessels plying the trade routes from Venice to Constantinople and Alexandria. Ships were often constructed by the government and leased out to private individuals. In the fourteenth century it was common for them to be organized into state convoys which set sail from the mother-city twice a year; one to Romania, the other to Cyprus, Syria, Palestine and Egypt.[21] In the context of the highly fragmented political situation in the Aegean, the extent of the Venetian possessions, coupled with the power of its maritime empire, meant that Venice wielded substantial influence in the region and committed great resources for the protection of its trade routes and outposts there. Crete, in particular, was the dominant island in the area and was the most prized of all Venetian colonies overseas. For this reason Venetian assistance in any crusade to the Aegean was highly valued, even if at times it conflicted with the Republic's commercial interests.[22]

[18] Jacoby, 'The economy of Latin Greece', pp. 208–11.

[19] The city of Euripos was called Negroponte by the Latins. It was the prominent city of the island of Euboea, which was divided into several lordships, some of which were ruled by the Venetians. For the purposes of this study 'Negroponte' will refer to the areas of Venetian-ruled Euboea. See Lock, *Franks in the Aegean*, pp. 150–1; D. Jacoby, 'La consolidation de la domination de Venise dans la ville de Négrepont (1205–1390): un aspect de sa politique coloniale', in *Bisanzio, Venezia e il mondo franco-greco (XIII-XV secolo)*, ed. C.A. Maltezou and P. Schreiner (Venice, 2002), pp. 151–89 (repr. in Idem, *Latins, Greeks and Muslims: Encounters in the Eastern Mediterranean, Tenth–Fifteenth Centuries*, Variorum Reprints (Farnham, 2009), IX).

[20] For the Sanudi dukes of the Archipelago, see Lock, *Franks in the Aegean*, pp. 146–9; Vionis, *A Crusader, Ottoman and Early Modern Aegean Archaeology*, pp. 35–6.

[21] See F.C. Lane, *Venice: A Maritime Republic* (London, 1973), pp. 68–78, 124–34; Idem, 'Venetian merchant galleys, 1300–1334: Private and communal operation', *Speculum* 38.2 (1963), 179–205.

[22] For a background to Venice in the Aegean, see Thiriet, *La Romanie vénitienne*; Lane, *Venice: A Maritime Republic*, pp. 30–43; Lock, *Franks in the Aegean*, pp. 135–60; J.E. Dotson, 'Venice, Genoa and control of the seas in the thirteenth and fourteenth centuries', in *War at Sea in the Middle Ages and Renaissance*, ed. J.B. Hattendorf and R.W. Unger (Woodbridge, 2003), pp. 119–36, at pp. 119–28.

After the Genoese were granted access to the Black Sea by Michael VIII in 1261, they also established colonies at Pera opposite Constantinople and at Caffa in the Crimea. Moreover, sometime between 1267 and 1275 the prominent Genoese merchant family of the Zaccaria were given control over the towns of Old and New Phokaia (Eski and Yeni Foça), situated on the Asia Minor coast some 50 kilometres northwest of the Gulf of Smyrna, and granted permission to mine alum in the mountains nearby.[23] In the first decade of the fourteenth century, the family were then granted rulership of the eastern Aegean island of Chios cementing their control over the waterways running to and from the Phokaias. Genoese dominance in the Aegean was enhanced after victory over its great maritime rival Venice at Curzola in 1298 and by the turn of the century it is said that the Commune of Genoa was at its prime.[24] It is important to understand that the Genoese in the eastern Mediterranean often acted independently of the mother-city; the colonies were usually governed with limited interference from the doge and administration of the homeland. This contrasted with the local Venetian administrations in Romania, which often maintained close contact with the government back in Venice. In addition, the Genoese state did not operate a regular convoy system and the ships used by Genoese sailors and merchants were usually constructed and owned by private individuals.[25] The Genoese often acted alone or as vassals of other states, making it far harder to establish a definitive Genoese 'policy' towards events in the Aegean. Nevertheless, they did maintain some form of unity in the area and often shared common interests and, more importantly, common enemies, especially the Venetians.

In addition to the lands held by the two great maritime republics, the Byzantines were also forced to relinquish possessions in the Aegean to other

[23] On the Zaccaria, see M. Carr, 'Trade or Crusade? The Zaccaria of Chios and crusades against the Turks', in *Contact and Conflict in Frankish Greece and the Aegean*, ed. M. Carr and N.G. Chrissis (Farnham, 2014), pp. 115–34; P.P. Argenti, *The Occupation of Chios by the Genoese and their Administration of the Island: 1346–1566*, 3 vols (Cambridge, 1958), vol. 1; L. Balletto, 'Les Génois à Phocée et à Chio du XIIIe au XIVe siècle', in *Byzance et le monde extérieur. Contacts, relations, échanges*, ed. M. Balard, E. Malamut and J.-M. Spieser (Paris, 2005), pp. 45–57; L. Gatto, 'Per la storia di Martino Zaccaria, signore di Chio', *Bullettino dell'Archivio Paleografico Italiano*, n.s., 2–3, part 1 (1956–7), 325–45, at 337–9; R. Lopez, *Benedetto Zaccaria: ammiraglio e mercante* (Milan, 1933; repr. with introduction by Michel Balard, Genoa, 1996). Also of interest, although now very dated, is W. Miller, 'The Zaccaria of Phocaea and Chios, 1275–1329', *The Journal of Hellenic Studies* 31 (1911), 44–55.

[24] See the comments of B.Z. Kedar, *Merchants in Crisis: Genoese and Venetian Men of Affairs and the Fourteenth-Century Depression* (London, 1976), p. 5. For a background to the Genoese in the Aegean, see ibid., pp. 1–20; and also Balard, *La Romanie génoise*; S.A. Epstein, *Genoa and the Genoese, 958–1528* (Chapel Hill, 1996), pp. 141–87.

[25] This point is emphasized in A. Agosto and A.M. Salone, *Mostra Documentaria Genova e Venezia tra i secoli XII e XIV* (Genoa, 1984), p. 9; Kedar, *Merchants in Crisis*, pp. 5–9; Lane, 'Venetian merchant galleys, 1300–1334', 179–80, 202–3; R. Lopez, 'Venice and Genoa: two styles, one success', *Diogenes* 71 (1970), 39–47.

Latin powers. These included Rhodes and several islands of the Dodecanese archipelago, which were seized by the Knights Hospitaller in c.1306–10.[26] The Hospitallers were a military-religious order with considerable wealth from western estates, whose ostensible reason for occupying Rhodes was to help defend Latin territories and to provide support for future crusading endeavours, be they against the Greeks and Turks in Romania, or against the Saracens in the Holy Land.[27] This *raison d'être*, combined with the strategic importance of the island, meant that the Hospitallers became a significant power in the Aegean and integral to crusading in the region, although they too became enmeshed in the rivalries and conflicts which characterized relations between the resident Latin powers.

In mainland Greece the Franks had held territories since the Fourth Crusade, but in the early fourteenth century another western power, the Catalans, emerged on the scene. The arrival of the Catalans in Romania can also be linked back to the inherent weakness of Byzantium in these years, especially the increasing reliance of the emperors on foreign mercenaries to defend their borders. The Catalans were employed in this way by Andronikos II to fight against the Turks in Asia Minor, but in 1305 they turned against their paymaster and in alliance with the Turks began ravaging the regions of Constantinople, Thrace and Macedonia, before marching into Thessaly.[28] In 1311, the Catalans then turned their attention from the Byzantines to the Franks of the Morea and seized the duchy of Athens, after killing Duke Walter I of Brienne at the battle of Cephissus. Until then Athens was technically a vassal state of the principality of the Achaia, which came under the suzerainty of the Angevin king of Naples, who at this point was Robert the Wise, along with his younger brothers Philip of Taranto and John of Gravina.[29] The Catalans had strong links to the rival Crown of Aragon and consequently posed a threat to Angevin and Brienne interests in

[26] The Hospitaller conquest of Rhodes is discussed in more detail in Chapter 3, pp. 66–7.

[27] Hospitaller Rhodes has been the focus of numerous studies by Anthony Luttrell, many of which can be found in five volumes of Variorum Reprints: *The Hospitallers in Cyprus, Rhodes, Greece, and the West, 1291–1440: Collected Studies* (Aldershot, 1978); *Latin Greece, the Hospitallers and the Crusades, 1291–1440* (Aldershot, 1982); *The Hospitallers of Rhodes and their Mediterranean World* (Aldershot, 1992); *The Hospitaller State on Rhodes and its Western Provinces, 1306–1462* (Aldershot, 1999); *Studies on the Hospitallers after 1306: Rhodes and the West* (Aldershot, 2007).

[28] R.I. Burns, 'The Catalan Company and the European powers, 1305–1311', *Speculum* 29 (1954), 751–71; S. Kyriakidis, 'The employment of large groups of mercenaries in Byzantium in the period ca. 1290–1305 as viewed by the sources', *Byzantion* 79 (2009), 208–30, at 216–30. The most comprehensive treatment of the Catalans still remains that of Setton, although this is now very dated and at times erroneous: K.M. Setton, *The Catalan Domination of Athens: 1311–1388* (Cambridge, MA, 1948).

[29] For more on Frankish possessions in Greece during the fourteenth century, see Lock, *Franks in the Aegean*, pp. 68–108; P. Topping, 'The Morea, 1311–1364', in *A History of the Crusades*, ed. K.M. Setton, 6 vols (Madison, 1969–1989), vol. 3, pp. 104–40, at pp. 104–7.

the area. On the other hand this meant that they were no longer the natural enemies of the Byzantines and slowly their relationship with the emperor at Constantinople improved. The rulers of the Latin possessions in Greece were thus in regular conflict with the main Greek and Turkish protagonists in the region, with the result that their territories were also inextricably linked to crusading in the Aegean.[30]

Finally, although not Aegean states, it is worth commenting on the two kingdoms of Cyprus and Cilician Armenia. They were closely linked to Byzantium and also played an important role in crusading in the region. Cyprus lay on the trade routes running from the Black Sea and western Europe to the Levant and was the furthest east of all Latin holdings in the Mediterranean. The position of the island had always allowed the Lusignan rulers to play an important role in the crusades and, as the Turks grew in strength, the Cypriot kings once again found themselves on the crusading frontier, this time in opposition to the Turcoman principalities of south-eastern Anatolia. Because of this, expeditions were regularly planned with the aim of providing aid to Cyprus, and the kings of the island became active participants in campaigns against the Turks, especially the naval leagues of the 1330s and 1340s.[31] Cilician Armenia, sandwiched between the Turks in Anatolia and the Mamluks in northern Syria, also occupied a strategic posi-tion in the East, with the city of Lajazzo (Ayas) constituting the last impor-tant Christian port on the Levantine coast after the fall of Acre. During the fourteenth century the position of the kingdom became progressively more perilous as the incursions of the Turks, Mamluks and Mongols increased. Consequently, Armenia began to feature heavily in crusade proposals, even though aid from western Europe was rarely forthcoming. In many instances plans to lend assistance to Cyprus and Cilician Armenia were combined with larger projects to liberate the Holy Land, but at times they were also linked to expeditions which had the objective of limiting Turkish expansion into the Aegean region.[32]

---

[30]   D. Jacoby, 'Catalans, Turcs et Vénitiens en Romanie (1305–1332): Un nouveau témoignage de Marino Sanudo Torsello', *Studia Medievali* 15.1 (1974), 217–61 (repr. in Idem, *Recherches sur la Méditerranée orientale du XIIe au XVe siècle: peuples, sociétés, économies*, Variorum Reprints (London, 1979), V); E.A. Zachariadou, 'The Catalans of Athens and the beginning of Turkish expansion in the Aegean area', *Studia Medievali* 21.2 (1980), 821–38 (repr. in Idem, *Romania and the Turks, c.1300–1500* (London, 1985), V).

[31]   For Cyprus, see N. Coureas, *The Latin Church in Cyprus: 1313–1378* (Nicosia, 2010), pp. 97–179; P.W. Edbury, *The Kingdom of Cyprus and the Crusades: 1191–1374* (Cambridge, 1991), pp. 101–41; G. Hill, *A History of Cyprus*, 4 vols (Cambridge, 1940–52), vol. 2, pp. 192–303.

[32]   For Cilician Armenia, see M.-A. Chevalier, *Les ordres religieux-militaires en Arménie cilicienne: templiers, hospitaliers, teutoniques et Arméniens à l'époque des croisades* (Paris, 2009), esp. pp. 573–678; T.S.R. Boase 'The history of the kingdom', in *The Cilician Kingdom of Armenia*, ed. T.S.R. Boase (Edinburgh, 1978), pp. 1–33; A.T. Luttrell, 'The Hospitallers'

Western Hostility towards Byzantium after 1204

The Fourth Crusade shattered the Byzantine empire and also ushered in a period of crusading against the Greeks. At first this manifested itself in the form of campaigns to shore up the Latin empire and other states in Romania, but once Constantinople fell in 1261 plans were made to recover the city, sometimes as a preliminary to the eventual liberation of Jerusalem. The attitudes of the western powers towards Byzantium had a significant impact on the evolution of the idea of a crusade against the Turks which gradually came to the fore in the second and third decades of the fourteenth century. Therefore, before the emergence of an anti-Turkish crusade is discussed in the following chapters, it is first necessary to provide an overview of crusading against the Greeks from 1204.

Over the course of the thirteenth century, the Aegean region evolved into an active crusading frontier as the Franks, with the support of the papacy, struggled to preserve their territories against the exiled Greek claimants. As early as May 1205 Pope Innocent III granted the crusade indulgence to those who would help defend the Latin empire, followed by the launching of an unsuccessful expedition to Romania in 1207. His successor Honorius III increased these efforts, preaching crusades in 1217 and 1223, which in terms of the level of papal support equalled and at times even surpassed those being organized in the Baltic and southern France. Other campaigns followed under Pope Gregory IX, including a crusade against the Nicaean emperor John III Vatatzes. But despite these efforts the Latin empire became increasingly enfeebled until it was reduced chiefly to Constantinople and its environs.[33]

After Constantinople was captured by Michael VIII in 1261, crusades were then preached with the aim of restoring the Latin empire. Initially the impetus came from the powerful Angevin king of Naples and Sicily, Charles of Anjou, who was the brother of King Louis IX of France and also a claimant to territories in Greece. Michael VIII was, however, an astute diplomat who was able repeatedly to foil Angevin plans, despite the military weakness of his empire. The agreement with the papacy which led to the union of the Greek and Latin Churches in 1274 was one such measure, as was his role in helping foment the outbreak of the Sicilian Vespers in 1282. The war in Sicily developed into a wider confrontation between the

---

· interventions in Cilician Armenia: 1271–1375', *The Cilician Kingdom of Armenia*, ed. T.S.R. Boase (Edinburgh, 1978), pp. 118–44.

[33] On crusades against the Byzantines in the thirteenth century, see the recent studies by N.G. Chrissis, in particular: *Crusading in Frankish Greece: A Study of Byzantine-Western Relations and Attitudes, 1204–1282* (Turnhout, 2012); 'New frontiers: Frankish Greece and the development of crusading in the early thirteenth century', in *Contact and Conflict in Frankish Greece and the Aegean, 1204–1453*, ed. M. Carr and N.G. Chrissis (Farnham, 2014), pp. 17–41.

Aragonese and Angevin royal houses into which many of the main players in Mediterranean Europe were drawn, including the Italian Ghibellines and the Sicilians in support of Aragon, and the papacy and the Capetian house of France on the side of the Angevins. The conflict would rumble on for the next twenty years. It distracted the western powers from a crusade against Byzantium, while also permanently fragmenting the Angevin hegemony in the central Mediterranean.[34]

The war over Sicily finally came to an end with the Peace of Caltabellotta in 1302, after which projects to re-establish the Latin empire of Constantinople were revived. Chief amongst these was a crusade planned by Charles of Valois, the younger brother of Philip IV of France, which dominated crusade planning during the pontificate of Clement V. Charles had married the titular Latin empress of Constantinople, Catherine of Courtenay, in 1301 and began preparing a campaign which would both recover Constantinople and also pave the way for a general passage to the Holy Land to be led by his brother Philip IV.[35] The preparations for this campaign reached an advanced stage. In 1304 and again in 1306 the full crusade indulgence was granted to participants and extensive church tithes were levied.[36] Then in 1307 a ban of excommunication was pronounced against Emperor Andronikos II and his supporters, who were condemned as schismatics and usurpers of the imperial throne.[37] In December 1306, Venice concluded a treaty with Charles, which stipulated that the crusader fleet was to depart from Brindisi within a year from March 1307.[38] Charles also gained assistance from the prince of Achaia, Philip of Taranto, who would use the crusade to shore up his newly acquired Angevin lands in Greece.[39] As well as this, in 1307 Charles sought to recruit local factions in the Aegean, such as the Catalan

---

[34] On the Sicilian Vespers, see S. Runciman, *The Sicilian Vespers: A History of the Mediterranean World in the Later Thirteenth Century* (Cambridge, 1958); D.J. Geanakoplos, *Emperor Michael Palaeologus and the West, 1258–1282: A Study Into Byzantine-Latin Relations* (Cambridge, MA, 1959), pp. 335–67; J. Dunbabin, *Charles I of Anjou: Power, Kingship and State-Making in Thirteenth-Century Europe* (London, 1998), pp. 99–113.

[35] Laiou, *Constantinople and the Latins*, pp. 43–56; Geanakoplos, 'Byzantium and the Crusades: 1261–1354', pp. 42–5.

[36] *Le registre de Benoît XI*, docs 1006–7; Clement V, *Regestum*, vol. 1, docs 243–7; vol. 2, docs 1755, 1758.

[37] Clement V, *Regestum*, vol. 2, doc. 1759; Setton, *Papacy and the Levant*, vol. 1, pp. 163–8.

[38] For the treaty with Venice, see Clement V, *Regestum*, vol. 1, doc. 248 (14 Jan 1306); *DVL*, vol. 1, doc. 27; Laiou, *Constantinople and the Latins*, pp. 204–7.

[39] Clement V, *Regestum*, vol. 2, doc. 1604–5 (15 May 1307). Philip had led a campaign to consolidate his hold on Achaia in the summer of 1306: D.M. Nicol, *The Despotate of Epiros 1267–1479: A Contribution to the History of Greece in the Middle Ages* (Cambridge, 1984), pp. 59–61; Kunstmann, 'Studien über Marino Sanudo', 775 (letter 2); Roddy trans., p. 251 (letter 30).

Company, who by this point had turned against their erstwhile employer Andronikos II, and a number of Greek conspirators in Asia Minor, unhappy with the rule of the emperor.[40] In the same year Charles even managed to dispatch a small fleet under the command of the French knight Thibault of Cepoy to the Aegean to cement these alliances, but his actions ultimately proved fruitless.[41] Over the next few years the crusading project of Charles of Valois fell apart. The death of his wife Catherine of Courtenay in 1308 and the transfer of her claim to their daughter Catherine of Valois was a major setback, as were the constant delays in securing the funds needed to get the campaign underway. To add to this, support from the king of France began to waver as other events, such as the ongoing conflict with Flanders and the arrest of the Knights Templar (1307), took precedence.[42] Charles persuaded the Venetians to postpone the expedition until February 1310, but when he failed to make this new deadline, they concluded a peace treaty with the Byzantine government, effectively putting an end to the projected crusade.[43]

After the collapse of the crusade plans of Charles of Valois, attempts to recover Constantinople and launch a general expedition to the Holy Land were revived by Clement V at the Council of Vienne in 1311–12.[44] Here a new date was set for a crusade to liberate Jerusalem to be led by Philip IV, which would also be preceded by a preliminary campaign to protect the Angevin kingdom of Achaia from the incursions of the Greeks and Catalans and even to recover Constantinople itself. This was now to be commanded by Philip of Taranto, who it was agreed would marry Catherine of Valois in 1313 and thus inherit the claim to the Latin empire.[45] Although indulgences were issued and extensive church tithes decreed for these campaigns, neither Philip of Taranto, the French king nor the pope was able to get

---

[40] For the negotiations with the Catalans, see Ramon Muntaner, *The Catalan Expedition to the East*, pp. 102–4, 130–4; *DOC*, doc. 34, p. 42; Burns, 'The Catalan Company and the European powers', 751–71; Setton, *The Catalan Domination of Athens*, pp. 1–5; Laiou, *Constantinople and the Latins*, pp. 208–9. For the Greek conspirators, see Laiou, *Constantinople and the Latins*, pp. 212–20; J.L. Boojamra, 'Athanasios of Constantinople: a study of Byzantine reactions to Latin religious infiltration', *Church History* 48.1 (1979), 27–48, at 38–9.

[41] According to Sanudo, this flotilla numbered thirteen vessels and sixty cavalry: Kunstmann, 'Studien über Marino Sanudo', 774–5 (letter 2); Roddy trans., pp. 250–1 (letter 30); Ramon Muntaner, *The Catalan Expedition to the East*, pp. 130–1.

[42] Laiou, *Constantinople and the Latins*, pp. 233–5; Schein, *Fideles Crucis*, pp. 179–84,

[43] Setton, *The Papacy and the Levant*, vol. 1, p. 168; Laiou, *Constantinople and the Latins*, pp. 236–7.

[44] Tanner, *Decrees of the Ecumenical Councils: Nicaea I to Vatican II*, vol. 1, pp. 333–401; S. Menache, *Clement V* (Cambridge, 1998), pp. 112–18, 205–46, 279–305.

[45] Laiou, *Constantinople and the Latins*, pp. 238–9.

the expedition off the ground.[46] The deaths in 1314 of both Clement V and Philip IV made sure of this. Even though the Valois and Angevin plans to recover Constantinople in the first decades of the fourteenth century proved to be ultimately unsuccessful, they were indicative of western perceptions of the Byzantines at this time. These in many ways mirrored the attitudes born in the thirteenth century, which justified crusading against the Greeks on the grounds that they were schismatics and centred on the defence or recovery of Latin lands from them in Romania. However, increasingly these campaigns became intertwined with French affairs, and consequently they suffered when domestic issues distracted the attention of the king of France away from a crusade.

During the pontificate of John XXII, crusade plans against the Byzantines were intermittently revived, but no expedition on the scale of that planned by Charles of Valois ever came close to materializing. The intensification of the wars in Italy and the rising tensions between the French and their neigh-bours in northern Europe, in particular, diverted attention and resources from a crusade to Constantinople.[47] Projects were still discussed in the courts of the French Kings Philip V and Charles IV, but John XXII proved to be far less generous with church taxation than his predecessor and these negotiations repeatedly broke down over problems of finance.[48] Increasingly crusade negotiations began to focus less on the idea of liberating the Holy Land by going by way of Constantinople and instead plans for a smaller and

[46] Clement V, *Regestum*, vol. 7, docs 7759–65, 7893, 8863–8, vol. 8, docs 8897–8, 8913–6, 9276; Tyerman, 'Sed nihil fecit?', pp. 170–1; Menache, *Clement V*, pp. 112–18; Schein, *Fideles Crucis*, pp. 239–57.

[47] For Italy, see Housley, *Italian Crusades*, pp. 84–6, 106–10, 250–1; P. Partner, *The Lands of St Peter: The Papal States in the Middle Ages and Early Renaissance* (London, 1972), pp. 318–26; G. Mollat, *The Popes at Avignon: 1305–1378*, trans. J. Love (London, 1963), pp. 94–110; J. Leonhard, *Genua und die päpstliche Kurie in Avignon (1305 – 1378): politische und diplomatische Beziehungen im 14. Jahrhundert* (Frankfurt am Main, 2013), esp. pp. 79–160. For Northern Europe, see W.C. Jordan, *The Great Famine: Northern Europe in the Early Fourteenth Century* (Princeton, 1996); D. Nicholas, *Medieval Flanders* (London, 1992), pp. 186–208; N. Housley, 'France, England and the "national crusade", 1302–86', in *France and the British Isles in the Middle Ages and Renaissance*, ed. G. Jondorf and D.N. Dumville (Woodbridge, 1991), pp. 183–201, at pp. 186–8 (repr. in Idem, *Crusading and Warfare in Medieval and Renaissance Europe*, Variorum Reprints (Aldershot, 2001), VII); P. Chaplais, *The War of Saint-Sardos (1323–1325): Gascon Correspondence and Diplomatic Documents* (London, 1954), pp. ix–xiii.

[48] See, for example, Tyerman, 'Sed nihil fecit?', pp. 170–81; C.J. Tyerman, 'Philip V of France, the assemblies of 1319–20 and the crusade', *Bulletin of the Institute of Historical Research* 57 (1984), 15–34 (repr. in Idem, *The Practices of Crusading: Image and Action from the Eleventh to the Sixteenth Centuries*, Variorum Reprints (Farnham, 2013), II); N. Housley, 'The Franco-papal crusade negotiations in 1322–3', *Papers of the British School at Rome* 48 (1980), 166–85 (repr. in Idem, *Crusading and Warfare in Medieval and Renaissance Europe*, Variorum Reprints (Aldershot, 2001), XII); C.H. Taylor, 'French assemblies and subsidy in 1321', *Speculum* 43 (1968), 217–44.

more realistic *passagium particulare* to relieve Cyprus and Cilician Armenia began to take precedent.[49] In fact, from 1324 to 1327, (unsuccessful) negotiations for the union of the Greek and Latin Churches were undertaken at the behest of Andronikos II and the crusade theorist Marino Sanudo, who acted as an intermediary between the emperor, the pope and Charles IV of France.[50] However, while it is true that the 1320s became a period of diminishing western aggression towards the Byzantines, it was also a time in which the realization of any Franco-papal crusade project was severely hindered by external events, regardless of its target. It would therefore be misleading to interpret this decade as signifying a dramatic shift in Franco-papal perceptions of the Byzantines.[51] Apart from the short period of union negotiations, attitudes towards the emperor remained overwhelmingly hostile. For example, throughout the 1320s a series of smaller Angevin campaigns against the Greeks in the Morea were planned and launched which were sometimes awarded crusading privileges by the pope. Even in the early 1330s John XXII supported an Angevin-Brienne campaign to Greece and issued a number of bulls condemning the actions of the schismatic Greeks in the region.[52] This longstanding animosity towards the Byzantines would continue to influence papal policy in regard to a campaign in the Aegean, as will be discussed in the following chapters.

[49] As Laiou has suggested, very few of the Franco-papal crusade projects of the 1320s were focussed on Byzantium: Laiou, *Constantinople and the Latins*, pp. 315–18.

[50] For more on these church union negotiations, see Chapter 5 (pp. 96–8) and also Laiou, *Constantinople and the Latins*, pp. 308–29; Idem, 'Marino Sanudo Torsello, Byzantium and the Turks: the background to the anti-Turkish league of 1332–1334', *Speculum* 45 (1970), 374–92, at 381–3; G. Durrholder, *Die Kreuzzugspolitik unter Papst Johann XXII* (Strasbourg, 1913), pp. 30–57; J. Gill, *Byzantium and the Papacy, 1198–1400* (New Brunswick, 1979), pp. 191–2.

[51] This period of Byzantine-western relations is discussed in detail by: Laiou, *Constantinople and the Latins*, pp. 308–29.

[52] The papal-Angevin campaigns in Greece are discussed in more detail in Chapter 5 (pp. 94–6).

2

A New Enemy: The Emergence of the Turks as a 'Target' of Crusade

> Christianity endures the greatest danger in the remotest parts where Christians dwell: obviously the parts where they are neighbours with the Tartars, also in parts where they are neighbours with the Spanish Moors, and also where Christians have borders by the sea in the eastern region with the Turks, the most evil Saracens who rule almost all of Asia Minor.
>
> Marino Sanudo Torsello, letter to Cardinal Bertrand du Pouget, 10 April 1330.[1]

Marino Sanudo's words are characteristic of a Venetian writing in the early 1330s – a period of intense Turkish raids on the Republic's possessions in the Aegean, which eventually led to the formation of the first naval league in 1333. But Sanudo's words do not characterize all western views of the Turkish beyliks for the whole time-span of this study. Unsurprisingly, no single source can provide such a thing, as no uniform view ever existed. Instead the perception of the Turks in the eyes of western Christendom gradually evolved over time, from one of ambivalence and ambiguity to one of fear and aversion, as the beyliks emerged as the sole target of a crusade mid-way through the century. Still, even during this process of growing animosity, not all views of the Turks were necessarily negative; instead they remained complex and multifaceted, being constantly influenced by a plethora of external factors. It is these inconsistencies as well as the overlying trend of rising hostility that this chapter aims to map out.

The Emergence of the Turkish Beyliks in Anatolia

The expansion of Latin trade in the Aegean and Black Seas during the second half of the thirteenth century coincided with the emergence of Turkish warrior-nomads on the old Seljuk-Byzantine frontier. A pivotal point in this demographic transformation was the Mongol victory at the

---

[1]   Kunstmann, 'Studien über Marino Sanudo', 781 (letter 2); Roddy trans., p. 259 (letter 30).

battle of Köse Dağ in 1243, which resulted in the reduction and submission of the Seljuk Sultanate to the Mongols in Anatolia.[2] The gradual weakening of Mongol authority in the following decades led to the creation of numerous autonomous tribal domains in the area. These gradually evolved into a patchwork of Turkish principalities, known as emirates in Arabic, or beyliks in Turkish, centred around the ruling house of a head Turkish chieftain from which they often took their name.[3] The beyliks were usually ruled by a senior emir, or *ulu beg*, who delegated power to his younger sons who sometimes took the title of *beg* or *pasha*. By the end of the thirteenth century these beyliks, probably motivated by a hybrid holy war and tribal-warrior ethos, had firmly established themselves in the Aegean hinterland of Anatolia – something which had not been achieved since the initial Seljuk expansion of the eleventh century.[4]

The first of the beyliks to be established was that of Menteshe, situated to the south of the Meander valley, which by the last decades of the thirteenth century controlled the coastal region of classical Caria, commanding the cities of Milas (Mylasa), Balat (Palatia/Miletus) and Peçin. The early years of Menteshe remain obscure, but by 1311 it is known that the beylik was ruled by an emir, or *ulu beg*, called Masud.[5] In about 1307 a rival principality, that of Aydin, was formed to the north of Menteshe, under Emir Mehmed, who established his capital at Birgi (Pyrgion) and controlled the coastal cities of Smyrna and Ephesos.[6] Menteshe and Aydin were accompanied by the beyliks of Sarukhan and Karasi to the north, which occupied the coastal regions stretching from just north of New Phokaia to the Dardanelles, and

[2] C. Cahen, *Pre-Ottoman Turkey: A General Survey of the Material and Spiritual Culture and History c.1071–1330*, trans. J. Jones-Williams (London, 1968), pp. 268–360; P. Jackson, *The Mongols and the West, 1221–1410* (Harlow, 2005), pp. 74–5.

[3] On the establishment of the Anatolian beyliks, see R.P. Lindner, *Explorations in Ottoman Prehistory* (Ann Arbor, 2007), pp. 1–12; Kafadar, *Between the Two Worlds*, pp. 1–9; Zachariadou, *Trade and Crusade*, pp. 4–12, 105–21; Idem, *Studies in pre-Ottoman Turkey and the Ottomans* (Aldershot, 2007); Cahen, *Pre-Ottoman Turkey*, pp. 1–32, 64–72; W.L. Langer, and R.P. Blake, 'The rise of the Ottoman Turks and its historical background', *American Historical Review* 37 (1932), 477–80. For a Byzantine perspective: S. Vryonis Jr., *The Decline of Medieval Hellenism in Asia Minor and the Process of Islamization from the Eleventh through the Fifteenth Century* (Berkeley, 1971), esp. pp. 135–42.

[4] For the motivations of the beyliks see, for example, P. Wittek, *The Rise of the Ottoman Empire: Studies into the History of Turkey, Thirteenth-Fifteenth Centuries*, ed. C. Heywood (London, 2012), pp. 56–9 (= *The Rise of the Ottoman Empire* (London, 1938), pp. 33–7); H.W. Lowry, *The Nature of the Early Ottoman State* (Albany, 2003), esp. pp. 5–13.

[5] On the establishment of Menteshe, see P. Wittek, *Das Fürstentum Mentesche, Studie zur Geschichte Westkleinasiens im 13.-15. Jahre* (Istanbul, 1934), pp. 58–87; Zachariadou, *Trade and Crusade*, pp. 105–12.

[6] On the establishment of Aydin see Lemerle, *L'émirat d'Aydin*, pp. 19–26; H. Akin, *Aydın Oğulları tarihi hakkında bir araştırma* (Istanbul, 1946), pp. 15–28; Zachariadou, *Trade and Crusade*, pp. 108–9, 112–16.

by Hamid and Karaman on the southern coast of Asia Minor, extending
from the southerly border of Menteshe, near Makre, to beyond Candelore
in the east.[7] In addition, there were the principalities of Germiyan and the
Ottomans which were both initially landlocked and sandwiched between
the maritime beyliks and the remaining Byzantine lands in north-western
Anatolia (see Maps 1 and 2).[8] By the late 1270s there is evidence that the
coastal beyliks had begun trading with the Venetians and by the end of the
century they were encroaching upon both Latin and Greek possessions in
the Aegean Sea.[9]

There are few Muslim sources relating to the beyliks from this period,
especially those written by the Turks themselves. Because of this, it can be
difficult to get a sense of the inner workings of the different ruling fami-
lies and their relations with one another. Fortunately however, the famous
fourteenth-century travel writer Ibn Battuta journeyed through Anatolia in
the early 1330s, leaving an invaluable account of the beyliks, packed with
colourful anecdotes and details about the different Anatolian emirs, their
lands and their dynastic struggles, which would increasingly come to the
attention of European writers in the fourteenth and fifteenth centuries.
Battuta first reached the south coast of Anatolia at the end of 1330, aiming
to cross the peninsula on a somewhat roundabout route to India. He arrived
by sea at the port of Alanya (Candelore) in the beylik of Karaman, from
where he proceeded westward to Antalya and, after a brief detour into Cilician Armenia, northwards through the Aegean hinterland to the lands of
Menteshe, Aydin, Sarukhan, Karasi and finally Osman.[10] On the whole
Battuta was very impressed with these regions and their rulers, many of
whom he met in person and who will come to feature prominently in
this study. In particular, Battuta spoke highly of the emir of Menteshe,
Orkhan (c.1319–37), the son of Masud, whom he considered to be an especially honourable ruler, handsome in both figure and conduct. Battuta was

[7]   That is, from modern-day Fethiye (Makre) to Alanya (Candelore).
[8]   More information on the formation of these beyliks is given in C.E. Bosworth, *The New
Islamic Dynasties: A Chronological and Genealogical Manual* (Edinburgh, 1996), pp. 213–42;
Kafadar, *Between the Two Worlds*, pp. 1–9; Lindner, *Explorations in Ottoman Prehistory*, pp.
1–12; Zachariadou, *Trade and Crusade*, pp. 105–16; C. Cahen, 'Les principautés turcomanes au
debut du XIVe siècle d'après Pachymere et Gregoras', *İstanbul Üniversitesi Edebiyat Fakültesi
Tarih Dergisi* 32 (1979), 111–16; E.A. Zachariadou (ed.), *The Ottoman Emirate (1300–1389):
Halcyon Days in Crete I: A Symposium Held in Rethymnon, 11–13 January 1991* (Rethymnon,
1993).
[9]   Zachariadou, *Trade and Crusade*, pp. 3–7; H. Theunissen, 'Ottoman-Venetian
diplomatics: the Ahd-names. The historical background and the development of a category of
political–commercial instruments together with an annotated edition of a corpus of relevant
documents', *Electronic Journal of Oriental Studies* 1.2 (1998), 1–698, at 68–9.
[10] For Battuta's itinerary see R.E. Dunn, *The Adventures of Ibn Battuta: A Muslim Traveler
of the 14th Century* (Berkeley, 1986), pp. 137–58.

Figure 2. The castle of Peçin, built by the emirs of Menteshe.

particularly impressed by the court Orkhan held, which was attended by scholars, amongst them doctors of law and philosophy. Apparently Orkhan had recently taken up residence in the city of *Barjin* (Peçin), on the hill overlooking Milas, which according to Battuta had many fine buildings and mosques.[11] Today the extensive ruins of the castle of Peçin and the surrounding city, although mostly dating from the later fourteenth century, are still evidence of a sizeable urban area – one which must have been founded by an emir with considerable resources (see Fig. 2).

Next on his journey was Aydin, situated to the north of Menteshe. Here Battuta visited the founder of the Aydin-oglus, Mehmed Beg (c.1313–34), at the town of Birgi. The traveller was well looked after and entertained, leading him to praise his host as 'one of the best, most generous and worthy of sultans'. As with Orkhan, Mehmed also held a court of scholarly sophistication, where Battuta was pleased to meet many intellectuals, as well as the emir's eldest sons, Hizir and Umur Pasha, the rulers of Ephesos and Smyrna respectively. However, not everything was harmonious amongst the Aydin-oglus; one of Mehmed's youngest sons Suleymanshah had recently angered his father by fleeing to Orkhan at Peçin, who was also his father-in-law; a sign of the strife between the beyliks at this time.[12] The town of Birgi was situated inland from Smyrna and had been made the capital by the Aydin-oglus some years before where they had built (in c.1312) a large

---

[11] Ibn Battuta, *The Travels*, vol. 2, pp. 429–30; Wittek, *Das Fürstentum Mentesche*, pp. 135–7.
[12] Ibn Battuta, *The Travels*, vol. 2, pp. 438–44.

Figure 3. Ulu Cami, Birgi, built by Mehmed Aydin-olgu in c.1312.

architectural complex centred on an *ulu cami*, or great mosque, which still stands today.[13] This structure was grander than anything undertaken by the other beyliks in these years and is an indication of the comparative power and wealth of Aydin. Certainly, in terms of architectural achievement Aydin surpassed many of its rivals, including even the early Ottomans (see Fig. 3).

Battuta and Hizir had already met whilst at Birgi, but an over-familiarity, or lack of common courtesy on the part of the former, seems to have strained relations between the two when they crossed paths again at Ephesos. Here Battuta failed to dismount when greeting the Turkish lord on the outskirts of the city, giving such offence that no kindness was extended to him during his stay. The traveller understandably did not dwell in Ephesos and instead proceeded to Smyrna where he met the emir's other son Umur, whom he had also first encountered at Birgi. In contrast to Hizir, the lord of Smyrna was very generous, at one point even giving Battuta a Greek slave girl as a gift. Not surprisingly Umur made a very good impression on Battuta whose account resounds with praise for the emir, not least for his pious military

---

[13] For photographs and descriptions, see R.M. Riefstahl, *Turkish Architecture in Southwestern Anatolia* (Cambridge, MA, 1931), pp. 26–30, 105; G. Goodwin, *A History of Ottoman Architecture* (London, 1971), p. 17. See also Kafadar, *Between the Two Worlds*, pp. 134–5; Lemerle, *L'émirat d'Aydin*, pp. 89–90.

endeavours against the Christians.[14] This view of Umur was also shared by other writers, both Muslim and, more surprisingly, Christian; a reflection of the impact he had on contemporaries of all faiths and cultural backgrounds. Umur also features heavily in western sources, in fact more than any other Anatolian lord of the period, making him a significant player in the changing perception of the Turks. His portrayal in contemporary European literature will be discussed later in this chapter.

Finally, Battuta worked his way through the northern beyliks, where he met the emir of Sarukhan at Manisa (Magnesia), travelled past Christian-held Phokaia, and into Karasi, visiting the son of the emir Yakhshi at Bergama (Pergamum). He then ventured inland, reaching Bursa (Proussa), where he stayed for some days with the Ottoman emir, Orkhan (c.1324–62), the son of Osman, known as the legendary founder of the Ottoman dynasty. By this time the Ottomans had already conquered large swathes of Byzantine Asia Minor and were beginning a period of expansion which would see them dominate the region over the next half-century. Battuta was clearly impressed with their military achievements, and especially those of Orkhan whom he claimed was 'the king of all the Turkmens and the richest in wealth, lands and military resources'. Such was the disaster wrought on the region by the Ottomans, remarked Battuta, that a vast stretch of wasteland, of eighteen days' march across, extended eastward from their border to the remaining Greek-ruled territories in Anatolia. Less than fifteen years after Battuta had left the region, Orkhan annexed the neighbouring beylik of Karasi and brought his armies across the Dardanelles into Thrace. By the time of the emir's death in 1360, the Ottomans were poised for the conquest of south-eastern Europe.[15]

Early Western Views of the Turks

Amity, Ambiguity and a Period of Transition

Emperor Alexios I's appeal to the pope for military aid at the Council of Piacenza in 1095, which led to the preaching of the First Crusade, was in many ways a result of the Turkish domination of eastern Asia Minor, characterized by the Byzantine defeat at Manzikert in 1071.[16] Consequently, the crusading movement was closely linked to the Turks from the outset, with the result that even before the fourteenth century and the rise of the Ottomans, a vague and rather amorphous idea of the Turks existed in the

[14] Ibn Battuta, *The Travels*, vol. 2, pp. 444–7.

[15] Ibn Battuta, *The Travels*, vol. 2, pp. 447–52, 499–500; Dunn, *The Adventures of Ibn Battuta*, pp. 151–23.

[16] See Hillenbrand, *Turkish Myth and Muslim Symbol*, pp. 3–25; P. Frankopan, *The First Crusade: The Call from the East* (London, 2012), esp. pp. 87–100.

West. However, many of the ruling Turkic elites of Anatolia in the four-teenth century were ethnically and linguistically different from those of the eleventh century, having arrived on the second great wave of Turkish migration from Central Asia, in the wake of the Mongol onslaught of the thirteenth century. To further complicate things, the inhabitants of *Turchia*, as the region was known in the West, or Rūm to other Muslims, were often divided into communities of differing religious, linguistic and political affiliations. The Ottoman ruling class, for example, was predominantly but not exclusively Muslim, and mostly Turkish speaking, although not all as a native tongue; consequently 'Turk' was only one of many ethnicities ruled by that class.[17] Confusingly, throughout the period these peoples were, with few exceptions, referred to as *Turchi* in Latin sources – a rather nebulous phrase which did not reflect the ethnoreligious complexity of the region – or alter in accordance with the political changes in the peninsula which occurred on either side of the rise and fall of the Seljuk empire; begin-ning with the influx of various Turkmen peoples in the eleventh century and ending with the establishment of the Turkish beyliks at the end of the thirteenth.[18]

The armies of the First Crusade fought these *Turchi* (predominantly the Seljuks) on many occasions. Peter the Hermit's undisciplined force was routed by them in 1096, whilst the main crusader army famously defeated the Seljuk Sultan Kilij Arslan at Dorylaeum a year later.[19] During the Second and Third Crusades, Latin armies also crossed Asia Minor, coming into conflict with the Seljuk Turks once again. In 1147, for example, the German contingent led by Emperor Conrad III was crushed at Dorylaeum, but on the Third Crusade, Frederick Barbarossa fared better, capturing the Seljuk capital of Konya in 1190 before his death a few months later.[20] It is inter-esting to note that many of the crusade chroniclers understood the difference

---

[17] See Kafadar, *Between the Two Worlds*, pp. 1–4; Zachariadou, *Trade and Crusade*, pp. 117–21.

[18] The exceptions being the twelfth- and thirteenth-century works of William of Tyre and Simon of Saint-Quentin, who together provide a great deal of information on the Seljuks, from the time of their migration into Asia Minor until the advances of the Mongols: William of Tyre, *Chronicon*, ed. R.B.C. Huygens, 2 vols (Turnhout, 1986), vol.i, pp. 114–17; Simon of Saint-Quentin, *Histoire des Tartares*, ed. J. Richard (Paris, 1965), pp. 62–86. See also G.G. Guzman, 'Simon of Saint Quentin as historian of the Mongols and the Seljuk Turks', *Medievalia et Humanistica* 3 (1972), 155–78, at 161–7; A.V. Murray, 'William of Tyre and the origin of the Turks: On the sources of the *Gesta Orientalium Principum*', in *Gesta Dei per Francos: Etudes sur les croisades dédiés à Jean Richard*, ed. M. Balard, B.Z. Kedar and J. Riley-Smith (Aldershot, 2001), pp. 217–29; Meserve, *Empires of Islam*, p. 150.

[19] T.S. Asbridge, *The First Crusade: A New History* (London, 2004), pp. 89–113.

[20] J.P. Philips, *The Second Crusade: Extending the Frontiers of Christendom* (London, 2007), pp. 177–84, 195–206; C.J. Tyerman, *God's War: A New History of the Crusades* (London, 2006), pp. 417–30.

between the Anatolian Turks and other Muslim groups, such as the Saracens (*Saraceni*), who occupied lands outside of Anatolia.[21] In fact, the Turk was occasionally described as a lesser kind of infidel in crusade chronicles, one who was sometimes praised in battle and whose character was preferred to the perfidious Greek or Saracen. One well-known example comes from the anonymous author of the *Gesta Francorum* who, when narrating the battle of Dorylaeum in 1097, commended the Turks for their military prowess and even compared their lineage to that of the Franks.[22] Similarly, the principal chronicler of the Second Crusade, Odo of Deuil, also commended the Turks on occasion, although this was often to emphasize the comparatively evil behaviour of the Byzantine Greeks, whom he blamed for the failure of the Second Crusade.[23]

In general, however, the reaction of the Latin writers towards the *Turchi* of the eleventh and twelfth centuries was overwhelmingly negative. They were usually labelled as pagans, heathens or idolaters, despite their mono-theist beliefs, and were condemned for the damage they inflicted on the crusader armies passing through Anatolia.[24] In the later fourteenth and fifteenth centuries, the use of the earlier crusades as a motif for inspiring a new crusade against the Ottoman Turks was a popular one, especially by Renaissance humanist writers who were keen to draw parallels between the two eras.[25] This was a method also adopted by some writers of the early fourteenth century. The crusade theorist William of Adam, for example, sought to justify his recommendation that a crusade should travel through Anatolia by stating that 'no crusade has ever been made in which the Turks did not attack our army'.[26] The anonymous author of the *Directorium ad Passagium Faciendum*, who was heavily influenced by William of Adam, also believed (mistakenly) that Peter the Hermit had easily subjugated the Turks on his way to Jerusalem, thus setting a precedent for his plan.[27] Still, apart from these writers, it is surprising to find that few other authors

[21] See, for example, *Gesta Francorum et Aliorum Hierosolimitanorum*, ed. and trans. R. Hill (London, 1962), pp. 18–21. However, it was still rare for other medieval chroniclers to make ethnic and geographic distinctions between different Muslim groups: J.V. Tolan, *Saracens: Islam in the Medieval European Imagination* (New York, 2002), pp. 105–34.

[22] *Gesta Francorum et Aliorum Hierosolimitanorum*, pp. 20–1.

[23] See, for example, Odo of Deuil, *De Profectione Ludovici VII in Orientem*, ed. and trans. V.G. Berry (New York, 1948), pp. 140–1.

[24] See, for example, Tolan, *Saracens*, pp. 105–34.

[25] Bisaha, *Creating East and West*, pp. 19–30; P. Orth, 'Papst Urbans II. Kreuzzugsrede in Clermont bei lateinischen Schriftstellern des 15. und 16. Jahrhunderts', in *Jerusalem im Hoch- und Spätmittelalter. Konflikte und Konfliktbewältigung – Vorstellungen und Vergegenwärtigungen*, ed. D. Bauer, K. Herbers and N. Jaspert (Frankfurt a. Main, 2001), pp. 367–405.

[26] William of Adam, *How To Defeat the Saracens*, p. 75.

[27] 'Directorium ad Passagium Faciendum', pp. 502–5; Leopold, *How To Recover the Holy Land*, pp. 149–50.

directly linked military action against the Anatolian beyliks in the fourteenth century to the famous conflicts between the Seljuks and the crusaders
in the eleventh and twelfth centuries, despite the clear parallels that existed
between them. Maybe writers of the fourteenth century were aware of the
differences between the beyliks and the Seljuks, even if they referred to them
both as *Turchi*.

In fact, the few sources which do mention the beyliks at the turn of the
fourteenth century, rather than describing them in terms of overt hostility,
instead refer to them as friends and allies, influenced by a mixture of admiration and political expediency, or, in the case of the papacy, with an attitude of ambivalence, stemming from a general ignorance of who the Turks
of the beyliks were and an underestimation of their military potential. In
these years, the focus of the crusading powers in western Europe was also
firmly set on those groups of the eastern Mediterranean which had previously been the target of a crusade, namely the Byzantine Greeks and the
Mamluks, with the result that the Turks were often regarded in a positive
light in comparison to these older and, seemingly more dangerous, foes.

A combination of these factors, and the underlying pragmatism of a mercenary company operating on the fringes of Christendom, helps to explain
the remarkably pro-Turkish attitude of the chronicler Ramon Muntaner, a
member of the Catalan Company who served in Anatolia during the early
1300s. The Catalans allied with a band of Anatolian warriors under the
command of a warlord known as Xemelic whom Muntaner remembered
with much fondness:

> [I]f ever any people have shown obedience to a lord, these Turks showed it
> to us; and if ever people had been loyal and true, these Turks were always so
> towards us. They were also very skilled at arms and in many other matters,
> and thus did they stay amongst us as brothers; and at all times did they form
> a separate army at our side.[28]

Of course Muntaner's views, although probably genuine, were heavily influenced by external political factors, not least his strong feelings of animosity
towards the Byzantines and their emperor, who he claimed had betrayed
the Catalan Company by killing their leader Roger of Flor. Although the
Catalans had avenged themselves on the empire, it is not surprising that
Muntaner, echoing Odo of Deuil some two centuries earlier, portrayed the
Turks as worthy adversaries in contrast to the Greeks, whom he considered
to be the real enemies of his people. Nevertheless, on reading Muntaner's
account, one is left with an impression of the author's genuine regard for the
Turks, even during the periods at which the Catalans were engaged in war
with them; proof that relationships between different cultural groups in the

---

[28] Ramon Muntaner, *The Catalan Expedition to the East*, p. 110.

eastern Mediterranean were as often divided along the lines of pragmatism as along those of faith.

A similar viewpoint is also provided by the early work of Marino Sanudo, someone who like Muntaner had first-hand experience of the East, but was writing about the beyliks from a far more detached perspective. Sanudo's point of view is especially important because he had spent much of his life travelling in the eastern Mediterranean and later advising the papacy and the nobility of western Europe on the best way to liberate the Holy Land.[29] In his proposal for a crusade against Mamluk Egypt, found in book two of the *Liber Secretorum Fidelium Crucis*, written in 1312–13, Sanudo advocated a deal in which the crusaders could enter into friendly negotiations with the Turks of the Asia Minor littoral (*Turchis qui morantur in Turchiae maritima*). In particular, he believed that the crusaders could purchase provisions and war materials from the beyliks of Karaman, Hamid and Menteshe, who occupied the southern coast from the ports of Candelore to Makre (*Clandeloro usque Macrum*).[30] Sanudo was probably influenced by Venetian merchants in the Aegean, who had been intermittently trading with the Turks of these regions, in particular from Makre, which was part of the Menteshe principality by that time.[31] His proposal is interesting on two accounts: first, in the context of the period, Sanudo is unusual in specifying which Turks the crusaders should deal with. As shall be seen, papal sources were very vague in this regard and even the Venetian archives more often refer to *Turchi* and *Turchia* without any further elaboration. Secondly, as someone familiar with both eastern Mediterranean and European politics, Sanudo was especially well placed to judge how the Turks could fit into attempts to liberate the Holy Land. In this sense, his opinions must be taken as representative of those who were trading in the Levant, even if his idea of an alliance with the beyliks gained no particular support in the papal curia or other European courts at the time.

The views of the papacy towards the Turks in these early years, although never as positive as those expressed by Muntaner and Sanudo, still shared the common belief that the Greeks and Mamluks were the real enemies of the Roman Church in the East. Consequently, papal sources remain surprisingly ambivalent, and also ambiguous, in their representations of the Turks, especially in comparison to the Byzantine Greeks who remained the principal target of a crusade in the Aegean region. Although it is fair to say that the *Turchi* found in papal documents in these early years – being infidels – were never looked upon in a positive manner by the popes,

---

[29] On Sanudo's life, see Marino Sanudo, *Book of the Secrets*, trans. Lock, pp. 1–20.

[30] Marino Sanudo, 'Liber Secretorum', p. 67; Lock trans., p. 117.

[31] See, for example, *Pietro Pizolo, notaio in Candia*, ed. S. Carbone, 2 vols (Venice, 1978–85), vol. 1, pp. 70–1 doc. 141, pp. 139–40, doc. 293, vol. 2, pp. 114, doc. 936, pp. 159–60, doc. 1040, p. 161, doc. 1042; Zachariadou, *Trade and Crusade*, pp. 3–7.

they were rarely represented in distinct terms and were clearly not regarded as an important component of crusade preaching. Take, for example, the planned French and Angevin crusades to Greece and Constantinople in the early fourteenth century, which dominated crusade negotiations during the pontificates of Popes Benedict XI and Clement V.[32] These expeditions were being planned at a time when the papacy and other western powers were well aware of Turkish incursions into Byzantine-ruled Asia Minor, yet they remained strictly crusades against the Byzantine Greeks, with the aim of re-establishing the Latin empire and paving the way for a later expedition to the Holy Land. This is illustrated by the crusade bulls issued for these missions which justified them on the grounds that the Greek emperor and his people were schismatics and usurpers of the imperial throne. The crusade army would thus be used specifically to liberate Greece and Constantinople, with indulgences only being granted to those who fought against the Byzantines and not the Turks, to whom no reference is made.[33]

Still the proposed crusades against the Byzantine empire do mark the first important step in the evolution of a more hostile perception of the Turks in western literature, one in which *Turchi* began to feature in the papal crusading documents, even though these promoted expeditions overwhelmingly anti-Greek in focus and justification. Evidence of this can be found in the acknowledgement of the Turkish threat to Christian lands in two bulls issued in connection with the crusade of Charles of Valois in 1304 and 1306. In these documents the pope called on the crusaders to seize Constantinople from the weakened Greek emperor, in case it should fall to the Turks:

> If (which God forbid!) it should happen that that same empire fell to the Turks and other Saracens and infidels, by whom the said Andronikos is being continually attacked, it would not thereafter be easy to rescue [the empire] from the hands of those same peoples. O what serious danger and huge confusion the whole Roman mother Church and the whole Christian religion would suffer if (which may God avert!) such a loss were to occur![34]

In a letter asking Venice to join the expedition, Clement V even stated that the 'souls of the Parthians or the Turks' would be broken at the appearance of the crusading armies.[35] This acknowledgement of the danger posed by

---

[32] These projects are discussed in more detail in Chapter 3, pp. 28–30.

[33] *Le registre de Benoit XI*, ed. C. Grandjean, Bibliothèque des Écoles françaises d'Athènes et de Rome (Paris, 1903), docs 1006–8; Clement V, *Regestum*, vol. 1, docs 243–8, vol. 7, doc. 7893, these indulgences are discussed in more detail in Chapter 5 (pp. 108–9). For a background of justifications for crusading against the Greeks see Chrissis, *Crusading in Frankish Greece*; Chrissis, 'New frontiers', pp. 17–41.

[34] *Le registre de Benoit XI*, doc. 1006; Clement V, *Regestum*, vol. 1, doc. 243.

[35] Clement V, *Regestum*, vol. 1, doc. 248. According to Laiou, an equivalent letter sent by the pope to Genoa made far more of the Turkish threat to the Byzantine empire than that sent to Venice: Laiou, *Constantinople and the Latins*, pp. 204–5. However, her references are

the Anatolian beyliks is important because it suggests that the papacy was willing to sanction a crusade against the Greeks as a means of defending Christian lands in the East from the Turks; a wholly original justification for a crusade against the Byzantine empire and a sign of the growing threat of the Anatolian beyliks, both in the Aegean region and in the consciousness of western Europe.

The same justification of protecting eastern Christians from the Turks was also probably used by Charles of Valois in an alliance he attempted to form with Greek rebels in 1307. These rebels were natives of Asia Minor and their letters to Charles reflect the need of a strong outside ruler to defend the eastern borders of the empire from the Turkish onslaught.[36] Unfortunately, the responses of Charles to the rebels do not survive, but the negotiations are nevertheless evidence that a crusade to recover Constantinople could be promoted as a mission to defend eastern Christians from the advances of the Turks.

This method of using the threat posed by the Anatolian beyliks to justify a campaign against Greeks can also be found during the Hospitaller conquest of Rhodes, where once again, Greek territories were the primary target, but in which *Turchi* also featured. Although the Hospitaller campaigns were almost certainly not envisaged by the pope as a means of defending the Latins of the Aegean from the Anatolian beyliks, some evidence of anti-Turkish motivations in the sources do exist, usually justified along the lines they had colluded with Greek 'schismatics'.[37] For example, contemporary accounts stated that the island was inhabited by the 'impious Turks' who were living there under the rule of the emperor of Constantinople.[38] Similarly, a papal document of 1307 confirming the possession of Rhodes to the Hospitallers also made mention of the 'schismatics and infidels' who

---

unclear and the manuscripts she cites do not seem to show this: Paris, Archives Nationales, J509, docs 16, 16bis.

[36] Laiou, *Constantinople and the Latins*, pp. 212–20; Boojamra, 'Athanasios of Constantinople', 38–9. The relevant letters are published in H. Moranvillé, 'Les projets de Charles de Valois sur l'Empire de Constantinople', *Bibliothèque de l'École des chartes* 51 (1890), 63–86, at 82–6; Laiou, *Constantinople and the Latins*, Appendix II, pp. 341–3; summaries in C. du F. Du Cange, *Histoire de l'Empire de Constantinople sous les empereurs français jusqu'à la conquête des turcs*, ed. J.A. Buchon, 2 vols (Paris, 1826), vol. 2, p. 344, doc. 22.

[37] Collaboration with enemies of the faith as a justification for a crusade could cut both ways. For example, crusades against the Byzantines had often been justified on the grounds that they had colluded with the infidel, see J. Harris, 'Collusion with the infidel as a pretext for western military action against Byzantium (1180–1204)', in *Languages of Love and Hate: Conflict, Communication and Identity in the Medieval Mediterranean*, ed. S. Lambert and H. Nicholson (Turnhout, 2012), pp. 99–117.

[38] See Bernard Gui, 'E Floribus Chronicorum (Quarta Vita)', in *Vita Paparum Avenionensium*, ed. S. Baluze and G. Mollat, 4 vols (Paris, 1914), vol. 1, pp. 59–80, at pp. 62–9; Amalric Auger, 'Actus Romanorum Pontificum (Sexta Vita)', in *Vita Paparum Avenionensium*, ed. S. Baluze and G. Mollat, 4 vols (Paris, 1914), vol. 1, pp. 89–106, at p. 93.

opposed the Order during the invasion.[39] It is unlikely that the Turks had actually settled on Rhodes before 1306, but they had raided the island in the late thirteenth and early fourteenth centuries and some were employed by the Greeks to garrison the fortress of Phileremos in preparation for the Hospitaller invasion.[40] These references highlight the increasing threat which the maritime beyliks posed to the islands of the eastern Aegean by 1306; a situation recognized by Master Fulk of Villaret who tried unsuccessfully to negotiate a treaty by which the Hospitallers could hold Rhodes as subjects of the Greek empire on condition that they defended it from Turkish attack.[41]

The Maritime Beyliks as the *inimicus Christi* in the Aegean

Up until this stage, with the exception of the first-hand accounts of Muntaner and Sanudo, the western image of the Turks was a hazy one, particularly that expressed in papal sources. However, after the Hospitaller conquest of Rhodes, which brought the Order into contact with the Anatolian beyliks and soon led to conflicts with Menteshe and later Aydin, the image of the Turks came more sharply into focus in European literature as individual emirs and dynasties began to emerge slowly from the indistinct references to *Turchi* found in earlier sources. As this image became more defined, the instances where the Turks were condemned for colluding with the Greeks also decreased, as the Anatolian beyliks began to transform exclusively into the new 'enemy' in the East in contrast to the Greeks who began to be considered as an ally.

The first example of this came in 1311, in a papal letter dispatched to Genoa, where Pope Clement V revealed that certain Genoese traders operating in the Aegean had allied themselves with *Madachia*, a powerful Turkish lord, and had paid him 50,000 gold florins to make various assaults on the newly established Knights Hospitallers on Rhodes.[42] A few months after the letter was dispatched, envoys reported to the pope at the Council of Vienne that the Order had defeated a Turkish fleet at Amorgos, probably sent by

---

[39] Clement V, *Regestum*, vol. 2, doc. 2148.

[40] *Cronaca del Templare di Tiro: 1243–1314*, ed. L. Minervini (Naples, 2000), p. 326; A.T. Luttrell, *The Town of Rhodes: 1306–1356* (Rhodes, 2003), p. 76.

[41] George Pachymeres, *Relations historiques*, vol. 4, bk. 13, ch. 33, pp. 698–701; A.T. Luttrell, 'The Hospitallers of Rhodes confront the Turks: 1306–1421', in *Christians, Jews and Other Worlds: Patterns of Conflict and Accommodation: the Avery Lectures in History*, ed. P.F. Gallagher (Lanham, 1988), pp. 80–116, at p. 83 (repr. in Idem, *The Hospitallers of Rhodes and Their Mediterranean World*, Variorum Reprints (Aldershot, 1992), I).

[42] Clement V, *Regestum*, vol. 7, doc. 7631, cf. doc. 7632. See also A.T. Luttrell, 'The Genoese at Rhodes: 1306–1312', in *Oriente e Occidente tra Medioevo ed età moderna: studi in onore di Geo Pistarino*, ed. L. Balletto, 2 vols (Genoa, 1997), vol. 1, pp. 743–61, at pp. 758–9 (repr. in Idem, *The Hospitaller State on Rhodes and its Western Provinces, 1306–1462*, Variorum Reprints (Aldershot, 1999), I).

this same *Madachia*.[43] A year after this, in 1313, Master Fulk of Villaret claimed in a document that the Knights had captured a number of fortresses in *Turchia*, most likely in the coastal lands belonging to this *Madachia*.[44] The Turkish lord was Masud, the emir of Menteshe. His naming in the letter is the first specific reference to an emir of the fourteenth-century Anatolian beyliks in a papal document and one of the first to be found in any source of western European origin.[45]

The letter and the subsequent communications over the conflict between Masud and the Hospitallers are especially important as they reveal a network of international correspondence stretching between the Latin Aegean powers and the papacy which helped to shape a new image of the Turks. At the time of these events, the pope was presiding over the Council of Vienne – one of the greatest ecclesiastical gatherings of its day. This was crucial as the Council was called primarily to suppress the Knights Templars, who had been arrested in France and put on trial on the orders of Philip IV in 1307.[46] Despite protestations from the pope, Philip had pressured the papacy to condemn the Order and to ensure that Templar goods in France were transferred to the French Crown. At the Council of Vienne Clement resisted calls to condemn the Templars, but instead agreed to suppress the

[43] The battle at Amorgos is also discussed in Chapter 4 (pp. 88–91). It is reported in H. Finke, *Papsttum und Untergang des Templerordens*, 2 vols (Münster, 1907), vol. 2, pp. 298–302, doc. 146; *Chroniques d'Amadi et de Strambaldi*, ed. R. de Mas Latrie, 2 vols (Paris, 1891–3), vol. 1, p. 391.

[44] The letter is published in A.T. Luttrell, 'Feudal tenure and Latin colonization at Rhodes', *The English Historical Review* 85 (1970), 755–75, at 757, 771–3 (repr. in Idem, *The Hospitallers in Cyprus, Rhodes, Greece, and the West, 1291–1440: Collected Studies*, Variorum Reprints (Aldershot, 1978), III). The capture of castles in Turkey is also mentioned in various versions of the *Brief Lives of the Masters of the Hospital*, see A.T. Luttrell, 'Notes on Foulques de Villaret, Master of the Hospital 1305–1319', in *Guillaume de Villaret, 1er recteur du Comtat-Venaissin 1274, Grand Maître de l'Ordre des hospitaliers de Saint-Jean de Jerusalem, Chypre 1296* (Paris, 1985), pp. 73–90, at pp. 82–7 (repr. in Idem, *The Hospitallers of Rhodes and their Mediterranean World*, Variorum Reprints (Aldershot, 1992), IV) and also by Ludolf of Sudheim, who claims that the Hospitallers had also forced the Menteshe Turks to pay them tribute: Ludolph of Sudheim, 'De itinere Terre Sancte', ed. G.A. Neumann, in *Archives de l'Orient Latin*, 2 vols (Paris, 1881–4), vol. 2, part 2, pp. 305–77, at p. 331–2; Stewart trans., pp. 34–7; Luttrell, *Town of Rhodes*, pp. 214–19.

[45] Other early references to the Anatolian emirs include Ramon Muntaner, who mentions the beyliks of *Sesa* (Sasa or Karaman) and *Tin* (Aydin) and Marino Sanudo, in his *Istoria*, who talks of Masud and two of his sons Orkhan and *Strumbrachi*. However, these accounts were written some years after the death of Masud, unlike the papal letter of 1311: Ramon Muntaner, *The Catalan Expedition to the East*, p. 55; Marino Sanudo, *Istoria di Romania*, p. 209.

[46] On the trial of the Templars, see M. Barber, *The Trial of the Templars*, 2nd edition (Cambridge, 2006).

Order and to transfer its goods to the Hospitallers.[47] The events of the Council were thus of direct relevance to the Hospitallers, who were eager to demonstrate that they were actively defending the faith overseas. Bearing this in mind, it seems likely that Fulk of Villaret deliberately portrayed the defence of the Aegean against the Anatolian beyliks – of which Masud was the main protagonist – as the new *raison d'être* of the Hospital. Indeed the dates of the reports from the Rhodes support this. The Hospitaller emissaries who first reported the Menteshe–Genoese alliance to the pope, did so during the opening weeks of the Council, probably in October or November 1311. Similarly, a crusade proposal from King Hugh of Cyprus, which also mentioned the Genoese conflict with the Hospital, reached the pope while he was at Vienne in 1311.[48] Finally, and most crucially, the report of the Hospitaller victory over Masud's fleet off Amorgos in early 1312 was delivered to the pope on or just before 22 April – barely twenty days after the Templars had been suppressed, and just ten days before the decision was made to transfer the goods of the Temple to the Hospital.[49]

The Council of Vienne therefore gave the Hospitallers a pan-European audience and meant that the key players in a crusade were all aware of the conflict between Menteshe and the Order. Representatives were invited to the Council from all over western Christendom: from Italy, France, Germany, the Iberian Peninsula, the British Isles, Scandinavia and Eastern Europe.[50] The sources mentioning the conflict between Masud and the Hospitallers reflect this international scope – they include papal letters dispatched to Genoa, Cyprus and Rhodes, an Aragonese ambassador's report, and a French chronicle written on Cyprus. Consequently, what may have previously been regarded as a trivial and obscure conflict between the Hospitallers and a little-known beylik, was in fact blown into international significance by the crucial role it played in ensuring the future of the Order at the Council of Vienne. The repeated references to Masud and Menteshe during such a momentous occasion thus helped to raise the profile of the Turks within the collective consciousness of western Christendom at this time.

The feelings of trepidation towards the Turks fostered during the Council of Vienne were further augmented a few years later by the first reports of Turkish raids on Venetian colonies in the Aegean and Greece, which reached the mother-city with increasing frequency after the summer of 1318. From this point, defending the Republic's possessions from these attacks became

---

[47] N.P. Tanner, *Decrees of the Ecumenical Councils: Nicaea I to Vatican II*, 2 vols (London, 1990), vol. 1, pp. 333–5.

[48] See M.L. de Mas Latrie, *Histoire de l'île de Chypre sous le regne des princes de la maison de Lusignan*, 3 vols (Paris, 1852–61), vol. 2, pp. 118–25, esp. 119–20.

[49] Luttrell, 'The Hospitallers of Rhodes confront the Turks', pp. 85–6; Barber, *The Trial of the Templars*, pp. 270–2.

[50] See Barber, *The Trial of the Templars*, p. 221.

a common topic of debate in the Senate and Great Council, the archives of which provide a vivid testimony to the threat which the maritime beyliks now posed to Venetian colonies and trade in the region. In one letter, dated June 1318, the duke of Crete wrote to the doge with alarm that the Turks, in alliance with the Catalans of Athens, had inflicted 'damage, depredation and much plunder on the islands of the Archipelago', including a raid on Santorini where 'many beasts and other things' had been seized, and the sack of Karpathos where a fleet of sixteen armed ships had captured around three hundred men and animals and taken them back to Asia Minor.[51] The perpetrators of these raids are not identified specifically in the sources; they are referred to as indistinct *Turchi*, originating from *Turchia*, with no reference to a particular Turkish lord, unlike the Hospitaller reports of Masud. Still, judging from a letter from the duke of Crete – which commented that the Turks in question had broken a treaty by attacking Venetian possessions, probably in reference to a previous trade agreement between Crete and Menteshe – it is reasonable to assume that the Turks in this instance were from Menteshe as well.[52] Also, it may be the case that *Turchia* in this instance was understood to mean more specifically the regions of Menteshe, as was the case in Venetian and Cretan administrative documents written twenty years later.[53] On many occasions, however, the identity of the Turks would have been hard to determine for the Venetian authorities as they originated from various regions of Anatolia and were not affiliated to one particular beylik; it is known that many Turks were shipped across the Aegean by the Catalans to serve with them against the Venetians and others launched raids on their own volition, thus partly explaining the generic allusions to 'Turks' and to 'Turkey' in the Venetian sources.[54]

The same ambiguity is not found in the next major encounter, this time between the Latin rulers of the eastern Aegean islands of Chios and Rhodes (the Genoese Zaccaria family and the Hospitallers) and the Turks of Ephesos (i.e. Aydin). The first conflicts occurred towards the end of the second decade of the century, especially in 1319 when a sizeable Turkish fleet from Ephesos was defeated by an allied Hospitaller and Zaccaria force. Two letters survive written to the pope reporting the Christian victory, one by the captain of the Hospitaller fleet, Albert of Schwarzburg, and the other by

---

[51] *DVL*, vol. 1, doc. 61; *DOC*, doc. 96, see also *DVL*, vol. 1, doc. 63; *DOC*, docs 98, 101; Zachariadou, 'The Catalans of Athens', 826–9.

[52] See Zachariadou, 'The Catalans of Athens', 825–6.

[53] See Zachariadou, *Trade and Crusade*, pp. 118–19.

[54] See, for example, *DOC*, doc. 98, where it is reported that two Turkish ambassadors will be taken to Turkey by the Catalans to recruit a number of Turks: *habuimus etiam per ipsam fidedignam personam quod armatur Athenis etiam unum aliud lignum quod deferre debet duos ambaxatores ipsius domini Alfonsi [...] cum duobus ambaxatoribus Turchorum in Turchiam, qui vadunt pro accipiendo Turchos in bona quantitate, a mille usque ad mille et quingentos.*

the temporary governor of the Order overseas, the papal *vicarius* Gerard of Pins. These letters provide a remarkable account of events: they describe in detail the preparations of the Hospitallers and the Zaccaria after they had heard of news from Ephesos; the tense waiting game once the Turks had set sail from the port; and the final encounter in the waters off Chios. Here, after a hard-fought battle lasting the whole day, the Christians emerged victorious, apparently killing or wounding over two thousand Turks and destroying twenty of their ships with only a handful escaping in the night.[55]

As was the case with the Hospitaller victories over Masud, the news of this battle spread rapidly throughout Christendom. It reached Florence where the chronicler Giovanni Villani wrote of a Turkish admiral attacking Rhodes, and also Cyprus, where it featured in an anonymous sixteenth-century Italian source, probably an adaptation of a contemporary French original.[56] Other victories won by the Zaccaria over the Turks also began to reach western Europe in these years, further fuelling the growing awareness and trepidation of the emerging maritime beyliks. This is demonstrated by the garbled references to their exploits in a diverse variety of sources, such as in the crusade treatise of William of Adam. He makes numerous mentions of the lords of Chios, at one point writing that without their vigorous persecution of the Turks 'no man, woman, dog, cat, or any living creature' could remain on any of the nearby islands.[57] This was a view mirrored by Marino Sanudo and the author of the *Directorium ad Passagium Faciendum*, as well as the Anonimo Romano who later wrote that Martino Zaccaria was a 'noble and talented master of war'.[58] Even the German pilgrim Ludolf of Sudheim, who journeyed through the East between 1336 and 1341, wrote of Martino Zaccaria (*Nycolao de Sya*) sailing to the rescue of a Hospitaller force stranded on Kos (*Lango*) and killing over six thousand Turks on the island.[59] Contemporary Greek writers and a later Ottoman source also allude to these

[55] Delaville le Roulx, *Hospitaliers à Rhodes*, pp. 365–7, doc. 2; Gatto, 'Martino Zaccaria', 337–9, doc. 1. For more on this battle, see Chapter 4, pp. 88–9, and also Carr, 'Trade or crusade?', pp. 122–5.

[56] Giovanni Villani, *Nuova cronica*, vol. 2, bk. 10, ch. 120, p. 323; *Chroniques d'Amadi et de Strambaldi*, vol. 1, p. 400. These accounts of the battle vary slightly from those given in the letters, but they probably refer to the same event, see Carr, 'Trade or crusade?', pp. 123–5.

[57] William of Adam, *How To Defeat the Saracens*, pp. 53–5, 65–7, 81.

[58] Marino Sanudo, 'Epistolae', in *Gesta Dei per Francos*, ed. J. Bongars, 2 vols (Hannover, 1611; repr. Jerusalem, 1972), vol. 2, pp. 289–316, at pp. 297–8 (letter 5); Roddy trans., pp. 156–60 (letter 15); 'Directorium ad Passagium Faciendum', pp. 457–8; Anonimo Romano, *Cronica*, p. 74.

[59] Ludolph of Sudheim, 'De itinere Terre Sancte', p. 333; Luttrell, *Town of Rhodes*, pp. 214–15.

encounters; a testament to their importance and their widespread dissemination at the time.[60]

An Aegean Legend: Umur Pasha and His Impact in the West

The account of Ibn Battuta given at the start of this chapter provides a vivid confirmation of the growth in confidence and authority of the Turkish maritime beyliks, demonstrated in particular by the Aydin-oglu Mehmed beg who, as seen earlier, had launched numerous raids from his ports into the heart of Venetian, Hospitaller and Genoese territories. After the capture of Chios by the Byzantines in 1329, which was followed by the seizure of the harbour-fortress at Smyrna from the Genoese, the fleets of Aydin were able to launch raids into the Aegean with even more regularity and destructiveness.[61] The situation became so desperate that by April 1332 the duke of Naxos, Niccolò Sanudo, had concluded a treaty with the Aydin Turks.[62] Two months later, in June, the Venetian Senate discussed whether Negroponte as well should conclude 'some arrangement with the Turks'.[63] These were undoubtedly those of Aydin as it is known from a later Ottoman source that the island became a tributary of the Aydin-oglus later in that year.[64]

At this point, the Cretan authorities also consulted the Knights Hospitaller about the possibility of forming an alliance with rival Turkish emirs against Aydin. In one instance, it was suggested that an agreement should be formed with Orkhan of Menteshe (*Orchani Turcus*), and in another it was recommended that the Venetians ally themselves with *Carmignanus*, the emir of Germiyan or possibly Karaman.[65] The Venetian government, the *Serenissima*, even wrote to the pope about the inability of the Turks to unite in defence of themselves: 'although the power of the perfidious Turks is great, nevertheless there are several Turkish states in those regions, of which each one is distinct from the others, and one could not quickly render aid

---

[60] See, for example, Nikephoros Gregoras, *Byzantina Historia*, vol. 1, bk. 8, ch. 10, p. 438; Enveri, *Le destān d'Umūr Pacha*, pp. 51, 55–6.

[61] See Lemerle, *L'émirat d'Aydin*, pp. 56–9; H. Inalcik, 'The rise of the Turkish maritime principalities in Anatolia, Byzantium and the Crusades', *Byzantinische Forschungen* 9 (1985), 179–217, at 190–1.

[62] ASVen, *Misti del Senato*, reg. 15, fol. 7 (2 Apr 1332); summary in Thiriet, *Sénat*, vol. 1, doc. 2.

[63] ASVen, *Misti del Senato*, reg. 15, fol. 17v (13 Jun 1332); R.-J. Loenertz, *Les Ghisi: Dynastes vénitiens dans l'Archipel, 1207–1390* (Florence, 1975), doc. 39, pp. 213–4; Thiriet, *Sénat*, vol. 1, doc. 15.

[64] Enveri, *Le destān d'Umūr Pacha*, pp. 69–73 (verses 599–744, esp. 685–90). The baillie Petro Zeno agreed to pay a tax to Umur: *Il s'engagea à payer le harac* (verse 689).

[65] ASVen, *Misti del Senato*, reg. 16, fols 38v–39v, 43 (November–December 1333); Theotokes, *Thespismata*, vol. 2.1., pp. 129–30, 138, docs 13, 23; summaries in Thiriet, *Sénat*, vol. 1, docs 38–9; Zachariadou, *Trade and Crusade*, p. 28.

to another'.[66] Nevertheless, the divisions amongst the Turks did little to dampen the concern over the threat which they posed, as was expressed in numerous papal letters written in these years, which demonstrate that the Turks could no longer be easily subjugated.[67] Marino Sanudo confirmed the danger which the beyliks now posed and went so far as to warn that they were on the brink of expanding into the Adriatic Sea and the European kingdoms beyond.[68] Even Giovanni Villani, writing in Florence at the time, commented on the tribute being exacted by the Turks on the Latins in the Aegean.[69] By the early 1340s they had reduced many more of the Aegean islands to tributary status and had devastated Thrace, Macedonia, central Greece and the Peloponnese.[70]

By this time, the former Byzantine port-cities of Smyrna and Ephesos, where many raids were launched from, had grown into prosperous trade centres under the house of Aydin.[71] Greek slaves were numerous and cheap in these markets, whilst the cost of Turkish slaves in the region had rock-eted because of their comparative scarcity.[72] Two western pilgrims, William of Boldensele and Ludolf of Sudheim, who journeyed in the East between 1335 and 1341 both commented on the wealth and prosperity of Ephesos and its Turkish inhabitants, in contrast to the impoverished Christian minority who still resided there.[73] Another eyewitness, Matthew, the Orthodox arch-

---

[66] *DVL*, vol. 1, doc. 124; Setton, *Papacy and the Levant*, vol. 1, pp. 181–2.

[67] For example John XXII, *Lettres secrètes*, vol. 4, docs 5207, 5247, 5269–76, 5324, 5329, 5404, 5423, 5429, 5438, 5442, 5485, 5486, 5495. See also *DVL*, vol. 1, doc. 115; *AE*, vol. 24, pp. 292–3, ch. 31, pp. 499–500, ch. 22–4, pp. 511–14, ch. 13–16; vol. 25, pp. 7–11, ch. 3–5.

[68] Writing to Bertrand, the bishop of Ostia and papal legate, in 1330: Kunstmann, 'Studien über Marino Sanudo', 755–89 (letter 2); Roddy trans., pp. 222–70 (letter 30). Sanudo expressed his concerns over the Turkish incursions in many other letters, for example, 'Epistolae', ed. Bongars, pp. 291–4, 297–8, 304–7, 312–16 (letters 3, 5, 16, 20–3); A. Cerlini, 'Nuovo lettere di Marino Sanudo il vecchio', *La bibliofilia* 42 (1940), 321–59, at 349–54 (letter 2); Kunstmann, 'Studien über Marino Sanudo', 791–813 (letters 5–7); C.B. de la Roncière and L. Dorez, 'Lettres inédites et mémoires de Marino Sanudo l'ancien (1334–1337)', *Bibliothèque de l'École des chartes* 56 (1895) 21–44, at 43–4 (letter 9); Roddy trans., letters 7, 15, 18, 23, 26–8, 33–5, 42.

[69] Giovanni Villani also recounted the same event but without distinguishing who the Turks were: *Nuova cronica*, vol. 2, bk. 2, ch, 201, p. 765.

[70] John Kantakouzenos, *Ioannis Cantacuzeni eximperatoris Historiarum libri IV*, vol. 1, bk. 2, ch. 38, p. 537; Nikephoros Gregoras, *Byzantina Historia*, vol. 2, bk. 12, ch. 7, p. 597.

[71] See C. Foss, *Ephesus after Antiquity: A Late Antique, Byzantine and Turkish City* (Cambridge, 1979), pp. 144–5; Pryor, *Geography, Technology and War*, pp. 170–2.

[72] Ibn Battuta, *The Travels*, vol. 2, pp. 444–5. See also Fleet, *European and Islamic Trade in the Early Ottoman State*, p. 49.

[73] William of Boldensele, 'Des Edelherrn Wilhelm von Boldensele Reise nach dem gelobten Lande', in *Die Edelherren von Boldensele oder Boldensen*, ed. C.L. Gotefend (Hannover, 1855), pp. 18–78, pp. 31–3; Ludolf of Sudheim, 'De itinere Terre Sancte', p. 33; Stewart trans., pp. 30–1.

THE TURKS AS A 'TARGET' OF CRUSADE 51

bishop of Ephesos, remarked on the extensive size of Smyrna which he said provided the ideal refuge for pirates.[74] In economic terms Aydin was booming at this time; coins were struck at Ephesos for the first time in a thousand years and the beylik regularly featured in the trading manual of Florentine merchant Francesco Pegolotti, one of the first European commentators to provide specific information about trade with the Anatolian principalities.[75] He described the weights and measures used by the Aydin-oglus and compared them to those used in Italy and the Aegean islands. From his handbook it is known that at Altoluogo, an Italian name for Ephesos, the Turks sold raw materials, such as alum, grain and rice, and bought finished products, especially dyed European fabrics of azure, vermillion and emerald.[76]

Although the reign of Mehmed Beg saw the establishment of Aydin as a major Anatolian power, it was his son Umur Pasha, famed for his audacious attacks on the Latins in the Aegean, who became regarded as the greatest Turkish warrior of his generation. Umur's exploits became so legendary that an epic poem was written documenting his life, probably reproduced from a lost contemporary source in around 1465 by the Ottoman poet-chronicler Enveri. His *Düstūrnāme*, or 'Book of the Grand Vizier', was dedicated to Mahmud Pasha, the grand vizier of Mehmed the Conqueror and contains a whole section (Book 18) devoted to Umur's heroic exploits against the Franks.[77] In it the emir is depicted as a brave jihad warrior, commanding a warship named *Gāzī*, who wrought terrible afflictions on the Latins of the Aegean.[78] One particular passage gives a dramatic example of how many Turks during Umur's lifetime and afterwards regarded his feats:

---

[74] Matthew, Archbishop of Ephesus, *Die Briefe des Matthaios von Ephesos im Codex Vindobonensis Theol. Gr. 174*, ed. D. Reinsch (Berlin, 1974), p. 344. For more on Matthew and his visit to Smyrna and Ephesos, see Vryonis Jr., *The Decline of Medieval Hellenism*, pp. 342–8.

[75] The coins were Latin imitations, a silver coin minted in Ephesos was modelled on the *gigliati* of Robert of Naples. Similar coins were also struck by the emirs of Sarukhan and Menteshe: Foss, *Ephesus after Antiquity*, pp. 150–1; J.T. Wood, *Discoveries at Ephesus: Including the Site and Remains of the Great Temple of Diana* (London, 1877), pp. 181–3.

[76] Francesco Balducci Pegolotti, *La Pratica Della Mercatura*, pp. 55–7, 92, 104, 367–70; *Medieval Trade in the Mediterranean World: Illustrative Documents*, ed. and trans. R. Lopez, and I.W. Raymond (New York, 1967), pp. 353–5.

[77] The author followed closely the lost work of Hadji Selman, who may have been a contemporary of Umur and perhaps a comrade-in-arms: Enveri, *Le destān d'Umūr Pacha*, pp. 27–33; Lemerle, *L'émirat d'Aydin*, p. 9.

[78] Enveri, *Le destān d'Umūr Pacha*, pp. 52–5 (verses 145–224); Kafadar, *Between the Two Worlds*, pp. 78–80; E.A. Zachariadou, 'Holy war in the Aegean during the fourteenth century', in *Latins and Greeks in the Eastern Mediterranean after 1204*, ed. B. Arbel, B. Hamilton and D. Jacoby (London, 1989), pp. 212–25, at pp. 219–20 (repr. in Idem, *Studies in pre-Ottoman Turkey and the Ottomans* (Aldershot, 2007), XVII).

Arriving in Izmir, the Pasha [Umur] planned a new holy war.
He prepared to fight day and night. For which the Lord was pleased.
He still wished to see his sword shedding blood,
he still wished to make his enemies groan,
he even wished to boil the sea
and to make his horse leap into the country of the Franks.[79]

Such were his deeds that the cult of Umur, which sprung up after his death and was especially promoted by the Ottomans, continued amongst Turkish sailors of the Aegean for many centuries.[80] Even the Byzantine contemporary Nikephoros Gregoras awarded Umur the highest praise by stating that he was more civilized than barbarian and possessed some Hellenic culture.[81] The appearance of Umur in such a work as the *Düstūrnāme* is a testament to his reputation as a *gāzī* warrior as held by the Ottoman sultans of the late fifteenth century. In a similar manner, the *türbe* (tomb) of the emirs of Aydin at Birgi contains a dedication to Mehmed Beg, dated to 1334, which reads 'This turbeh has been constructed for the Grand-Emir, the wise, the warlike, the defender of the faith, the founder of pious works, the Sultan of the Gāzīs, Murbāriz ed-duala wa'd-dīn Muhammed b. Aydin – may God enlighten his resting place!'.[82] This too has been used to provide further confirmation of the *gāzī* ethos of the House of Aydin.[83]

In the end, Umur's aggression triggered the Crusade of Smyrna, a response from the Latins which became as legendary as the emir's original deeds. For the most part the Crusade was a success, as it managed to restrict the piratical activities of Aydin and eventually led to the death of Umur in 1348. The Crusade captured the imagination of contemporaries. It featured in a number of northern Italian chronicles as well as a host of miracle stories and other apocrypha which circulated in the West at the time.[84] It was also recounted on occasion in the writings of the French knight Philippe de

[79] Enveri, *Le destān d'Umūr Pacha*, p. 55 (verses 225–35).

[80] Kafadar, *Between the Two Worlds*, p. 69.

[81] Nikephoros Gregoras, *Byzantina Historia*, vol. 2, bk. 13, ch. 4, pp. 649–50; D.M. Nicol, *The Reluctant Emperor: A Biography of John Cantacuzene, Byzantine Emperor and Monk, c.1295–1383* (Cambridge, 1996), pp. 34–5. Umur Pasha was, however, understandably vilified in the pro–Latin speech of Demetrius Kydones, written in 1366, who wrote of the emir that 'while living, no evil was unexpected': J. Ryder, 'Demetrius Kydones' "History of the Crusades": reality or rhetoric?', in *Contact and Conflict in Frankish Greece and the Aegean*, ed. M. Carr and N.G. Chrissis (Farnham, 2014), p. 105.

[82] P. Wittek, 'Turkish architecture in southwestern Anatolia. Part II', *Art Studies* (1931), 173–212, at 201; Riefstahl, *Turkish Architecture in Southwestern Anatolia*, p. 105.

[83] The most famous example being that by Wittek, *The Rise of the Ottoman Empire*, pp. 33–7; ed. Heywood, pp. 56–9.

[84] See, for example, Giovanni Villani, *Nuova cronica*, vol. 3, bk. 13, ch. 39, pp. 390–1; 'Cronica di Bologna', in *RIS* 18 (Milan, 1731), cols. 242–792, at 393–4, 399; *Storie pistoresi (1300–1348)*, ed. S.A. Barbi, *RISNS* 11.5 (Città di Castello, 1927), pp. 214–16; N. Jorga, 'Une lettre apocryphe sur la bataille de Smyrne', *Revue d'orient Latin* 3 (1895), 27–31. This is

Mézières, who fought at Smyrna as a young man and wrote fifty years later that Umur (*Morbaissant*) was the most powerful of the Turkish lords at that time.[85] As a result of the Crusade of Smyrna, the emir began to feature more heavily in western sources than any other Turk. He is referred to in person by his Latin name, *Morbasanus*, rendered in Italian as *Morbasciano* and in French as *Morbaissant* (a corrupted form of 'Umur' plus 'Bassanus', a common Latin transliteration of 'Pasha').

One Italian source, the Anonimo Romano, provides a rather fictitious but colourful description of this *Morbasciano*, recounted during the story of a Venetian embassy sent to him to try and negotiate a truce during the Crusade of Smyrna. According to the source, the envoys found Umur sitting on the ground, leaning on his left arm in a thoughtful mood. He was elegantly clad in silk and enormously fat, his stomach protruding like a barrel. He drank almond milk and was served sweetmeats, eggs, rice and spices, served on richly painted earthenware dishes, which he ate in great quantities with a golden spoon. When asked if he was afraid of the imminent arrival of a crusading army led by Humbert of Viennois, Umur replied that he had nothing to fear as long as his two friends were thriving. When the ambassadors asked, 'Who are these friends of yours?', Umur nonchalantly replied 'they are Guelph and Ghibelline!'.[86] This highly fictitious account was undoubtedly intended to reflect more on the policies of the Venetians and the factional infighting that hindered the Crusade of Smyrna than Umur's actual character, but the lively description nevertheless provides a good example of the impact which *Morbasciano* had made upon the European imagination at this time.

However, the ultimate step in the definition of Umur Pasha in the West came after the wide circulation of a apocryphal epistle allegedly written by *Morbasanus* to Pope Clement VI which circulated probably just after the Crusade of Smyrna, at a similar time as the Anonimo Romano.[87] In this epistle *Morbasanus* wrote that the Venetian people, who 'live with neither law nor morals', had tricked the pope into launching a crusade against him,

---

discussed in more detail in Chapter 6 (pp. 116–17) and also by Housley, *Avignon Papacy*, pp. 146–9.

[85] Philippe de Mézières, *Une epistre lamentable et consolatoire*, pp. 213–14; Idem, *Le songe du Vieil Pelerin*, ed. G.W. Coopland, 2 vols (Cambridge, 1969), vol. 2, p. 501.

[86] Anonimo Romano, *Cronica*, pp. 84–5; Setton, *Papacy and the Levant*, vol. 1, p. 207.

[87] The date at which the epistle was first composed and circulated is extremely difficult to determine, although in the salutation it is said that *Morbasanus* and his brothers were *imperatoris Organi collaterales pugiles*, suggesting that they fought on the side of Emperor Orkhan, who is most likely the Ottoman sultan who died in 1360. Aydin was not subordinate to the Ottomans until 1390, but they began to attract the attention of the Christian world in 1354 after their capture of Gallipolli. The circulation of the epistle in the later 1350s, at a similar time to that of the *Aninomo Romano*, written in c.1357–60, therefore seems plausible. See the background to these events in Zachariadou, *Trade and Crusade*, pp. 63–75.

based on unfounded accusations of Turkish raids. What is more, the Turks were also descendants of the Trojans, thus making them bound to the Italians by ties of blood and the true inheritors of the lands of Romania, unlike the Venetians who had seized them illicitly. This shared ancestry, coupled with the fact that the Turks were innocent of shedding Christ's blood and of occupying the holy places, wrote *Morbasanus*, made the Crusade against him both unnecessary and against the tenets of the Christian faith.[88] The *Epistola Morbasiani* periodically reappeared throughout the fifteenth century, finally being considered as the answer of the Ottoman sultan Mehmed II to the famous letter of conversion written to him by Pope Pius II.[89] These versions continued to circulate into the sixteenth century and beyond, appearing in German and French translations, as well as in Latin and Italian, the language of the original fourteenth-century variants.[90] As was seen earlier, during the reign of Mehmed II Umur also resurfaced as the protagonist in the biographical poem of Enveri, evidence of his impact on both Christian and Muslim writings. The wording of the *Epistola Mobasiani* was even echoed in an account of the Crusade of Smyrna added to the chronicle of Guglielmo Cortusi.[91] The influence of *Morbasanus* on the European imagination was so strong that Giovanni Boccaccio himself drew his inspiration from him for the character of Bassano, king of Cappadocia, in the *Decameron*. This character makes only a brief appearance in Boccaccio's tale,

---

[88] A fourteenth-century Latin version of the letter has been published by J. Gay, *Le Pape Clément VI et les affaires d'Orient (1342–1352)* (Paris, 1904), pp. 172–4 and an Italian version, most probably from the first quarter of the fifteenth century, by G. Toffanin, *Lettera a Maometto II: (Epistola ad Mahumetem)* (Napoli, 1953), pp. 181–2.

[89] See, for example, Weimar, Herzogin Anna Amalia Bibliothek, Q 108, fols 314v–315v; Q 109/9, fol. 62r–v.

[90] Along with Dr Cristian Caselli, I have identified over eighty manuscripts variants of the *Epistola Morbasiani* although they have not yet been edited. Examples of the later variants, include: Vatican City, Biblioteca Apostolica Vaticana, Vat. lat. 2915, fol. 114r–116v (fifteenth–sixteenth century); Munich, Bayerische Staatsbibliothek, Ital. 90, fols 1–4 (seventeenth century). German translations include: Munich, Bayerische Staatsbibliothek, Cgm 216, fols 162v–163r; Cgm 317, fols 142r–v; Cgm 4692, fols 10v–13v; Clm 9503 [Ob. Alt. 3], fol. 353v. Some (but not all) of the manuscripts have been identified by Meserve, *Empires of Islam*, pp. 35–7 and also by B. Wagner, *Die 'Epistola Presbiteri Johannis': Lateinisch und Deutsch* (Tübingen, 2000), pp. 20–4; B. Wagner, 'Sultansbriefe', *Die deutsche Literatur des Mittelalters. Verfasserlexikon* 11 (2004), 1463–4.

[91] These are the words: *Morbassan, qui se scribit dominum Achaie et imperatoris Organi colateralem et pugilem, cum multitudine equitum supervenit*: Guglielmo Cortusi, *Chronica de novitatibus Padue et Lombardie*, ed. B. Pagnin, *RISNS* 12.5 (Bologna, 1941–9), p. 109. They are clearly influenced by the salutation of the *Epistola Morbasiani*, which reads: *Morbasianus hebenesi cum fratribus Cerabi et Inbahit imperatoris Organi collaterales pugilles et in partibus Acaie domini*. Guglielmo finished writing his chronicle in the 1350s and was living at a very advanced age in 1361: Setton, *Papacy and the Levant*, p. 190, n. 135.

where he marches on Smyrna, slaying its ruler Osbech, before entering the city in triumph.[92]

Given Umur's widespread appearance in a range of sources during the time of the Crusade of Smyrna, it is both surprising and unfortunate that references to him in papal documents remain minimal. In fact, he seems to feature in just two of the many letters concerning the Crusade. The first occasion was in January 1345, when the pope wrote that *Marbassanus* 'the chief commander of the Turks' had been 'completely defeated and triumphantly put to flight' by the crusaders during the capture of the harbour-fortress of Smyrna. The second was three years later, in August 1348, when the pope expressed his joy at the reports that *Marbasanus*, 'the leader of the Turks', had been killed during an assault on the fortress.[93] Unfortunately these two references provide no extra clue as to the papal view of Umur and can be seen as extremely limited in comparison to the rich descriptions found in the Anonimo Romano and the *Epistola Morbasiani*. In a sense, these laconic allusions are characteristic of papal correspondence, which rarely refers to a Turkish lord by name, or in much detail. Having said that, a fleeting reference to a certain 'lord of the Turcomans' known as *Haramanus* was made in papal documents of the early 1320s (probably in reference to the emir of Karaman), and Umur's older brother Hizir (*Chalabus*) is mentioned during the negotiations for a truce at Smyrna after 1348.[94] However, along with Umur and Masud, these individuals remain the exception.

Rhetoric and Justification for Crusading against the Turks

By the mid-point of the fourteenth century, descriptions of the Turks, although at times still vague, were beginning to become more clearly articulated than in earlier years; specific references had been made to the emirs of Menteshe (Masud and Orkhan) and to those of Aydin (Umur and Hizir), whilst the lords of Germiyan and Karaman had also been alluded to. In addition, the beyliks of Menteshe and Aydin were regularly identified, in

[92] Giovanni Boccaccio, *The Decameron*, pp. 124–5 (II.7). Boccaccio refers to Osbech as the 'King of the Turks'. He has traditionally been linked to Uzbek, the khan of the Golden Horde, although Kinoshata and Jacobs, who have studied this story in detail, suggest that Osbech is in fact Umur Pasha. However, they do not make the obvious link between Bassano and *Morbasanus*: S. Kinoshita and J. Jacobs, 'Ports of call: Boccaccio's Alatiel in the medieval Mediterranean', *Journal of Medieval and Early Modern Studies* 37.1 (2007), 163–95, at 179–81. A hundred years earlier the term *Turchia* could refer to Cappadocia: Zachariadou, *Trade and Crusade*, p. 117, n. 505.

[93] Clement VI, *Lettres à la France*, vol. 1, doc. 1397; Clement VI, *Lettres autres que la France*, doc. 1697.

[94] John XXII, *Lettres secrètes*, vol. 2, docs 1571–3, 1691; Clement VI, *Lettres autres que la France*, doc. 2078.

one way or another, as those responsible for the attacks on Venetian, Hospitaller and Zaccaria territories in Romania.

The Avignon popes granted numerous spiritual and economic privileges in response to the growing menace of the Anatolian beyliks, both in order to encourage participation in military action against them and to legitimize them fully as a target of holy war. These concessions were first issued by Pope John XXII and included grants of indulgences for fighting against the Turks in various locations at different times and 'trade licences', which supposedly facilitated the maintenance of a defence force to be used against the Turks on Chios.[95] Benedict XII, the successor of John XXII, was altogether far less favourable towards a crusade against the Turks than his predecessor, but he also granted indulgences for fighting against them in 1335, but at no other time.[96] The final pope to feature in this study, Clement VI – whose pontificate was dominated by the Crusade of Smyrna – was the most proactive of all the Avignon popes in this regard. He issued numerous extensive spiritual and economic privileges, including the full 'Holy Land' crusade indulgence for participation in the Crusade of Smyrna and trade licences to the Venetians and many others.[97]

The motivations of the popes, merchants and crusaders who granted and received these privileges will be the focus of Chapters 5 and 6 of this book, so the composition and makeup of these mechanisms will not be discussed here in detail. Even so, from the brief description of the privileges outlined above, a corollary pattern can be drawn between the evolving image of the Turks in the West and the papal response to it. In basic terms, as the beyliks became regarded as more of a threat, more privileges were granted for resisting them and, as shall be shown later in this book, these privileges became increasingly generous. Also, the earliest grants of indulgences connected to the Turks, issued in 1322, included other non-Latin groups, specifically the Greeks, Alans, Bulgars, Mongols and Mamluks, and not just the Turks. As was noted earlier, the Turks had been mentioned as colluding with the Greeks during the Hospitaller conquest of Rhodes and in the grants of indulgences of 1322 a similar pattern can be seen at work; at first the Turks were regarded as one of many threats in Romania by the Church, but within a year they began to feature in indulgence grants as the primary non-Latin 'enemy' – a further reinforcement of the hardening attitudes towards them at the papal curia during the 1320s.[98]

---

[95] These are discussed in detail in Chapter 6, pp. 120–3, 132–7.

[96] ASVat, *RA* 48, fols 194–194v; *RV* 119, fols 132v–133, ep. 343–7 (20 Apr 1335); summary in Benedict XII, *Lettres communes*, vol. 1, doc. 2250.

[97] See, for example, *Documents on the Later Crusades*, pp. 78–80, doc. 22; *DVL*, vol. 1, doc. 144.

[98] This is discussed in more detail in Chapter 5, pp. 109–11.

However, when addressing the western image of the Turks, the most important feature of these privileges was the distinct 'anti-Turkish' rhetoric which accompanied them, most strikingly expressed in the actual documents granting the privileges and the other letters of the Avignon popes, or in the writings of the crusade theorists. In the main, the popes justified the need to carry out military action against the Turks on the grounds that their piratical raids into the Aegean and Greece were leading to the widespread and evil enslavement of the Christian population of Romania, a factor which, if left unchecked, would lead to the permanent eradication of the Latin colonies in the region. The great Levantine slave trade had traditionally been carried out between the Black Sea regions and Egypt or western Europe, but since the emergence of the beyliks at the end of the thirteenth century a subsidiary trade had been established from the western Anatolian coast to Crete and then to Europe, with the Turks raiding the Aegean islands and selling their captives, who were usually Orthodox Greeks, to the Latins.[99] Mentions of Turkish piratical acts and of the general 'oppression' of the Christians in the East was a common feature in the correspondence of John XXII and was also a motif he expressed when calling for resistance against the Catalans in Greece, who it was claimed were in the practice of selling Moreote slaves to the Turks.[100] It was, however, Clement VI who utilized enslavement most heavily as a motivation tool for confronting the Turks. This is most vividly expressed in the bull proclaiming the Crusade of Smyrna in 1343, where he wrote that:

> For some time past [the Turks] have mobilised the strength of their nation and used a great number of armed vessels to invade by the sea the Christian territories in the region of Romania, and other neighbouring places in the hands of the faithful. Raging atrociously against the Christians and their lands and islands, they have taken to roaming the seas, as they are doing at present, despoiling and depopulating the settlements and islands of the Christians of those parts, setting them ablaze, and what is worse, seizing the Christians themselves as booty and subjecting them to horrible and perpetual

[99]   The Levantine slave trade is discussed in detail by M. Balard, *La Romanie génoise*, vol. I, pp. 289–310, vol. 2, pp. 785–833, and with specific reference to the Aegean by Zachariadou, *Trade and Crusade*, pp. 160–3. Also see the studies by Epstein, *Purity Lost*, pp. 52–95, 162–6; B. Arbel, 'Slave trade and slave labour in Frankish and Venetian Cyprus (1191–1571)', in Idem, *Cyprus, the Franks and Venice, 13th–16th Centuries*, Variorum Reprints (Aldershot, 2000), IX, 151–90; G. Christ, 'Sliding legalities: Venetian slave trade in Alexandria and the Aegean', in *Slavery and the Slave Trade in the Mediterranean Region during the Medieval Period (1000–1500)*, ed. C. Cluse and R. Amitai (Turnhout, 2015), pp. 210–29; Barker, *Egyptian and Italian Merchants in the Black Sea Slave Trade*, esp. pp. 355–409.
[100]   See, for example, *DOC*, doc. 120; John XXII, *Lettres secrètes*, vol. 2, docs 1571–3, vol. 3, doc. 2410, vol. 4, docs 5247, 5404; John XXII, *Lettres communes*, vol. 4, doc. 16672, vol. 13, doc. 63890.

slavery, selling them like animals and forcing them to deny the Catholic faith.[101]

Condemnation of the Turks for enslaving Christians, especially the Greeks, also emanated from other circles. The Calabrian monk Barlaam, for example, made much of the endemic problem in his calls for a joint Byzantine and Latin campaign against the Turks, and even stated in the late 1330s that the liberation of Greek slaves was an essential prerequisite of church union.[102] A more distant commentator, the Dominican Riccold of Monte Croce, who spent ten years of his life in Baghdad and travelled extensively in western Asia, also noted the selling of many Greek captives by the Turks on his journey through Anatolia in 1288.[103] Even Francesco Petrarch, who was notoriously hostile towards the Byzantines, deplored the widespread enslavement of the Greeks in a letter to Cardinal Giovanni Colonna written mid-way through the century.[104]

The Turks were also condemned for their role in the slave trade by the crusade theorists, who used it to emphasize their barbarity and savageness.[105] An especially moving testimony is given by William of Adam, who recounted seeing bands of over two thousand Greeks, being led 'like flocks of sheep', to be sold in the markets of the East. Among these he regularly saw pregnant mothers clutching their children as they were dragged off to their doom. In his tract William also went to great lengths in attacking those Latin merchants who participated in the trade. In particular he condemned the Genoese, whom he referred to as the *Alexandrini*, because they sailed to and from Alexandria, where they sold slave children as well as prohibited merchandise. The prominent role of the Genoese in the slave trade was also depicted by others, namely Boccaccio in the *Decameron*.[106] In fact the Zaccaria of Chios, whom William mentioned often, were amongst the only traders to attempt to disrupt the evil activities of their countrymen, a factor which helps to explain William's admiration for them.[107] An image of the Turk enslaving helpless Christians was also a common theme adopted by Marino Sanudo when calling upon western rulers to unite in the face of the

---

[101] *Documents on the Later Crusades*, pp. 78–80, doc. 22. Other examples include Clement VI, *Lettres à la France*, vol. 1, docs 332–41, 360, 368, 433–4, 591, 1704.

[102] *AE*, vol. 25, pp. 160–1, ch. 22–3.

[103] Riccold of Monte Croce, *Pérégrination en Terre Sainte et au Proche Orient: Lettres sur la chute de Saint-Jean d'Acre*, ed. R. Kappler (Paris, 1997), pp. 76–9.

[104] N. Bisaha, 'Petrarch's vision of the Muslim and Byzantine East', *Speculum* 76 (2001), 284–314, at 312.

[105] For example, Kunstmann, 'Studien über Marino Sanudo', 797 (letter 5); Roddy trans., p. 280 (letter 33). On the theorists and the slave trade, also see Barker, *Egyptian and Italian Merchants in the Black Sea Slave Trade*, pp. 373–95.

[106] Giovanni Boccaccio, *The Decameron*, p. 356 (V.7).

[107] William of Adam, *How To Defeat the Saracens*, pp. 9, 49–51, 79–83.

Turkish advances.[108] In a letter to the king of France of 1332 he even wrote that the Turks had captured 25,000 people from Greek and Latin lands in their piratical raids of the previous year.[109] Clearly, the enslavement of Christians in the East was a very real problem and one which weighed heavily on the consciousness of the crusading powers in the West. Even hatred of the Greeks, as Petrarch and William of Adam demonstrated, could be put aside for the common good of the Christians in Romania.

As news of increasing Turkish raids into the Aegean began to reach Europe in the 1330s and 40s, the justification of protecting the Christians from enslavement by the Turks progressed to one which stressed the need to defend Christian lands, not just in Romania, but also in the Adriatic and kingdoms of western Europe from the advances of the Turks. As in many other instances, Marino Sanudo was one of the main propagators of this theme, warning in 1332 that the Turks would come into the Adriatic Sea 'ravaging the land and sea completely' unless aid was forthcoming.[110] Popes John XXII and Benedict XII did not share the same concern as Sanudo voiced at this time, but Clement VI, in a letter of 1345, wrote that the Turks would have advanced as far as Naples if it were not for the victories of the crusaders at Smyrna.[111] These prophetic warnings of course proved to be true, as was demonstrated in the late 1360s by Petrarch, who wrote with fear that the Turks were 'crossing over from there [Turkey] toward us and true Catholicism'.[112]

Running in parallel with this hardening of rhetoric was a gradual shift in the terminology used to identify the different ethnic groups of the Muslim eastern Mediterranean. By the second and third decades of the fourteenth century the term *Turchus* began to feature more heavily in the sources, replacing the ubiquitous *Saracenus*, which had hitherto dominated the diction of Latin writers.[113] On occasion also, the two terms began to be blended together, such as by William of Adam who used the word *Saraceni* to describe the Egyptians and as a modifier for the Turks, such as for the

---

[108] For example, *DOC*, docs 129, 136, 147; Cerlini, 'Nuovo lettere di Marino Sanudo', 348–5 (letter 22); Kunstmann, 'Studien über Marino Sanudo', 755–88 (letter 2); Roddy trans., pp. 127–36 (letter 7), 156–60 (letter 15), 173–82 (letter 18), 217–20 (letter 28), 222–70 (letter 30).

[109] Kunstmann, 'Studien über Marino Sanudo', 791–9 (letter 5); Roddy trans., pp. 272–81 (letter 33).

[110] Kunstmann, 'Studien über Marino Sanudo', 791–9 (letter 5); Roddy trans., pp. 272–81 (letter 33).

[111] Clement VI, *Lettres à la France*, vol. 1, doc. 1704.

[112] Francesco Petrarch, *Letters of Old Age: Rerum Senilium Libri I–XVIII*, ed. and trans. A.S. Bernardo *et al.*, 2 vols (Baltimore, 1992), vol. 1, p. 255 (7:1); Bisaha, 'Petrarch's vision of the Muslim and Byzantine East', 284. For the influence of these attitudes on crusading in the fifteenth century, see Housley, *Crusading and the Ottoman Threat*, pp. 22–4.

[113] S.C. Akbari, *Idols in the East: European Representations of Islam and the Orient, 1100–1450* (Ithaca, 2009), p. 285.

Turchi Saraceni, which could mean either the 'Turkish Saracens', or the 'Saracen Turks'.[114] The letters of Marino Sanudo also share this characteristic. In them the Turks are clearly distinguished from the Saracens or Agarene peoples, but in a letter of 1330, they are described as 'the worst Saracens', an indicator of Sanudo's conviction that they were the main threat to the Latins of Romania by the 1330s.[115] This method of denigrating the Turks by comparing them to other Muslim powers, albeit to less favourable ones, was also widely adopted by the Renaissance humanist writers of the fifteenth century.[116] By 1453 this literary and symbolic shift had gone full-circle, and Muslims were commonly considered as 'Turks' and not 'Saracens' as had been the norm in earlier centuries.[117]

In some senses, the more refined perception of Muslim groups expressed by fourteenth-century writers, especially of regional, political and ethnic difference, can be seen as one of the earliest examples of a shift from a medieval to an early modern form of Orientalism.[118] Indeed, the anti-Turkish rhetoric which was born in the fourteenth century directly influenced those Renaissance humanist writers of the later fourteenth and fifteenth centuries, especially in their portrayal of the Ottomans.[119] As Peter Lock has suggested, Marino Sanudo should be regarded as an important early humanist, like his contemporaries Dante, Petrarch and Boccaccio, even though he is rarely thought of in this way. He did not contribute to the development of the Italian language in the same manner, but his approach to knowledge, verbal presentation and sourcing, including Classical references, should earn him a place amongst the early humanists.[120] In terms of descriptions of the Islamic East, and of the Turks in particular, many later humanist writers were also undoubtedly influenced by authors such as Sanudo and William of Adam,

[114] William of Adam, *How To Defeat the Saracens*, pp. 18, 73.

[115] Kunstmann, 'Studien über Marino Sanudo', 778 (letter 2); Roddy trans., p. 255 (letter 30); P. Lock, 'Sanudo, Turks, Greeks, and Latins in the early fourteenth century', in *Contact and Conflict in Frankish Greece and the Aegean, 1204–1453*, ed. M. Carr and N.G. Chrissis (Farnham, 2014), pp. 135–49, at p. 139. Interestingly, in the 'Liber Secretorum' written earlier in the century, the Turks are on one occasion described as Agarenes ('those wicked Agarenes'): Marino Sanudo, 'Liber Secretorum', p. 29; Lock trans., p. 59. This blending of Turks and Agarenes was also an occasional feature of other diplomatic correspondence, for example in the Hospitaller document drawing up the provisional naval league in 1332: *DVL*, vol. 1, doc. 116.

[116] See, for example, Meserve, *Empires of Islam*, pp. 203–37.

[117] Orth, 'Papst Urbans II', pp. 367–405, esp. pp. 379, 386. See also Housley, *Crusading and the Ottoman Threat*, pp. 18–61.

[118] See Akbari, *Idols in the East*, pp. 19, 285.

[119] The Florentine humanist Benedetto Accolti, for example, used the 'Liber Secretorum' of Marino Sanudo in his work, alongside more traditional crusade sources: Orth, 'Papst Urbans II', pp. 382–3. See also Meserve, *Empires of Islam*, pp. 149–52; Trivellato, 'Renaissance Italy and the Muslim Mediterranean in recent historical works', 140–5.

[120] Marino Sanudo, *Book of the Secrets*, trans. Lock, p. 5.

especially in the complex distinctions they drew between different Muslim groups of the East. To suggest, for example, that medieval crusade rhetoric focused on a narrow strip of land in the Levant, whilst ignoring the wider Muslim world, would be to underestimate drastically the complex descriptions provided by those writers of the early fourteenth century and the impact they had.[121]

Moreover, in the same way that not all humanist writers drew a consistently negative picture of the Turks, neither did their late-medieval forebears. The best example of this can be found in the representation the Turkish lord Umur Pasha (*Morbasianus*) in the sources discussed earlier, especially the fourteenth- and fifteenth-century variants of the *Epistola Morbasiani* which bridge the gap between medieval and humanist representations of the Turks better than any other. In the letter, Umur became a legendary figure detached from the real individual, in which features of civility and prudence were articulated alongside those traditionally associated with the *inimicus Christi* as was commonly displayed in papal rhetoric. For example, *Morbasanus* was portrayed as a civilized lord who shared some values belonging to western culture; he was rational, tolerant and well-versed in the Classics – a noble descendant of the Trojans and kinsman of the Italians, for whom he had a 'hidden affection'. He was exacting just revenge for the blood of Hector by subjugating the Greeks and was lawfully attacking the Venetians who had wrongly seized his ancestral lands in Romania. He was also familiar with the Christian religion, complaining that crusaders with 'remission of their sins' had recently arrived in his lands, but had no justification for attacking the Turks as they revered Christ as a prophet and were innocent of shedding his blood. He even reminded the pope that Christians could not forcibly convert Muslims as it was against their faith.[122] In addition, *Morbasanus* expressed his hatred of the Jews for crucifying Christ, thus tapping into the prevailing anti-Semitic feelings of the time.[123]

It is, however, important to stress that the letter was written primarily as a piece of anti-Venetian progaganda. The author was someone who opposed Venice and its participation in the Crusade of Smyrna, most probably a commercial rival of the Republic, such as a Genoese or Florentine. The portrayal of *Morbasanus* in a positive light, and as an enemy of

---

[121] This is suggested by Bisaha, 'Petrarch's vision of the Muslim and Byzantine East', 285–6; Bisaha, *Creating East and West*, pp. 14–19.

[122] Gay, *Le Pape Clément VI*, pp. 172–4; *Lettera a Maometto II*, ed. Toffanin, pp. 181–2; Housley, *Avignon Papacy*, pp. 231–2.

[123] See R. Po-chia Hsia, 'Religion and race: Protestant and Catholic discourses on Jewish conversions of the sixteenth and seventeenth centuries', in *The Origins of Racism in the West*, ed. M. Eliav-Feldon, B. Isaac and J. Ziegler (Cambridge, 2009), pp. 265–75; R.I. Moore, *The Formation of a Persecuting Society: Power and Deviance in Western Europe, 950–1250* (Oxford, 2007), pp. 27–45.

Venice, must therefore be understood principally as a mechanism used by the author to criticize the policies of the Republic overseas. Likewise the anecdote discussed earlier of the Venetian embassy visiting Umur, found in the Anonimo Romano, can also be interpreted as a method to paint the Venetians in a bad light and more importantly, to deplore the infighting between the different Latin factions during the Crusade of Smryna and on the Italian peninsula.[124] This strategy of using Turkish rulers as a mouthpiece to underline the internal deficiencies within Christendom would become commonplace amongst the Renaissance humanists, for example, by Coluccio Salutati in 1397.[125] More than anything, the regard shown to Umur in the *Epistola Morbasiani* demonstrates that commercial rivalries and necessity regularly cut through faith-based prejudices in the Mediterranean. This may also partly explain the stance of Boccaccio; he was a writer who came from a merchant family and was highly aware of the necessities of trade, thus his portrayal of Muslims was perhaps more accommodating than most.[126] As will be shown later on in this book, the conflict between the image of the Turks as propagated by the papacy and the realities of cross-cultural interaction on the ground in the Aegean posed some significant difficulties for the implementation of a crusade in the region, where the commercial and spiritual interests of the emerging merchant crusaders were often difficult to reconcile.

---

[124] See above, note 86; Anonimo Romano, *Cronica*, pp. 84–5.
[125] Meserve, *Empires of Islam*, p. 74.
[126] Bisaha, *Creating East and West*, pp. 18–19.

3

Latin Response to the Turks:
The Naval Leagues

Twenty to thirty armed galleys should be sent to inflict damage on the Sultan and his lands and people, as well as on the ships and vessels of the Turks who are the most evil persecutors of the Christian faith [...] And truly, unless this fleet and protection are sent ahead, they do not see how the *passagium* can succeed, because the iniquity and audacity of the Turks increases daily.

> Doge Giovanni Soranzo of Venice, letter to King Philip VI of France advising him on a crusade to the Holy Land, 11 May 1332.[1]

During the crusades to the Holy Land of the eleventh to thirteenth centuries, western (primarily Italian) naval power had repeatedly triumphed against Muslim fleets in the waters of the eastern Mediterranean. Within a few decades most of the important ports on the Syrian coast had been seized by the Franks – largely thanks to the support of the Italian republics – and much of the significant Muslim naval presence in the region had been quashed. However, over the course of the thirteenth century the Latin grasp of the Levantine seaboard began to weaken significantly, culminating with the loss of Acre to the Mamluks in 1291. Although the Italians still remained the most active merchants in the eastern Mediterranean after this point, they had lost a major foothold on the Syrian coast. Within three decades after the fall of Acre, the presence of the Italian merchant colonies in the East – integral to western naval dominance in the region – was further compromised by a new Muslim foe, the Turks of the Anatolian maritime beyliks, who by then threatened Romania and the few remaining Latin possessions in the eastern Mediterranean.[2] As was noted in the previous chapter, the depredations of the Turks against the Latins of Romania were primarily carried out by sea, usually consisting of raids on the Aegean islands and the Greek mainland, the seizing of goods and, where possible, the enslavement of the Christian population. Over the course of the fourteenth century, a new strategy in crusading warfare would evolve to combat the Turkish

---

[1] *DVL*, vol. 1, doc. 110.

[2] For a background of naval warfare and the role of the maritime republics during the crusades, see E. Rose, *Medieval Naval Warfare: 1000–1500* (London, 2002), pp. 35–42 and also Carr, 'Between Byzantium, Egypt and the Holy Land', pp. 75–87.

menace: the naval league. This was an allied Christian fleet of galleys, usually formed by the local Latin powers with the help of the papacy, for which the participants were sometimes awarded crusader privileges. As can be seen from the advice of Doge Giovanni Soranzo above, the naval league was a strategy which reflected the realities of warfare in the Aegean, where the fragmented political situation led to a departure from grandiose plans to recover the Holy Land and more closely reflected the concerns of the local Latin protagonists.

Crusading after the Fall of Acre

The collapse of Byzantine power in Asia Minor and the rise of the Turks in the Aegean, although known in the West, was not the chief concern of the crusading powers at the end of the thirteenth century. Instead their minds were focussed on the recovery of the Holy Land, brought into sharp focus after the fall of Acre on 18 May 1291, which ended almost two hundred years of Latin settlement in the Levant. Not surprisingly, the news of the collapse of the city re-awakened crusading fervour in western Christendom and ushered in a period of heightened enthusiasm for the recovery of Jerusalem. This resulted in the formation of various military strategies and proposals which would profoundly influence crusade thinking throughout the four-teenth century.[3] One of the most significant developments in crusade plan-ning after 1291 was the growth of interest in the use of economic apparatus to facilitate the recovery of the Holy Land, as propagated by a number of the crusade theorists in their *De recuperatione terrae sanctae* treatises – memoranda written between 1291 and 1336 suggesting ways in which the Holy Land might be recovered.[4] These writers commonly advocated a strict economic blockade of Mamluk Egypt, similar to the papal trade embargo that had been in place in one form or another since at least the Third Lateran Council of 1179. The embargo prohibited trade in war materials, such as iron, timber and weapons, as well as slaves, and was punishable by excommunication.[5] The theorists believed that this blockade could be easily enforced by the superior naval forces of the crusading powers, and would

---

[3] Schein, *Fideles Crucis*, pp. 264–5; Housley, *Later Crusades*, p. 22.

[4] The most detailed assessment of the crusade theorists is given by Leopold, *How To Recover the Holy Land*. See also *Projets de croisade (v. 1290 – v. 1330)*, ed. J. Paviot (Paris, 2008); Atiya, *The Crusade in the Later Middle Ages*, pp. 47–154; J. Delaville le Roulx, *La France en Orient au XIVe siècle*, 2 vols (Paris, 1886), vol. I, pp. 13–27; Schein, *Fideles Crucis*, pp. 74–III; and the introduction to William of Adam, *How To Defeat the Saracens*, pp. 1–II.

[5] For a background to the embargo, see Stantchev, *Spiritual Rationality*, *passim*; Christ, *Trading Conflicts*, pp. 113–19.

starve the Mamluks of war provisions and pave the way for the easy liberation of the Holy Land.

Of the theorists, the Franciscan friar Fidenzio of Padua was amongst
the first to adopt this strategy. He wrote that the Mamluks were especially
vulnerable to a trade embargo as their strength depended on the import of
war materials and other goods from the West, as well as the tariffs levied
on Christian merchants, and slaves to sustain their army. According to
Fidenzio, a fleet of no less than thirty galleys would be needed to cut off
Egypt in preparation for a general crusade.[6] This idea of economic warfare
was henceforth adopted by other theorists writing immediately after the fall
of Acre, including Charles II of Anjou and Ramon Lull, as well as those
of the fourteenth century, such as William of Adam and Marino Sanudo.[7]

In August 1291, in an effort to gain the cooperation of the maritime
republics – essential for the effective enforcement of the trade embargo
– Pope Nicholas IV urged Genoa and Venice to make peace with one
another in order to prevent any trade with Egypt. This was followed by
the proclamation of a total ban on all trade with Muslims, which would
form the backbone of papal decrees for the rest of the Avignon period.[8] A
handful of small-scale expeditions were planned and launched to the East
after this point on the pretext of implementing the strategies of the theorists
by restricting trade with the Mamluks. For example, Nicholas IV ordered
that a fleet of twenty galleys, funded by the Templars and the Hospitallers,
should be raised to protect Cyprus and Cilician Armenia against an Egyptian attack and to prevent merchants from illegally trading with the infidel.
In 1292, the Genoese captain Manuel Zaccaria was placed in charge of this
fleet which, according to a report made by him, was to be used to protect
Cyprus and enforce the blockade on Egypt. A short time later, Zaccaria's
flotilla raided the ports of Candelore (Alanya) on the south-eastern coast
of Asia Minor and Alexandria in Egypt.[9] This was followed in 1304 when
Frederick III of Sicily, who had previously refused to spearhead a crusade

[6]   For Fidenzio of Padua see *Projets de croisade*, ed. Paviot, pp. 53–169; Leopold, *How To
Recover the Holy Land*, pp. 116–23; Schein, *Fideles Crucis*, pp. 91–102.

[7]   For more on these see Leopold, *How To Recover the Holy Land*, pp. 8–51, 119–35; Schein,
Fideles Crucis, pp. 91–111.

[8]   On Nicholas IV, see Stantchev, *Spiritual Rationality*, pp. 120–22, and see pp. 122–45
for the embargo after this point. See also Ashtor, *Levant Trade in the Later Middle Ages*,
pp. 17–71; G. Ortalli, 'Venice and papal bans on trade with the Levant: The role of the
jurist', *Mediterranean Historical Review* 10 (1995), 242–58; A. Cocci, 'Le projet de blocus
naval des côtes égyptiennes dans le *Liber secretorum fidelium Crusis* (1321c) de Marino Sanudo
il Vecchio (1279c.-1343)', in *La Méditerranée médiévale: Perceptions et représentations*, ed. H.
Akkari (Paris, 2002), pp. 171–88.

[9]   J. Richard, 'Le royaume de Chypre et l'embargo sur le commerce avec l'Egypte (fin
XIIIe-début XIVe siècle)', *Académie des Inscriptions et Belles-Lettres* (1984), pp. 120–34, at p.
123; Schein, *Fideles Crucis*, pp. 77–8. The report of Manuel Zaccaria is in ASVat, *RA* 54, fols

to Constantinople, asked for and received papal permission to send ten ships under the command of his half-brother Sancho of Aragon to capture Byzantine islands in the Aegean which he claimed were to be used as a base for enforcing the embargo.[10]

Origins of a Naval League

The earliest Latin naval operations in the Aegean, like the naval leagues which followed, tended to be undertaken by a coalition of resident Christian states. This was because none of the local Latin rulers in the Aegean were powerful enough to dominate the region alone and, as many of them shared common enemies such as the Greeks or Turks, it made practical sense for them to ally with one another. This was especially the case for the new arrivals in the Aegean – the Hospitallers on Rhodes and the Genoese on Chios – both of whom ruled islands inhabited by native Greeks which lay within eyesight of the Turkish coast. Their hold on these domains must have felt particularly fragile in these early years and the simple matter of self-preservation which led them to ally with one another goes some way to explain the genesis of a united Latin fleet in the Aegean.

One of the earliest coalitions to be struck up was that between the Knights Hospitallers and the Genoese, which would form the basic strategy for the defence of the eastern Aegean islands in the early 1300s. This began in May 1306 when the Hospitaller Master Fulk of Villaret made an agreement with the Genoese corsair Vignolo de Vignoli and his companions Baldo Spinola and Michael della Volta for an initial attack on Rhodes.[11] The details surrounding the conquest remain obscure but by 1306 the Knights, with the help of these Genoese captains, had managed to secure a foothold on the island.[12] At this stage it is unlikely that Pope Clement V knew of Fulk's intention to seize Rhodes, especially as no mention of the island had been made in previous Hospitaller correspondence with the papacy over a planned crusade.[13] Nevertheless, in September 1307, the pope granted

---

467v–468; it was copied into an appendix of the registers of Benedict XII. A summary is in Benedict XII, *Lettres communes*, vol. 2, doc. 8378.

[10] Laiou, *Constantinople and the Latins*, pp. 138, 145, 147.

[11] The text of the original Hospitaller agreement of 1306 is in J. Delaville le Roulx, *Les Hospitaliers en Terre Sainte et à Chypre: 1100–1310* (Paris, 1904), pp. 274–276.

[12] For details of the initial expedition, see Luttrell, 'The Genoese at Rhodes', pp. 745–9; Idem, *Town of Rhodes*, pp. 75–8; Zachariadou, *Trade and Crusade*, pp. 10–11.

[13] Such as in a treatise written by Fulk of Villaret for Clement V: *Projets de croisade*, ed. Paviot, pp. 189–98, 221–33; B.Z. Kedar and S. Schein, 'Un projet de "passage particuliare" proposé par l'ordre de l'Hôpital, 1306–7', *Bibliothèque de l'École des chartes* 137.2 (1979), 211–26, at 211–20. See also A.T. Luttrell, 'The Hospitallers and the papacy, 1305–1314', in *Forschungen zur Reichs-, Papst-, und Landesgeschichte: Peter Herde zum 65. Geburstag*, ed

Rhodes *in perpetuum* to the Order.[14] The Hospitallers clearly valued Genoese assistance, partly because they provided ships and were more familiar with Rhodian waters, but also because both considered the Venetians as their mutual rivals in the region. The corsairs, in return for their assistance, requested and received certain privileges from the Hospital. For Vignolo, these included the retention of a *casale* on Rhodes and the grant of another *casale* on the island, as well as one third of the revenue and produce from the surrounding islands.[15] After this point, the Knights entered into further negotiations with other citizens of Genoa, agreeing a formal pact with certain shipbuilders in the city in 1308–9 for the construction of some of the vessels for a planned *passagium* to be led by Fulk of Villaret; an important and lucrative contract which included the construction of twelve galleys and one *navis magna*.[16] This Hospitaller fleet departed for the East in 1310, and although the ostensible aim was to defend the kingdoms of Cyprus and Cilician Armenia, it was instead used to consolidate the conquest of Rhodes, probably without the prior knowledge or consent of the pope.[17]

Once the Hospitallers were established on the island they formed commercial links with the Turks from the coastal regions of nearby Menteshe, from where they shipped animals and provisions to Rhodes.[18] However, their relationship with Genoese merchants operating in the area soon began to deteriorate as the Knights began to seize Genoese vessels which had transgressed

K. Borchardt and E. Bunz, 2 vols (Stuttgart, 1998), vol. 2, pp. 595–622, at pp. 599–601 (repr. in Idem, *Studies on the Hospitallers after 1306*, Variorum Reprints (Aldershot, 2007), item V); J.S.C. Riley-Smith, *The Knights of St. John in Jerusalem and Cyprus, c.1050–1310* (London, 1967), pp. 220–2; C. Georgiou, 'Propagating the Hospitallers' *passagium*: Crusade preaching and liturgy in 1308–9', in *Islands and Military Orders, c.1291–c.1798*, ed. S. Phillips and E. Buttigieg (Farnham, 2013), pp. 53–63, esp. pp. 61–2.

[14] See S. Schein, 'Philip IV and the crusade: a reconsideration', in *Crusade and Settlement: Papers Read at the First Conference of the Society for the Study of the Crusades and the Latin East and Presented to R.C. Smail*, ed. P.W. Edbury (Cardiff, 1985), pp. 121–6, at pp. 123–4; A.T. Luttrell, 'The island of Rhodes and the Hospitallers of Catalunya in the fourteenth century', in *Els Catalans a la Mediterrània Oriental a l'Edat Mitjana*, ed. M.T. Ferrer i Mallol (Barcelona, 2003), pp. 155–65, at pp. 155–7 (repr. in Idem, *Studies on the Hospitallers after 1306*, Variorum Reprints (Aldershot, 2007), XVIII); Luttrell, *Town of Rhodes*, pp. 171–2.

[15] Luttrell, 'Feudal tenure and Latin colonization at Rhodes', pp. 756–7.

[16] *Cartulaire général des hospitaliers*, ed. Delaville le Roulx, vol. 4, nos. 4830, 4840–1; Luttrell, 'The Genoese at Rhodes', pp. 752–3. See also Thiriet, *Assemblées*, vol. 1, doc. 192.

[17] Much ambiguity surrounds the latter stages of the Hospitaller conquest of Rhodes, a full discussion is given by Luttrell, 'The Hospitallers of Rhodes confront the Turks', p. 83, n. 10; Idem, 'The Hospitallers of Rhodes: Prospectives, problems, possibilities', in *Die geistlichen Ritterorden Europas*, ed. J. Fleckenstein and M. Hellmann (Thorbecke, 1980), pp. 243–66, at p. 250 (repr. in Idem, *Latin Greece, the Hospitallers and the Crusades, 1291–1440*, Variorum Reprints (Aldershot, 1982), I); Idem, *Town of Rhodes*, pp. 75–8, 171–4; Idem, 'Hospitallers and the papacy', p. 603; Menache, *Clement V*, pp. 105–6.

[18] Clement V, *Regestum*, vol. 7, doc. 7631; Zachariadou, *Trade and Crusade*, p. 11.

the papal embargo on trade with Muslims; an action which also indirectly resulted in the earliest conflicts with the neighbouring Turkish beyliks. The first instance of this came in 1312 when a Genoese corsair named Antonio Spinola paid Masud, the emir of Menteshe, 50,000 gold florins to attack Rhodes and seize Hospitaller operatives in his ports. However, this ploy failed spectacularly when the Knights defeated Masud's forces off Amorgos and later seized a number of castles in the coastal regions of his lands.[19]

After Menteshe was initially beaten back, the bulk of Turkish maritime aggression towards the Latins in the Aegean shifted to the neighbouring beylik of Aydin to the north. In response to this, the Hospitallers made another pact with Genoese merchants in the Aegean, this time with the lords of Chios, Martino and Benedetto II Zaccaria, whose family had come into control of the island during the first decade of the century.[20] The Zaccaria were a natural target of the emirs of Aydin for two main reasons. First, Chios lay closest to the two principal ports of the beylik, Ephesos and Smyrna, making it both a threat and a convenient target. Secondly, the Zaccaria controlled the towns of Old and New Phokaia, situated on the Anatolian coast on the northern border of Aydin and with them the highly valuable alum mines nearby.[21] The Genoese presence at Phokaia was therefore a thorn in the side of the emirs of Aydin, but also a potentially valuable acquisition if it was conquered. Little is known of the exact terms of the agreement between the Hospitallers and the Zaccaria, except for a fleeting reference to a treaty made before 1319 'for a united fleet to be equipped against the Turks'.[22] This agreement evidently allowed the two sides to benefit from shared intelligence and enabled a network of communication to be established between Chios and Rhodes, a system that was put to good use when their combined forces crushed a fleet from Aydin in the encounter off Chios in the summer of 1319. In terms of the evolution of a naval league in the Aegean this encounter was especially significant. As was noted in the previous chapter, the reports of it were widely disseminated in the West, which brought it to the attention of both Pope John XXII, who was later to

---

[19]   Finke, *Papsttum und Untergang des Templerordens*, vol. 2, pp. 298–302, doc. 146; *Chroniques d'Amadi et de Strambaldi*, ed. Mas Latrie, vol. 1, p. 391; Zachariadou, *Trade and Crusade*, p. 12; Luttrell, 'The Genoese at Rhodes', pp. 758–9; Luttrell, 'The Hospitallers of Rhodes confront the Turks', p. 85; Luttrell, 'Feudal tenure and Latin colonization at Rhodes', 757; Luttrell, 'Notes on Foulques de Villaret', pp. 82–7.

[20]   Probably sometime between 1305 and 1307, see Carr, 'Trade or crusade?', pp. 118–19, n. 18.

[21]   In c.1310 the Phokaias passed to the stewardship of the Cattaneo della Volta family, although they still owed fealty to the Zaccaria on Chios: Mazarakis, 'A martinello of Manuele and Paleologo Zaccaria', 116–17.

[22]   Document in J. Delaville le Roulx, *Les Hospitaliers à Rhodes, 1310–1421* (Paris, 1913; repr. London, 1974), p. 365, doc. 2. See also M. Carr, 'The Hospitallers of Rhodes and their alliances against the Turks', in *Islands and Military Orders, c.1291–c.1798*, ed. S. Phillips and E. Buttigieg (Farnham, 2013), pp. 167–76, at pp. 168–9.

give his backing to the first naval league, and to the crusade theorists, many of whom already advocated the idea of a united fleet of Christian galleys to patrol the eastern Mediterranean and enforce the trade embargo.[23] Gradually this concept of a fleet to be used for the economic blockade began to be merged with a naval league against the Turks, as one united Christian fleet began to be regarded as sufficient for achieving both objectives.[24]

This idea was articulated by one of the main promoters of a naval league and of the economic blockade, Marino Sanudo, who wrote in a marginal note inserted into his crusade treatise, the 'Liber Secretorum Fidelium Crucis', in c.1322/3, that a fleet of galleys should be assembled to make the Aegean 'more secure from Turkish raids and the inroads of other Saracens, and [...] from the Catalan Company and other evil doers'. This flotilla was to be made up of one vessel each from Martino Zaccaria, Guglielmo Sanudo of Naxos, the titular Latin patriarch of Constantinople and the archbishop of Crete, as well as two from the Hospitallers, and four from the king of Cyprus.[25] This proposition reflected the situation in the Aegean Sea, where the Venetians were defending their possessions from the Turks and Catalans in the western regions and the Hospitallers and the Zaccaria were doing likewise along the eastern coast. At the time of writing this marginal note Sanudo was at the courts of Avignon and Paris advising the pope and French king on the best ways of launching a crusade to aid Cilician Armenia and to liberate the Holy Land. It was probably during this time that he first began to make tentative efforts to combine a crusade against the Turks in the Aegean with Franco-papal proposals to aid Cilician Armenia, probably airing his idea of a common anti-Turkish union.[26] A few years later, in March 1325, Sanudo's plan was adopted by the *Serenissima* which discussed the possibility of forming a *societas* against the Turks, presumably

---

[23] See, for example, the letters from the Hospitallers to the pope in Gatto, 'Martino Zaccaria', 337–9, doc. 1; Delaville le Roulx, *Les Hospitaliers à Rhodes*, pp. 365–7, doc. 2 (summaries in John XXII, *Lettres communes*, vol. 2, docs 8374, 10269), and the references to the Zaccaria in William of Adam, *How To Defeat the Saracens*, pp. 53–5, 65–7, 81; 'Directorium ad Passagium Faciendum', pp. 457–8. The dissemination of the reports of this battle and other encounters are discussed fully in Chapter 2, pp. 47–9.

[24] See Marino Sanudo, 'Liber Secretorum', pp. 22–33; Lock trans., pp. 49–67; William of Adam, *How To Defeat the Saracens*, pp. 49–53; Leopold, *How To Recover the Holy Land*, pp. 119–35; Cocci, 'Le projet de blocus naval des côtes égyptiennes', pp. 171–88.

[25] Marino Sanudo, 'Liber Secretorum', pp. 30–1 (marginal note); Lock trans., pp. 62–3 (who misses out the Hospitaller galleys). The dating of this note is uncertain, but most probably 1322/3, see Jacoby, 'Catalans, Turcs et Vénitiens en Romanie', 247, n. 181; Zachariadou, 'The Catalans of Athens', 823, n. 6; cf. A. Magnocavallo, *Marin Sanudo il Vecchio e il suo progetto di Crociata* (Bergamo, 1901), p. 85; Laiou, 'Marino Sanudo Torsello', 378. The titular patriarch of Constantinople was Nicholas, the archbishop of Thebes (1308–31), who could presumably raise money from his see for the galley.

[26] For example, Sanudo suggested that reinforcements for the Cilician *passagia* should be made available from Rhodes and Romania, see Tyerman, 'Marino Sanudo Torsello', 63–4.

for the protection of its possessions from the combined attacks of the Turks and Catalans.[27] From this point onwards these assaults became increasingly threatening and by April 1327 the situation had become so severe that Negroponte was on the brink of falling to the Catalans.[28] Probably because of the intensification of the war in Greece, the *Serenissima* began to act upon its decision to form an alliance against the Turks made two years earlier, dispatching letters in July 1327 to the duke of Crete and the baillies of Negroponte and Constantinople, instructing them to discuss with the Byzantine Emperor Andronikos II, Martino Zaccaria, the master of the Hospitallers and others about the possibility of forming 'a *societas* against the Turks for the defence of our lands'.[29] Unfortunately the text of the discussion has been lost, but it is known that in December of that year, ten galleys were dispatched from Venice for the protection of the Adriatic and Romania, which may have been connected to this union against the Turks.[30] Likewise, ambassadors were sent to and from Venice and Constantinople, but the sources are silent as to their specific mission.[31] Still, it is clear that the plans of the Venetian authorities for the defence of their territories in the 1320s centred on combining forces with the allied eastern Aegean powers and the Byzantines to form a pan-Aegean naval league.

The Naval League of 1333–1334

By the early 1330s the plans for a naval league began to progress more quickly and in 1331 the Venetian Senate ordered the baillies of Negroponte and the duke of Crete to unite in opposition to the Turks.[32] In the following July the doge urged the lords of Crete and Negroponte to form a union with the Hospitallers, Niccolò Sanudo the Duke of Naxos and Bartolommeo II Ghisi the Lord of Tenos and Mykonos, and also dispatched envoys to Constantinople to discuss the possibility of Byzantine involvement in a coalition.[33] Martino Zaccaria, who had previously featured in a potential

---

[27] *Le deliberazioni (Senato)*, vol. 1, p. 296, doc. 175; Laiou, 'Marino Sanudo Torsello', 379–80; idem, *Constantinople and the Latins*, pp. 313–14; Jacoby, 'Catalans, Turcs et Vénitiens en Romanie', 248; Zachariadou, *Trade and Crusade*, p. 15; Idem, 'The Catalans of Athens', 830.

[28] See Marino Sanudo, 'Epistolae', ed. Bongars, letters 3, 5, 16, 20; Cerlini, 'Nuovo lettere di Marino Sanudo', letters 2, 5; Roddy trans., letters 7, 15, 18, 21, 23, 26; Thiriet, *Assemblées*, vol. 1, docs 457–9; Zachariadou, 'The Catalans of Athens', 831–3.

[29] *Le deliberazioni (Senato)*, vol. 1, p. 341–2, docs 194, 202.

[30] *Le deliberazioni (Senato)*, vol. 1, p. 348, doc. 270.

[31] *Le deliberazioni (Senato)*, vol. 1, pp. 349, 51, docs. 284, 315; Laiou, *Constantinople and the Latins*, p. 314; Idem, 'Marino Sanudo Torsello', 381.

[32] *Le deliberazioni (Senato)*, vol. 1, pp. 434, 437, 444, 453, docs 264, 302, 36, 159, 159.

[33] Theotokes, *Thespismata*, vol. 2.1, pp. 108–9, doc. 5; *Le deliberazioni (Senato)*, vol. 2, pp. 46–7, doc. 158; Loenertz, *Les Ghisi*, pp. 157, 215–16.

league, was however absent: he had lost Chios to the Byzantines in 1329 and was imprisoned in Constantinople, although he was to feature again in a naval league after his release in 1337.[34] Shortly after communications had been sent to the potential participants, the baillie of Negroponte, Petro Zeno, and the captain of the Adriatic Gulf, Petro de Canale, were given full powers to create a union with all interested parties.[35] Provisions were then shipped to the East for the Venetian galleys, and the Greek emperor gave his assent to the alliance, informing the doge that Petro de Canale would act as his representative in the forthcoming discussions. On 6 September, Canale, now a representative of both Venice and Byzantium, met with the Master of the Hospitallers, Hélion of Villeneuve, and a number of Venetian plenipotentiaries at Rhodes to finalize the arrangements for the league. The record of the meeting reported that the envoys had entered mutually and harmoniously into a 'union, confederation, league and alliance' for the 'exaltation and praise of the divine name' and the confusion of the Turks. It was decided that twenty armed galleys would be furnished for a period of five years; of these the Greek emperor would provide ten, Venice six and the Hospitallers four. This fleet was to gather in the harbour of Negroponte by 15 April 1333, then it would be ready to proceed against the naval and land forces of the 'Agarenes and Turks'.[36] In addition, Canale and Villeneuve agreed that the captain-general of the fleet should be a Venetian.[37]

However, the date of the mobilization of the fleet at Negroponte came

---

[34] See Carr, 'Trade or crusade?', p. 132.

[35] *DVL*, vol. 1, docs 113–14, 116; Thiriet, *Sénat*, vol. 1, doc. 22; Laiou, 'Marino Sanudo Torsello', 384–6; Lemerle, *L'émirat d'Aydin*, pp. 91–2. In early 1332, the Senate also ordered emissaries to be sent to Naples in order to recruit King Robert for the alliance, although he never committed to a league: N. Housley, 'Angevin Naples and the defence of the Latin East: Robert the Wise and the naval league of 1334', *Byzantion* 51 (1981), 548–56 (repr. in Idem, *Crusading and Warfare in Medieval and Renaissance Europe*, Variorum Reprints (Aldershot, 2001), XIII); D. Abulafia, 'Venice and the kingdom of Naples in the last years of Robert the Wise: 1332–43', *Papers of the British School at Rome* 48 (1980), 186–204, at 189–90. Also the Catalans stated that they were willing to assist Venice against the Turks, but the Republic, probably suspicious of their motives, rejected the offer: Zachariadou, 'The Catalans of Athens', 834–5.

[36] *DVL*, vol. 1, doc. 116–17. This agreement has been studied in detail by many scholars. For a recent comprehensive narrative of events, see Ivanov, '*Sancta Unio*', 153–5. See also, Delaville le Roulx, *Les Hospitaliers à Rhodes*, pp. 87–8; Lemerle, *L'émirat d'Aydin*, pp. 91–2; Setton, *The Papacy and the Levant*, vol. 1, pp. 180–1; Loenertz, *Les Ghisi*, pp. 157–8; Zachariadou, *Trade and Crusade*, pp. 24–5; Housley, *Avignon Papacy*, pp. 25–6. For Byzantine, Hospitaller and Catalan perspectives, see Setton, *The Catalan Domination of Athens*, pp. 36; D.J. Geanakoplos, 'Byzantium and the Crusades: 1261–1354', in *A History of the Crusades*, ed. K.M. Setton, 6 vols (Madison, 1969–1989), vol. 3, pp. 27–68, at pp. 50–1; Nicol, *Last Centuries of Byzantium*, pp. 177–9; Laiou, 'Marino Sanudo Torsello', 386.

[37] *DVL*, i. doc. 117, p. 229.

and went with no sign of action. One factor for this delay was the outbreak of a revolt on Crete in the summer of 1333, which prevented the armament of two galleys of the league and diverted Venetian resources in the region.[38] In the meantime, the members of the coalition discussed the idea of allying with some of the beyliks against Aydin, before the Venetian Senate decided that the galleys for the league should be made ready for the following May (1334).[39] At this point, the *Serenissima* made efforts to extend the league to other interested parties, including Philip VI of France and Hugh IV of Cyprus.[40] Crucially, during the negotiations of the second half of 1333 and early 13334, Pope John XXII, who had not yet fully committed himself to the Venetian league, for reasons which are discussed in Chapter 5, also agreed to lend his support. In the following months the kings of France and Cyprus followed suit.[41] In early 1334, the participants agreed that the fleet would consist of a total of forty galleys: ten to be provided by Venice, ten from the Hospitallers, six from the Byzantines, six from Cyprus and eight from the papacy and France together. This fleet was to assemble at Negroponte in May and serve for five months.[42]

In the winter of 1333–4, whilst the Franco-papal flotilla was under construction in France, the Venetian galleys already in the Aegean engaged the united Turkish forces of Umur of Aydin and Suleiman, the emir of Sarukhan, near the Morea, as well as those of a Slavonic pirate named Zassi who was possibly in league with the Turks. Around this time the

---

[38] For the rebellion, see F. Thiriet, 'Sui dissidi sorti tra il Comune di Venezia e i suoi feudatari di Creta nel Trecento', *Archivio Storico Italiano* 114 (1956), 699–712, at 702–5; Zachariadou, *Trade and Crusade*, pp. 26–7.

[39] Thiriet, *Sénat*, vol. 1, doc. 37–9; Zachariadou, *Trade and Crusade*, pp. 28–9.

[40] John XXII, *Lettres secrètes*, vol. 4, doc. 5276; Thiriet, *Sénat*, vol. 1, doc. 37; Edbury, *The Kingdom of Cyprus and the Crusades*, p. 157; Coureas, *The Latin Church in Cyprus: 1313–1378*, p. 98.

[41] *AE*, vol. 24, pp. 511–16, ch. 13–19; John XXII, *Lettres secrètes*, vol. 4, docs 5247, 5324; John XXII, *Lettres communes*, vol. 12, doc. 60781, 60898–900; *DVL*, vol. 1, doc. 122, 124; Theotokes, *Thespismata*, vol. 2.1, pp. 136–41, docs 20, 27. This is discussed in detail by S.M. Theotokes, 'E prôte summachia tôn kuriarchôn kratôn tou aigaiou chata tês kathodou tôn tourkôn archomenou tou 14 aiônos', *Epeteris Etaireias Byzantinon Spoudon* 7 (1930), 283–98, at 287–8; Lemerle, *L'émirat d'Aydin*, pp. 93–6; Setton, *Papacy and the Levant*, vol. 1, pp. 181–2; Zachariadou, *Trade and Crusade*, pp. 30–1; Coureas, *The Latin Church in Cyprus: 1313–1378*, p. 98.

[42] 'Die Protokollbücher der päpstlichen Kammerkleriker: 1329–1347', ed. H. Schröder, *Archiv für Kulturgeschichte* 27 (1937), 121–286, at 256–62; *DVL*, vol. 1, doc. 126–7; John XXII, *Lettres secrètes*, vol. 4, doc. 5485; Theotokes, *Thespismata*, vol. 2.1, pp. 139–41, 44–7, docs 27, 36, 41. Some scholars, including Ivanov, have claimed that Robert of Naples also contributed galleys to the league. However, the silence of any contemporary sources attesting to the presence of Neapolitan galleys in the Aegean makes this highly unlikely. See Ivanov, 'Sancta Unio', 167, n. 131, and a more thorough discussion by Housley, 'Angevin Naples and the defence of the Latin east', 555.

Venetians may have also launched an assault on the harbour of Smyrna itself.[43] In the summer of 1334 the Franco-papal force joined with the fleet of the Venetians, Hospitallers and Cypriots in the Aegean, bringing the league, with the exception of the Byzantine galleys, up to full strength.[44] Thereafter, the fleet attacked the emirates of Aydin, Karasi and Sarukhan along the north-eastern coast of Asia Minor. In the autumn of 1334 a major battle took place near the Gulf of Adramyttion, opposite Lesbos, and on the land nearby, where a fleet belonging to Yakhshi, the emir of Karasi, was defeated. Marino Sanudo described several encounters during this time in a letter to Hugh of Cyprus. Unfortunately the letter is badly damaged and is undated, obscuring the events it describes. Nevertheless, it is apparent that Sanudo claimed that the crusaders destroyed a number of Turkish vessels on the feast of the Nativity of the Virgin (8 September), and again on the 11th, 14th and 17th of September, during which the son-in-law of Yakhshi was killed.[45] The battle was important enough to attract the attention of several western chroniclers, including Giovanni Villani in Florence and the French continuator of William of Nangis at St Denis.[46]

When compared with other crusade projects of the early fourteenth century, the league accomplished a great deal in a relatively short period of time. The numbers of sources which report the battle at Adramyttion suggest that it was undoubtedly an important Christian victory and in the months that the fleet patrolled the Aegean, the Latins enjoyed a level of

[43] The exact chronology of these events is obscure. See the discussions in Zachariadou, *Trade and Crusade*, pp. 29–30, and Ivanov, 'Sancta Unio', 166, n. 123.

[44] Andronikos III never contributed galleys to the naval league, although according to Nikephoros Gregoras he did furnish a number of galleys in 1335, but by this time the league had disbanded: Nikephoros Gregoras, *Byzantina Historia*, vol. 1, bk. 9, ch. 5, pp. 523–5; Zachariadou, *Trade and Crusade*, pp. 37–8; cf. H. Inalcik, 'The rise of the Turkish maritime principalities in Anatolia', 192.

[45] Kunstmann, 'Studien über Marino Sanudo', 811–12 (letter 7); Roddy trans., p. 296 (letter 35). In another letter written by Sanudo in Venice on 22 October (presumably before news of the battle had reached him), Sanudo mentioned that 200 Turkish vessels were at Adramyttion: de la Roncière and Dorez, 'Lettres inédites et mémoires de Marino Sanudo l'ancien', 35–6 (letter 3); Roddy trans., 301–2 (letter 37).

[46] Giovanni Villani, *Nuova cronica*, vol. 3, bk. 12, ch. 18, p. 58; William of Nangis and Continuator, *Chronique latine de Guillaume de Nangis de 1113 à 1300, avec les continuations de cette chronique de 1300 à 1368*, ed. H. Géraud, 2 vols (Paris, 1843), vol. 2, p. 145; Ludovico Bonconte Monaldesco, 'Fragmenta Annalium Romanorum', RIS 12 (Milan, 1728), cols. 527–42, at col. 537; AE, vol. 25, p. 5, ch. 11. The exact chronology of the battle remains obscure. See the different opinions given by Theotokes, 'E prōte summachia', 283–98; Lemerle, *L'émirat d'Aydin*, pp. 97–100; Laiou, 'Marino Sanudo Torsello', 387; Zachariadou, *Trade and Crusade*, pp. 29–33; Ivanov, 'Sancta Unio', 170–2; V. Laurent, 'Action de grâces pour la victoire navale remportée sur les Turcs à Atramyttion au cours de l'automne 1334', *Eis Mnemen K.I. Amantou* (Athens, 1960), pp. 25–41.

security not yet experienced in the fourteenth century.[47] This was primarily because the league took advantage of the maritime supremacy which the Latins enjoyed at the time and it built upon an established tradition of minor maritime alliances which had been in place since the early 1300s. The Hospitallers and the Zaccaria had demonstrated that when their resources and intelligence were pooled together they were capable of resisting even the greatest of attacks from the beyliks. When the two other major Latin players in the East – Venice and Cyprus – also consolidated their forces in alliance, the combined Latin forces were strong enough to go on the offensive against the Turks. Interestingly, as will be discussed in Chapter 5, it is the participation of the papacy and the French in the 1333–4 naval league that has attracted the most attention from scholars even though their contributions were belated and of less consequence to the overall achievements of the league than those of the Venetians, Hospitallers and Cypriots, whose galleys were already successfully patrolling the Aegean.

The Naval Leagues of the Smyrna Campaign (1343–1352)

No naval league materialized during the pontificate of Benedict XII, the reasons for which are discussed in Chapter 5, but his successor, Clement VI, oversaw the formation of two naval leagues, the first in 1343, which formed the preliminary wave of the Crusade of Smyrna, and the second in 1350. The first operation was officially proclaimed as a crusade by Clement VI in the summer of 1343, although negotiations between the Hospitallers, Cypriots and Venetians had been ongoing since 1341. In total it was decided that twenty galleys were to be fitted out for this league: six from Venice, six from the Hospitallers, four from the papacy, and four from Cyprus, a number slightly lower than the league of 1333–4 and with the absence of the French. The fleet was to gather at Negroponte on the Feast of All Saints (1 November) 1343.[48]

---

[47] This view is shared by Lemerle, *L'émirat d'Aydin*, p. 98, and Geanakoplos, 'Byzantium and the Crusades', p. 51.

[48] ASVat, *RV* 157, fols 1v–3, ep. 19, 23–4, *RV* 62 fols 48, 49v–50 (8 Aug 1343); Clement VI, *Lettres à la France*, vol. 1, doc. 341; summaries in Clement VI, *Lettres à la France*, vol. 1, docs 332, 336, 337. The campaign has also been the focus of many other studies, see in particular Delaville le Roulx, *La France en Orient*, vol. 1, pp. 103–12; N. Jorga, *Philippe de Mézières, 1327–1405, et la croisade au XIVe siècle* (Paris, 1896), pp. 33–62; Gay, *Le Pape Clément VI*, pp. 32–80; Atiya, *The Crusade in the Later Middle Ages*, pp. 293–318; Lemerle, *L'émirat d'Aydin*, pp. 180–203; Setton, *Papacy and the Levant*, vol. 1, pp. 195–223; Zachariadou, *Trade and Crusade*, pp. 41–62; Housley, *Avignon Papacy*, pp. 33–6; Housley, *The Later Crusades*, pp. 59–62; D. Wood, *Clement VI: The Pontificate and Ideas of an Avignon Pope* (Cambridge, 1989), pp. 184–91; Demurger, 'Le pape Clément VI et l'Orient', pp. 207–14; Coureas, *The Latin Church in Cyprus: 1313–1378*, pp. 102–9.

Figure 4. Engraving depicting the harbour fortress and acropolis of Smyrna.

Once the captains of the galleys were appointed and other logistical considerations taken care of, the fleet assembled in the Aegean in the winter of 1343–4. In the following spring naval operations were undertaken against the Turks, which initially achieved a similar level of success to those in 1333–4. In one encounter in May, the crusader galleys won a notable victory against the Turks at Longos, a harbour on Pallena (the western promontory of the Chalkidike peninsula), where they ambushed and burned a fleet of some sixty vessels and captured a close relative of a Turkish emir.[49] In October this was followed by an even more impressive feat when the crusaders launched a surprise attack on Smyrna, where they managed to capture the harbour and harbour fortress of the city from Umur Pasha, but not the acropolis overlooking the city which remained in his hands (see Fig. 4).[50] Thereafter,

[49] See John Kantakouzenos, *Historiarum Libri IV*, vol. 2, bk. 3, ch. 69, pp. 422–3; Guglielmo Cortusi, *Chronica de novitatibus Padue et Lombardie*, p. 109; John of Winterthur, *Chronica*, ed. C. Brun, *MGHSS*, n.s. 3 (Berlin, 1955), p. 250; Lemerle, *L'émirat d'Aydin*, pp. 187–8; Setton, *Papacy and the Levant*, vol. 1, pp. 190–2; Zachariadou, *Trade and Crusade*, p. 49; Leonhard, *Genua und die päpstliche Kurie in Avignon*, p. 173. It is probably this encounter which led Clement VI to send three letters, in July and August 1344, congratulating the crusaders on their progress oversees: Clement VI, *Lettres à la France*, vol. 1, docs 987–8, 1027.
[50] For the assault on Smyrna, see Enveri, *Le destān d'Umūr Pacha*, pp. 111–13 (verses 1913–68); Nikephoros Gregoras, *Byzantina Historia*, vol. 2, bk. 13, ch. 4, p. 689; John Kantakouzenos,

it is likely that some of the combatants on the galleys remained to garrison the fortress at Smyrna, but the league, presumably now somewhat depleted in strength, still managed to repel an assault from the Turks led by a high-ranking naval officer, Mustafa, who was captured.[51]

These initial successes, however, proved to be short-lived, as on 17 January 1345 the crusade leaders, including the papal legate Henry of Asti, and the captains of the papal and Venetian galleys, Martino Zaccaria and Petro Zeno, were killed outside the walls of the city.[52] The Venetians and the Hospitallers diverted reinforcements to Smyrna in the spring, but soon after the Aydin-oglus began launching new raids in the Aegean from their other ports, especially Ephesos.[53] In the wake of this setback and the ensuing stalemate, Clement VI looked to the West for a suitable commander to lead a relief army to Smyrna and revive the fortunes of the failing crusade. The most enthusiastic and possibly only response to Clement's call came from Humbert II, the young and wealthy Dauphin of Viennois. He took the cross and was officially named as captain-general of the Christian army in May 1345. After marching through northern Italy, where chronicles report many people taking the cross, Humbert, accompanied by an army of around one hundred knights and eight hundred footsoldiers, sailed from Venice for the Aegean, reaching Negroponte in December 1345, where he joined up with six galleys from the league; the four papal galleys and one each from the Hospitaller and Venetian contingents.[54] When in the Aegean, Humbert made several unsuccessful attempts to recruit allies to bolster his force before he was attacked by a Genoese fleet commanded by Simone Vignoso who went on to capture the island of Chios, which Humbert had been considering as a potential base for the crusaders.[55] After this setback, the dauphin sailed to Smyrna, arriving in July 1346. Despite Humbert's arrival, however, after this point the unity of the league began to crumble as the Venetians sought peace with the Turks and the Hospitallers sided with the Genoese, even preventing Venetian ships from entering the port at Smyrna.[56] This infighting, plus the outbreak of disease amongst the crusader camp, forced Humbert to withdraw to Rhodes, whence he soon

---

Historiarum Libri IV, vol. 2, bk. 3, ch. 68, pp. 419–20; and the various letters reporting the victory in Clement VI, *Lettres à la France*, vol. 1, docs 1350–1, 1395, 1397, 1462, 1464; *DVL*, vol. 1, doc. 150.

[51] Anonimo Romano, *Cronica*, p. 78; Zachariadou, *Trade and Crusade*, p. 50.

[52] This is also discussed in Chapter 4, p. 91.

[53] *Duca di Candia: Quaternus consiliorum (1340–1350)*, ed. P. Ratti-Vidulich (Venice, 1976), docs 34–5, 49–50, 53–4; Thiriet, *Assemblées*, vol. 1, doc. 513; Zachariadou, *Trade and Crusade*, p. 51.

[54] See Carr, 'Humbert of Viennois and the Crusade of Smyrna', 239–41; Housley, *Avignon Papacy*, pp. 146–8; Setton, *Papacy and the Levant*, vol. 1, pp. 197–202.

[55] Leonhard, *Genua und die päpstliche Kurie in Avignon*, pp. 176–9.

[56] See A.T. Luttrell, 'Crete and Rhodes: 1340–1360', in *Acts of the International Congress of*

after departed for western Europe.[57] Fortunately for the crusaders, by 1347 the Hospitallers and the Venetians had managed to settle their differences and in the following spring the galleys of the league, combined with Hospitaller reinforcements, won a notable victory against the Turks of Aydin and Sarukhan off the island of Imbros.[58] In the spring of 1348 the Latins were given another boost when Umur was killed at Smyrna, apparently shot by an arrow when assaulting the walls of the harbour fortress.[59]

However, the progress of the crusaders was quickly put on hold by the arrival of the Black Death. The great pandemic had been contracted by the Genoese during the siege of Caffa by the Mongols of the Golden Horde in 1346, after which it was carried to Constantinople the following May and then to the western coast of Asia Minor and the European side of the Straits in autumn.[60] By 1348 it had spread to most parts of Anatolia and the Aegean, where it reportedly killed more than in any other area.[61] The disease also reached Italy and southern France, where it is estimated that up to half the population of Avignon died during a seven-month period.[62] The Florentine chronicler Giovanni Villani, who is one of the most reliable informants on both western European and Aegean affairs, leaves a vivid testimony of the progress of the plague from the eastern Mediterranean:

> Having grown in strength and vigour in Turkey and Greece and having spread thence over the whole Levant and Mesopotamia and Syria and Chaldea and Cyprus and Rhodes and all the islands of the Greek archipelago, the said pestilence leaped to Sicily, Sardinia and Corsica and Elba, and from there

---

Cretan Studies II (Athens, 1974), pp. 167–75, at pp. 170–3; Zachariadou, *Trade and Crusade*, pp. 52–3. This is discussed in more detail in Chapter 6, pp. 129–32.

[57] For Humbert's crusade at Smyrna see Carr, 'Humbert of Viennois and the Crusade of Smyrna', 245–6; J.-P. Valbonnais, *Histoire du Dauphiné et des princes qui ont porté le nom de dauphins*, 2 vols (Geneva, 1721–2), vol. 1, pp. 334–44; M.C. Faure, 'Le dauphin Humbert II à Venise et en Orient (1345–1347)', *Mélanges d'archéologie et d'histoire* 27 (1907), 509–562; Setton, *Papacy and the Levant*, vol. 1, pp. 195–223.

[58] Clement VI, *Lettres à la France*, vol. 2, docs 3336–7; *Duca di Candia: Quaternus consiliorum*, docs 164–5; Delaville le Roulx, *Hospitaliers à Rhodes*, p. 108; Zachariadou, *Trade and Crusade*, pp. 53–4; cf. J. Sarnowsky, 'Die Johanniter und Smyrna 1344–1402 (Teil 2: Quellen)', *Römische Quartalschrift* 87 (1992), 47–98, at 50, doc. 3.

[59] Nikephoros Gregoras, *Byzantina Historia*, vol. 2, bk. 16, ch. 7, pp. 834–5; Lemerle, *L'émirat d'Aydin*, pp. 227–9.

[60] O.J. Benedictow, *The Black Death, 1346–1353: The Complete History* (Woodbridge, 2004), pp. 57–74; M.W. Dols, *The Black Death in the Middle East* (Princeton, 1977), 52–5; S. Barry and N. Gualde, 'La Peste noire dans l'Occident chrétien et musulman, 1347–1353', *Canadian Bulletin of Medical History* 25.2 (2008), 461–98.

[61] See the account of Giovanni Villani, *Nuova cronica*, vol. 3, bk. 13, ch. 84, p. 486.

[62] G. Mollat, *The Popes at Avignon: 1305–1378*, trans. J. Love (London, 1963), p. 40; Setton, *Papacy and the Levant*, vol. 1, p. 187.

soon reached all the shores of the mainland [...] And many lands and cities were made desolate. And the plague lasted till –.[63]

Here Villani deliberately left a blank space after the word 'till' to be filled in once the disease had been lifted from Florence – a task that was never fulfilled: Villani too fell victim to the Black Death before completing his work.

Considering the virulence of this pandemic, it comes as no surprise to learn that crusading operations were severely hampered by this outbreak. To add to this, Romania was suffering a severe shortage of grain caused by the closure of the Black Sea markets, discussed fully in Chapter 6. The crusaders were thus forced to seek a truce with Aydin, the negotiations for which dragged on for some years.[64] By the time the leaders of the league met at Avignon in 1350 to discuss its future, the Turks had begun launching new raids into the Aegean, which led to the renewal of the league and not the agreement of a truce. This new league was officially confirmed in August 1350, when it was decided that a small flotilla of eight galleys was to be assembled in the Aegean; three each provided by Venice and the Hospitallers, and two more from Cyprus. However, only a few weeks later war broke out between Venice and Genoa, thus ending any hopes of a Venetian contribution to this league. Due to the Venetian-Genoese war, the lack of funds and the ravages of the Black Death, less than a year after it was re-formed, this second naval league was officially dissolved by Clement VI in the summer of 1351.[65] A year later the pope, who had done so much to facilitate the formation of two naval leagues, died.

[63] Giovanni Villani, *Nuova cronica*, vol. 3, bk. 13, ch. 84, p. 487; F. Schevill, *A History of Florence: From the Founding of the City through the Renaissance* (New York, 1936), pp. 238–40; Benedictow, *Black Death*, p. 69.

[64] The economic crisis in the Black Sea is discussed in more detail in Chapter 6, pp. 127–9.

[65] Clement VI, *Lettres à la France*, vol. 3, docs 4661, 5051–4, 5056; Clement VI, *Lettres autres que la France*, doc. 2193; Setton, *Papacy and the Levant*, vol. 1, pp. 219–23; Zachariadou, *Trade and Crusade*, pp. 56–60.

4

Logistics and Strategies

The battle was hard and cruel between them [...] at the first strike our galleys seized four of the aforementioned vessels of the Turks; of the rest they in fact had only their retreat. They all fled to the land of the island of Chios, with the exception of twelve ships, which our galleys could not overcome or seize at all in view of the fact that night had now come upon them; of the aforementioned vessels we finally overcame and seized twenty, on which we took more than two thousand Turks, living or dead, and this not through our own merits, but by divine grace. Indeed, the rest, who fled to the land, were all killed or captured, with the result that finally not a single one of them escaped.

Gerard of Pins, papal *vicarius* of the Hospitallers, letter to Pope John XXII reporting a naval victory against the Turks, 1 September 1319.[1]

Now that an overview of the evolution of the naval leagues has been given, it is time to make some observations on the logistics and strategies adopted during the campaigns. This will help to place the leagues within the wider context of medieval naval warfare and also to explain the overwhelming supremacy which the Latins enjoyed at the time. Fortunately the communications preserved in the papal and Venetian archives between the Latin powers over the formation of a league contain enough detail to draw some conclusions regarding the assembly of the fleets and their activities in the East. This includes information on their composition, in terms of both vessels and manpower, the types of tactics they adopted in combat, and the numbers of the enemy they faced.

Ship Types

Since the time of the First Crusade, the shipyards of the Italian maritime cities were producing some of the largest and most technologically advanced vessels in the Mediterranean.[2] These consisted of two basic varieties, which

---

[1]   Gatto, 'Martino Zaccaria', 337–9, doc. 1.

[2]   There are a great many studies into medieval ship types. For an introduction to those used from the twelfth to fourteenth centuries, see in particular J.E. Dotson, 'Ship types and fleet composition at Genoa and Venice in the early thirteenth century', in *Logistics of Warfare in the Age of the Crusades*, ed. John H. Pryor (Farnham, 2006), pp. 63–75; Idem,

were often (but not always) utilized for contrasting roles: sail-powered ships for commerce and oar-powered ships for war. The most well-known versions of these two ship types were the *navis* and the *galea*, which were also regularly mentioned by authors reporting on naval conflicts in the Aegean. By the thirteenth century, the Venetians, Genoese and others were commonly using the *navis* for commercial purposes. *Navis* corresponded to the English 'ship', but invariably meant a capacious, broad-beamed cargo vessel, separated by two or three decks and carrying sails on two or three masts. The primary oared vessel was the *galea* (galley), which was understood to be a long, narrow-beamed vessel capable of being sailed occasionally but designed primarily for propulsion by oars. In very basic terms the *navis* and the *galea* had obvious contrasting characteristics: galleys were fast, slender-hulled vessels, but they had limited capacity and were very demanding in terms of crew numbers and provisions. Broad sail-powered ships, on the other hand, were slower, less manoeuvrable and reliant on wind, but they had a much greater capacity for cargo and men. As well as this, sources reporting on the Aegean frequently mention *husserium*, *barcha* and *ligna*, the latter of which literally meant 'plank' and was analogous to the English word 'vessel', referring to water craft in a general sense. *Barchae* were smaller craft, sometimes considered as lifeboats kept on board larger vessels (such as *barcha de parascelmo*).[3] *Husseria* (*cum equis*) were horse transports. These came in various forms and could be large sailed transports or oared transports. The ones used in the Aegean are specified in the sources as those powered by oars, some of which would have probably been fitted with a horse port at the stern to allow both horse and rider to disembark.[4] Hybrid

---

'Merchant and naval influences on galley design at Venice and Genoa in the fourteenth century', in *New Aspects of Naval History: Selected Papers Presented at the Fourth Naval History Symposium, United States Naval Academy*, ed. C.L. Symonds (Annapolis, 1981), pp. 20–32; Idem, 'Everything is a compromise: Mediterranean ship design, thirteenth to sixteenth centuries', in *The Art, Science, and Technology of Medieval Travel*, ed. R.O. Bork and A. Kann (Farnham, 2008), pp. 31–40; Pryor, *Geography, Technology and War*, pp. 25–86; Idem, 'The naval architecture of crusader transport ships: A reconstruction of some archetypes for round-hulled sailing ships', in Idem, *Commerce, Shipping and Naval Warfare in the Medieval Mediterranean*, Variorum Reprints (London, 1987), VII, pp. 171–219, 275–92, 363–86. Other useful studies include F. Ciciliot, 'Sources for medieval nautical archaeology: Genoese notarial records', *International Journal of Nautical Archaeology* 25/3–4 (1996), 239–42; L.V. Mott, 'Serving in the fleet: crews and recruitment issues in the Catalan-Aragonese fleets during the war of the Sicilian Vespers (1282–1302)', *Cross-cultural Encounters on the High Seas (Tenth–Sixteenth Centuries)*, ed. K.L. Reyerson = *Journal of Medieval Encounters* 13 (2006), 56–77; R. Gertwagen, 'Nautical technology', in *A Companion to Mediterranean History*, ed. P. Horden and S. Kinoshita (Chichester, 2014), pp. 154–69, esp. pp. 161–4.
[3] Dotson, 'Ship types and fleet composition at Genoa and Venice', p. 65.
[4] On horse transports, see L.R. Martin, 'Horse and cargo handling on medieval Mediterranean ships', *The International Journal of Nautical Archaeology* 31 (2002), 237–47; Pryor, 'The naval architecture of crusader transport ships', pp. 171–219, 275–92, 363–86; Idem,

ships combining features of both oared and sailing vessels also existed, as
well as sailing ships which used oars on occasion.

In military terms, over the course of the thirteenth century the composition of western war fleets in the Mediterranean changed considerably,
evolving from the mixture of galleys, smaller oared vessels and sailing
ships seen in earlier decades to fleets dominated primarily by the galley in
the latter half of the century. The galleys used at this point were typically
biremes, which had two men on a rowing bench, each with an oar. Biremes
usually had twenty-seven benches to a side, making 108 rowers in total. The
oarsmen could only fight once contact had been made with an opposing
vessel, so they were complemented by twenty to thirty crossbowmen or
marines, as well as officers and other crew, bringing the full number of
men to around 165 per ship. The change to largely galley-based war fleets
does not, however, mean that biremes were the only fighting vessels used
during this period; large *naves* (the round-hulled sailing ships mentioned
above) could also be effective fighting ships. They were virtually immune
to oared vessels because of their high freeboard and could also carry significantly more fighting men on board, sometimes as many as five hundred.
However, their lack of speed and agility made them impractical for offensive
operations. Moreover, large sailed ships were considerably more expensive to
produce than galleys, making them less common in Mediterranean waters.[5]

Over the course of the fourteenth century the Genoese in particular
would pioneer the use of even heavier cargo ships, and eventually carracks,
but when resisting the Turks in the Aegean the galley remained the vessel of
choice for the Latin naval powers.[6] The lower cost of galleys was one reason
for this, but also the natural conditions of the Aegean meant that galleys
were more suited to the region. Although the sea was interspersed with
many islands and ports, sailing could be made difficult because of strong
seasonal winds, currents and stretches of treacherous coast. For example, the
Meltemi winds, known as the Etesian in Antiquity, blow steadily from May
to September from the north-east and could slow down voyages considerably, especially when sailing against the winds from the south west of
the sea to the Dardanelles and on to Constantinople.[7] The waters of the

'The naval architecture of crusader transport ships, revisited', *The Mariner's Mirror* 76 (1990),
255–73.

[5]   On the comparison between galleys and round ships, see Dotson, 'Ship types and fleet
composition at Genoa and Venice', pp. 63–75; Idem, 'Everything is a compromise', pp. 33–5.

[6]   S. Stantchev, '*Devedo*: The Venetian response to Sultan Mehmed II in the Venetian-
Ottoman conflict of 1462–79', *Mediterranean Studies (The Journal of the Mediterranean Studies
Association)* 19 (2010), 43–66, at 46–9; Rose, *Medieval Naval Warfare*, pp. 85–8.

[7]   On the Meltemi winds, see Pryor, *Geography, Technology and War*, p. 20. Despite the
strength of the Meltemi winds, sailing against them was unavoidable in the Aegean and
therefore commonplace: Gluzman, 'Between Venice and the Levant', 272–3.

eastern coast of Asia Minor were also strewn with islands, reefs and shoals, making sailing treacherous, and ships often had to wait to enter the Dardanelles from Tenedos because of the currents in the straits and the prevailing winds.[8] These are only a few examples of the natural conditions which posed difficulties to sailors in the Aegean. Considering these factors, the galley, with its superior manoeuvrability, low draft and oared propulsion, was a far more suitable vessel for offensive operations.

In terms of ship production, Venetian fleets were constructed at the famous state Arsenal in the lagoon, whilst Genoese fleets consisted of a mixture of communal and private vessels. Up until the mid thirteenth century this had always been a disadvantage to Genoa, whose system was administratively more cumbersome than that of Venice, but in later years the greater technical innovation of the Genoese system became an advantage.[9] This led to two important developments at the end of the thirteenth century: the introduction of the compass (allowing winter navigation) and, significantly, the birth of a new breed of fighting vessel – the trireme – which came to replace the lighter biremes of the earlier years. Unlike the bireme, the trireme sat three oarsmen per bench, each with an oar. Because of this, it had to be built with a wider hull (roughly 5 metres, compared with 3.7 metres for a bireme), but it remained the same length (approximately 40 metres). A broader hull would usually result in a reduction in speed, but the additional oarsmen meant that a trireme was capable of about the same speed as its predecessor, or even slightly swifter. This resulted in a heavier and more stable vessel, with a capacity at least three times greater at the cost of a 50 per cent increase in crew size. The larger capacity for marines and mechanical artillery, coupled with greater stability – at little or no cost to speed and manoeuvrability – made this a far more effective fighting vessel.[10] Furthermore, the increased capacity made triremes more economical when not used for fighting, resulting in their regular employment as cargo vessels in the fourteenth century, especially for the shipment of high value merchandise.[11] The galleys of the first naval league, for

---

[8]　The natural conditions of the Aegean are discussed in detail by Pryor, *Geography, Technology and War*, pp. 97–9.

[9]　See Chapter 1 (pp. 23–4) and also Dotson, 'Venice, Genoa and control of the seas', pp. 123–4; Rose, *Medieval Naval Warfare*, pp. 6–12.

[10]　Dotson, 'Everything is a compromise', pp. 33–5; Idem, 'Merchant and naval influences on galley design', pp. 23–5; Pryor, *Geography, Technology and War*, pp. 64–7. By the middle of the fourteenth century, the governments of the merchant republics had introduced detailed regulations on the sizes of their galleys. Reproductions of these, including a Genoese galley of Romania from 1333 and a galley described by Marino Sanudo, can be found in Dotson, 'Merchant and naval influence on galley design', pp. 26–30.

[11]　Dotson, 'Everything is a compromise', pp. 34–7.

example, were initially permitted to carry merchandise, although this was later forbidden by the pope in order to expedite their progress.[12]

Manpower

The galleys used in the Aegean during the fourteenth century would have been mostly triremes, holding in the region of twenty-five to twenty-eight benches per side, with three oarsmen on each bench, giving around 150–168 oarsmen on each galley. The rowers were free men who were employed primarily to propel the vessel, but they were also expected to fight in boarding actions or even on land if required. Sometimes the third oarsmen on each bench were also used as archers, known as *terzaroles*, who could either fight or row according to what was necessary.[13] The usefulness of oarsmen for land-based fighting or as *terzaroles* was, however, questionable. Philip de Mézières complained that all of the Christian sailors fled 'in a cowardly manner' after being attacked by the Turks when returning to their galleys at Lampsakos in 1359 and Ramon Muntaner declared that the advantages *terzaroles* gave in terms of speed were far outweighed by the use of professional crossbowmen in battle.[14] In addition to this, galleys would have had a number of specialist marines, sailors, medics and officers on board, possibly in the range of thirty to forty men, increasing the total numbers onboard to around 180–208 men.[15] This fits roughly with the figures given by the Venetians to Pope John XXII in preparation for the league of 1333–4, where the doge advised that forty armed galleys be equipped 'in each of which there should be two hundred men', as well as fifty horse transports, each carrying 'at least 120 oarsmen and twenty horsemen'.[16] For the papal galleys contracted for the same league the numbers were similar, at 174–180 oarsmen, with twenty-five crossbowmen or marines, as well as retinues, scribes, other officials and the ship's manager (*patronus*). Suitable provisions and equipment were also listed for each of these papal galleys, such as biscuit, sails, cordage and anchors, as well as arms, including 130 cuirasses, 150 helmets, 180 shields, 130 gorgets, 4,000 crossbow bolts, 250 lances and

[12] John XXII, *Lettres secrètes*, vol. 4, doc. 5495; *Documents on the Later Crusades*, p. 73, doc. 20.

[13] J.H. Pryor, 'The naval battles of Roger of Lauria', in Idem, *Commerce, Shipping and Naval Warfare in the Medieval Mediterranean*, Variorum Reprints (London, 1987), VI, pp. 179–216, at pp. 186–7; Dotson, 'Merchant and naval influences on galley design', p. 24.

[14] *Documents on the Later Crusades*, pp. 83–5, doc. 25; Pryor, 'The naval battles of Roger of Lauria', p. 187. See also Marino Sanudo, 'Liber Secretorum', pp. 57; Lock trans., pp. 102–3.

[15] A description of the specific duties involved for these other crewmen is given by Mott, 'Serving in the fleet', 60–1.

[16] DVL, vol. 1, doc. 124, p. 241; Theotokes, *Thespismata*, vol. 2.1, p. 140, doc. 27; Setton, *Papacy and the Levant*, vol. 1, pp. 181–2, n. 88; Theotokes, 'E prote summachia', 287–8.

500 small javelins.[17] For the naval league of 1343, the Venetians maintained these numbers when advising Clement VI. On this occasion, they recommended that thirty galleys, each carrying up to 200 men, along with sixty horse transports each of 120 oarsmen and twenty horsemen, be assembled for use against the Turks.[18] The exception to these numbers can be found in the 'Liber Secretorum' of Marino Sanudo, where the author advocated the use of larger galleys with four oarsmen per bench. He consequently recommended that those equipped for his provisional league in the early 1320s should carry up to 250 men, but no other sources suggest that these bigger galleys were ever used against the Turks.[19]

From the figures given above, it is possible to make some estimations regarding the numbers of men serving in each of the naval leagues and their galley strength, so that they can be compared with other campaigns of the period. In terms of the numbers of vessels used in the leagues, it is safe to assume that the documents outlining the final agreements can be trusted, as on both occasions they are corroborated by other independent sources.[20] If this is the case, then officially the 1333–4 league was made up of thirty-four galleys (not including the six promised by the Byzantines which never turned up) and the league that captured Smyrna was made up of twenty.[21] If the numbers of men on board each galley are taken to be around 200, then the galley-strength of the leagues was made up of roughly 6,800 and 4,000 men respectively. When compared with the greatest maritime campaigns of the period, namely the Genoese-Venetian wars, in terms of galley strength this was not particularly large. For example, in the first war of the mid thirteenth century, the average fleet size was around thirty galleys, so not dissimilar to the first naval league. However, in the second and third wars, which spanned the end of the thirteenth and most of the fourteenth century,

[17] *Documents on the Later Crusades*, p. 72, doc. 20.

[18] Full text in Theotokes, *Thespismata*, vol. 2.1, pp. 216–19, doc. 9; summary in Thiriet, *Sénat*, vol. 1, doc. 142; Setton, *Papacy and the Levant*, vol. 1, p. 183, n. 95.

[19] Marino Sanudo, 'Liber Secretorum', pp. 30–1 (marginal note); Lock trans., pp. 62–3. For his general crusade Sanudo also recommended smaller galleys with fewer men, as well as larger ones with five men per bench: 'Liber Secretorum', pp. 5, 30, 56–7, 60, 63–6, 75–8; Lock trans., pp. 26, 61, 102–3, 107–8, 111–15, 128–32.

[20] See the accounts of the leagues discussed in the previous chapter as well as Zachariadou, *Trade and Crusade*, pp. 21–62 and Setton, *The Papacy and the Levant*, vol. 1, pp. 180–223.

[21] The 1334 league was made up of ten galleys from Venice, ten from the Hospitallers, six from Cyprus and eight from the papacy and France together, see Chapter 3, note 42. The 1343 league was made up of six from Venice, six from the Hospitallers, four from the papacy and four from Cyprus, see Chapter 3, note 48. The provisional league of 1332, agreed between the Venetians, Hospitallers and Byzantines, was the same size as that of 1343 and significantly smaller than that of 1334. It was to consist of 20 galleys; ten from Byzantium, six from Venice and four from the Hospitallers, see Chapter 3, note 36. The smaller league of 1350, which never materialized, was meant to be formed of only eight galleys; three each provided by Venice and the Hospitallers, and two from Cyprus, see Chapter 3, note 65.

the average fleet size was double, at around sixty galleys. On one occasion, in 1295, the Genoese even constructed a fleet of 165 galleys, but this was an exception for the period. The wars between the two cities should be considered as representing the pinnacle of galley numbers at this time.[22]

On the other hand, if the naval leagues are compared with other maritime engagements of this period in the Mediterranean, such as during the war of the Sicilian Vespers, the sizes of the fleets are not dissimilar. For example, in 1283 and 1284 the famed Calabrian admiral Roger of Lauria won two notable victories over the Angevins at Malta and at Naples with fleets numbering around twenty to twenty-nine galleys. Later in the war, the fleets would grow in size, but nevertheless those equipped for the leagues against the Turks are not insubstantial when compared with those used in the Sicilian war.[23] Moreover, when compared with other fleets assembled or proposed for action in the Aegean at this time, the fleets for the leagues are far greater in size. For example, the combined Hospitaller–Zaccaria fleet of 1319 had only four galleys along with other vessels and the league proposed by Marino Sanudo in the early 1320s numbered ten.[24] Even the large forces equipped by Hugh of Cyprus in the late 1330s, which were said to have numbered twenty-one galleys on one occasion and twelve on another, were less substantial than the combined forces of the first league.[25]

It is also worth noting that the total numbers of men and vessels involved in the naval leagues would have been far greater than the galley-strength alone. Venice, for example, advised that fifty horse transports be equipped for the first naval league and sixty for the second. These were each to consist of 120 oarsmen and twenty horsemen, equating to an extra 6,000 oarsmen and 1,000 horsemen for the first league, and 7,200 oarsmen and 1,200 horsemen for the second.[26] It is not known whether all of these horse transports were constructed, but if they were then the numbers of men serving in the leagues would have more than doubled, to 13,800 in 1333–4 and 12,400 in 1343 – a significant number indeed. It is also highly likely that other ships, such as smaller *barchae*, necessary for successful amphibious warfare, would have been equipped by the various members of the league even if they were not mentioned in the official agreements; the success the leagues enjoyed

[22] These fleets are discussed in Dotson, 'Venice, Genoa and control of the seas', esp. pp. 125–6.

[23] Detailed descriptions of the fleet sizes used by Roger of Lauria in the Sicilian war are provided by Pryor, 'The naval battles of Roger of Lauria', esp. pp. 184, 190–2, 195–6, 201–2, 205, 209.

[24] Delaville le Roulx, *Hospitaliers à Rhodes*, pp. 365–7, doc. 2; Gatto, 'Martino Zaccaria', 337–9, doc. 1; Marino Sanudo, 'Liber Secretorum', pp. 30–1 (marginal note); Lock trans., pp. 62–3.

[25] *Le Liber pontificalis: Texte, introduction et commentaire*, ed. L. Duchesne, 3 vols (Paris, 1886–92), vol. 2, p. 527; Coureas, *The Latin Church in Cyprus: 1313–1378*, p. 100.

[26] See above, notes 16, 18.

on land certainly suggests that this was the case. Similarly, it was expected that armed merchant galleys trading in the Aegean would have assisted the leagues when called upon to do so, especially if they owed allegiance to one of the member states.[27] These composite fleets and informal alliances were, after all, common features of maritime warfare in the Aegean. This was the case with the allied fleet assembled by the Hospitallers and Zaccaria in 1319, which was made up of four war galleys, but also included two horse transports and around twenty-five other smaller vessels. Moreover, on the eve of the battle against the Turks the numbers of this fleet were bolstered by the arrival of eleven more Genoese galleys which ultimately resulted in a victory for the Latins.[28]

There is also specific evidence of the leagues increasing in size during the period in which they were at sea. This is especially the case for the second naval league when, after the capture of Smyrna in 1344, even more galleys and recruits flocked to the Aegean. These included a flotilla of Peter of Arborea in western Sardinia who, as part of a pilgrimage to the Holy Land, had pledged to travel with four galleys to the East to spend six months fighting against the Turks.[29] A year later, the force led by Humbert of Viennois sailed to the Aegean, which consisted of four galleys and probably a number of other smaller vessels.[30] These additions, which could have feasibly numbered over eight galleys and 2,000 men, would have increased the size of the second league to something similar to that of 1334, without even factoring in others who took the cross at this time, especially those from northern Italy where the response to crusade preaching was especially great.[31] When these unofficial contributions are added to the numbers of men serving on the galleys and horse transports, it is quite feasible that each of the leagues could have had a total fighting strength of over 15,000 men, with perhaps three-quarters of those being oarsmen. These are considerable numbers, even if they do not match the great Genoese-Venetian wars of the period.

It is also worth considering the strength of the Turkish fleets which the leagues faced. According to the sources, these numbered twenty-three vessels at Amorgos in 1312;[32] twenty-nine or thirty-two at Chios in 1319;[33] 150–250

[27] This was suggested by Marino Sanudo, 'Liber Secretorum', pp. 30–1 (marginal note); Lock trans., pp. 62–3.

[28] Delaville le Roulx, *Hospitaliers à Rhodes*, p. 366, doc. 2.

[29] ASVat, *RS* 7, fol. 79v (30 Nov 1344).

[30] For the numbers of Humbert's expedition, see Carr, 'Humbert of Viennois and the Crusade of Smyrna', 240, n. 8; Setton, *Papacy and the Levant*, vol. 1, pp. 195–7.

[31] Recruitment and participation in the Crusade of Smyrna is also discussed in Chapter 5, pp. 114–18.

[32] *Chroniques d'Amadi et de Strambaldi*, ed. Mas Latrie, vol. 1, p. 391.

[33] Delaville le Roulx, *Hospitaliers à Rhodes*, pp. 365–6, doc. 2; Gatto, 'Martino Zaccaria', 337–9, doc. 1.

at Adramyttion in 1334;[34] fifty-two or sixty at Longos in 1344;[35] and 118 at Imbros in 1347.[36] The sources should probably be treated cautiously in regard to these figures, but nevertheless it seems that the Turks often outnumbered the Latins, sometimes by more than four to one. In terms of ship types, it is likely that the Turkish fleets were made up of smaller craft, such as light galleys and transports.[37] One reason for this was that the Turks were concerned primarily with raiding in order to seize captives and livestock, or to create a buffer-zone in the eastern Aegean, rather than engaging the Latins at sea. This is certainly the impression given by sources reporting on their raids at the turn of the fourteenth century.[38] As the century progressed, the Turks became more ambitious and their fleets became stronger. The flotilla from Aydin that attacked Chios in 1319 allegedly contained ten galleys, while Ibn Battuta later reported that Umur used war-galleys to raid as far afield as the environs of Constantinople.[39] However, these were probably exceptions and Turkish fleets were still mostly made up of lighter vessels, which were ideal for raiding and piracy, but were no match for the heavier triremes of Latins when confronted at sea. Also, as Marino Sanudo was eager to point out in the 'Liber Secretorum', it was the quality of the crews of the galleys, and not their quantity, which ultimately resulted in success.[40] The Turks were inexperienced sailors and although some Greeks living in Anatolia undoubtedly crewed Turkish ships as well, their Latin opponents were invariably highly-skilled mariners, led by experienced captains.[41] This was especially the case with the Hospitallers under Fulk of Villaret and Albert of Schwarzburg, and even more so with merchant crusaders, such as Martino Zaccaria, and those who fought on the galleys of the Venetian Republic.

[34] Various sources report the battle of Adramyttion, see Chapter 3, p. 73.

[35] John Kantakouzenos, *Historiarum Libri IV*, vol. 2, bk. 3, ch. 69, pp. 422–3; Guglielmo Cortusi, *Chronica de novitatibus Padue et Lombardie*, p. 109.

[36] Clement VI, *Lettres à la France*, vol. 2, doc. 3336.

[37] On vessels used by the Turks, see Pryor, *Geography, Technology and War*, pp. 67–8, 167–70; Zachariadou, 'Holy war in the Aegean during the fourteenth century', pp. 215–17.

[38] See, for example George Pachymeres, *Relations historiques*, vol. 4, bk. 10, ch. 29, pp. 376–7; Ramon Muntaner, *The Catalan Expedition to the East*, p. 52; Marino Sanudo, 'Liber Secretorum', p. 29; Lock trans., p. 59. The nature of the Turkish raids is also discussed in Chapter 1, pp. 21–2 and Chapter 2, pp. 44–9.

[39] Delaville le Roulx, *Hospitaliers à Rhodes*, pp. 365–6, doc. 2; Ibn Battuta, *The Travels*, vol. 2, pp. 446–7; Zachariadou, 'Holy war in the Aegean during the fourteenth century', pp. 215–17.

[40] Marino Sanudo, 'Liber Secretorum', pp. 30–1; Lock trans., pp. 61–2.

[41] Pryor, *Geography, Technology and War*, pp 69, 145–6, 154.

Tactics

From the sources it is likely that the Latins of Romania won at least eight major sea-battles over the Turks in the first half of the fourteenth century. Three of these were by the forces of the Knights Hospitallers of Rhodes and the Zaccaria of Chios from 1312–1328 (including the victories at Amorgos and Chios); at least one significant victory was won at Adramyttion by the first naval league in 1334; Hugh of Cyprus defeated the Turks twice in 1336–7; and the second naval league was victorious at Longos and Imbros in 1344 and 1347 (see Map 4). However, to piece together a detailed picture of these maritime conflicts is an extremely difficult task, primarily because of the vagueness and unreliability of many of the sources which are scant on specific or accurate information regarding maritime combat. This is not surprising considering that most of the accounts we have were recorded by those unfamiliar with naval warfare and distant from events in the Aegean, such as papal letters and chroniclers in the West. Nevertheless, by analysing these accounts in the wider context of medieval naval warfare, some tentative observations on the strategies employed by the captains of the leagues can be made.

In regard to naval tactics, to quote John Pryor, galley warfare in the Middle Ages was 'not naval warfare in the modern sense, but rather amphibious warfare, in which skilful use of coastal geography and the nexus of the fleet to the land was equally important as mastery of the sea itself'.[42] This close relationship between land and sea was mostly a result of the relatively small capacity of galleys and the high numbers of oarsmen they required, which meant that they could not stay out at sea for long. Typically galleys of the period could last for no more than two weeks at sea without re-provisioning their water supplies, with the result that they needed to dock for provisioning frequently and hugged the coast most of the time.[43] The

---

[42] See Pryor, 'The naval battles of Roger of Lauria', pp. 185–6. For a discussion of galley warfare in a later period, see J.F. Guilmartin Jr., *Gunpowder and Galleys: Changing Technology and Mediterranean Warfare at Sea in the Sixteenth Century* (London, 1974), pp. 57–84, and for amphibious warfare in particular: D.J.B. Trim and M.C. Fissel, 'Amphibious warfare, 1000–1700: Concepts and contexts', in *Amphibious warfare 1000–1700: Commerce, State Formation and European Expansion*, ed. D.J.B. Trim and M.C. Fissel (Leiden, 2011), pp. 1–50.

[43] Oars dominated galley design and little space was left for anything but oarsmen and benches. If raised platforms and light projections extending from the hull etc., are neglected then around 95 per cent of a galley's deck space was devoted to oarsmen and benches. A typical Mediterranean galley of the early sixteenth century, of 144 oarsmen and thirty to forty soldiers, sailors and officers, would need about ninety gallons of water per day. Twenty days at sea would require around 1,800 gallons, or 100 eighteen-gallon barrels – a considerable amount considering the size of the galleys. See Guilmartin Jnr., *Gunpowder and Galleys*, pp. 62–3, 71; Rose, *Medieval Naval Warfare*, pp. 19–21. It is worth noting that most medieval

repeated successes of the Latins in the Aegean suggests that their captains had mastered this relationship between land and sea far better than their Turkish counterparts. In particular, they exploited the geographical makeup of the Aegean to far greater effect, especially in surprising the enemy, which explains why the majority of their victories were achieved on land, where the Latin marines and other crewmen pursued and defeated the Turks who had fled from their boats.

Evidence of the effectiveness of Latin amphibious warfare can be found in the earliest encounters in the Aegean. This was the case in 1312 when the Hospitallers defeated a Turkish fleet of twenty-three vessels from Menteshe and pursued the remaining Turks onto the island of Amorgos, where they apparently killed eight hundred, with the loss of only fifty-seven knights and three hundred infantrymen.[44] Similarly, in 1319, the Hospitallers and the Zaccaria hunted down a number of Turks who had fled to the shore of Chios after a defeat at sea, with the result that 'not a single one of them escaped'.[45] In the second naval league, the captains utilized their greater geographical understanding of the region to such good effect that they completely surprised a numerically superior Turkish fleet on two occasions, in both instances forcing the Turks to flee from their boats before the crusaders could engage them. This was the case in 1344 when the league came upon around fifty to sixty Turkish vessels laying at anchor in the harbour of Longos. Here the crusaders captured and destroyed their vessels, before chasing the Turks onto land and slaughtering them.[46] Finally, at Imbros in 1347 the galleys of the league again surprised a large fleet situated off the island, this time numbering 118 vessels. The Turks were taken by surprise and fled to land for safety. But they were soon surrounded on the island by the crusaders, who received reinforcements of two galleys and

galleys would have had slightly larger crews than those used for the calculations above, suggesting that the number of days they could spend at sea would have been even lower. See the comments by Marino Sanudo, 'Liber Secretorum', p. 28; Lock trans., pp. 57–8; Pryor, *Geography, Technology and War*, pp. 74–80. It should also be noted that the oarsmen required significant amounts of food to maintain their high level of activity, which also put a strain on the provisioning of galleys, see Mott, 'Serving in the fleet', 67–8.

[44] *Chroniques d'Amadi et de Strambaldi*, vol. 1, p. 391. A report of an Aragonese ambassador at the Council of Vienne, dated 22 April 1312, also recounts the Hospitaller victory, but with inflated numbers of the dead. It states that 1,500 Turks and seventy-five Knights were killed: H. Finke, *Papsttum und Untergang des Templerordens*, vol. 2, pp. 298–302 (doc. 146).

[45] Delaville le Roulx, *Hospitaliers à Rhodes*, p. 366, doc. 2; Gatto, 'Martino Zaccaria', 338, doc. 1.

[46] John Kantakouzenos, *Historiarum Libri IV*, vol. 2, bk. 3, ch. 68, pp. 422–3; Guglielmo Cortusi, *Chronica de novitatibus Padue et Lombardie*, p. 109; a rather fantastical account puts the number of Christian dead at only 300, compared with over 18,000 on the Turkish side: John of Winterthur, *Chronica*, p. 250.

one *ligna* from the Hospitallers on Rhodes, and then captured them.[47] Even during the assault on Smyrna – which was not strictly a maritime encounter – the forces of the league managed to make another impressive land-based victory by seizing the harbour fortress from the powerful Umur Pasha.[48] The league may have been fortunate on this occasion, as Umur was absent from Smyrna with his main force at the time, but considering the crusaders' habit of surprising the Turks, the timing of the attack may well have been deliberately planned and based on prior intelligence.[49]

Considering that most encounters with the Turks ended on land, it would be useful to reconstruct the details of the confrontations which took place on the Aegean islands. However, unfortunately the sources are very vague in this regard, and apart from the numbers of Turks killed, they yield almost no information about the tactics or strategies employed. From the above, we can glean that the Turks were often surprised and forced to flee in panic onto land, after which they were pursued by the Latin crews who had disembarked from their ships. Typically the beyliks, like the Seljuks before them, relied on formidable light cavalry, especially horse archers, which were best suited to open conditions where rapid movement and fire-power could break up the formations of their enemies.[50] Clearly amphibious warfare and combat on the mountainous, rocky and wooded interiors of the Aegean islands, probably with few or no horses, was the antithesis of the preferred Turkish style of combat. A good example of this is given at Amorgos in 1312, where the Turks were forced to flee to the mountains and to throw rocks down at the Hospitallers in a vain attempt to halt their advance.[51] Considering that the primary objective of the Turks was to carry out surprise raids, which were intended to avoid direct combat with an opposing army, it is not surprising that the crews of the Turkish ships, as well as the vessels themselves, were not suited to direct confrontation with experienced Latin opponents. This contrasts markedly with the successes of the Turks in Anatolia and Greece, where they proved to be formidable,

---

[47] Clement VI, *Lettres à la France*, vol. 2, docs 3336–7; *Duca di Candia: Quaternus consiliorum*, docs 164–5; Delaville le Roulx, *Hospitaliers à Rhodes*, p. 108, n. 2; Sarnowsky, 'Die Johanniter und Smyrna (Teil 2)', 50, doc. 3.

[48] No detailed description of the capture of the harbour-fortress of Smyrna exists, but a vivid account of a similar engagement, the assault and capture of the fortress of Lampsakos in 1359, is given by Philippe de Mézières: *Documents on the Later Crusades*, pp. 83–5, doc. 25.

[49] Enveri, *Le destān d'Umūr Pacha*, pp. 111–13 (verses 1913–68); Nikephoros Gregoras, *Byzantina Historia*, vol. 2, bk. 13, ch. 4, p. 689; John Kantakouzenos, *Historiarum Libri IV*, vol. 2, bk. 3, ch. 68, pp. 419–20.

[50] J. France, 'Philippe de Mézières and the military history of the fourteenth century', in *Philippe de Mézières and His Age: Piety and Politics in the Fourteenth Century*, ed. R. Blumenfeld-Kosinski and K. Petkov (Leiden, 2012), pp. 283–93, at pp. 285–6.

[51] *Chroniques d'Amadi et de Strambaldi*, vol. 1, p. 391.

especially against Byzantine armies.[52] This may explain why the Aydin Turks were far more effective at resisting the crusaders once the latter had seized the harbour fortress of Smyrna and combat had moved onto the land. In this instance Umur was able to lay siege to the harbour fortress and successfully hem the crusaders in, despite repeated reinforcements.[53] In January 1345 he also won a significant victory when he managed to kill a number of Latins, including the crusade leaders, at the abandoned church of Saint John outside the city walls. The exact details of the encounter are obscure but it seems that Umur secretly led his army to the church, where they fell upon the crusaders during mass. Some of the crusaders saw the approaching Turks and managed to escape back to the harbour fortress, but the majority were slain.[54] Evidently the Turks were most effective against the Latins when ships were not involved.

Of the encounters reported in the sources, only one of the sea battles is described in any detail, that off Chios in 1319. Unfortunately, a letter of Sanudo describing the battle of Adramyttion in 1334 is now badly damaged and little information is given about the two victories won by Hugh of Cyprus in 1336 and 1337.[55] In addition, although the Hospitaller victory at Amorgos in 1312 began as a conflict at sea, the accounts provide only rudimentary details of the engagement before the Turks were pursued onto the island.[56] In terms of battle tactics, galley warfare in the Middle Ages was a highly complex and skilful art. One of the most common tactics adopted was to ram an enemy ship so that marines could board it, hopefully leading to its capture. Typically a battle would commence with a bombardment from archers or crossbowmen, followed by the advance of the fleet, which commonly went into battle in crescent moon formation, as was advocated by Marino Sanudo.[57] Galleys were strongest at the prow or stern, where

---

[52] Muntaner, for example, regularly praised the martial prowess of Turks: Ramon Muntaner, *The Catalan Expedition to the East*, pp. 46–63, 109–10.

[53] Enveri, *Le destān d'Umūr Pacha*, p. 114 (verses 1997–2012); Lemerle, *L'émirat d'Aydin*, p. 190.

[54] Several sources recount this event: Enveri, *Le destān d'Umūr Pacha*, pp. 114–15 (verses 2013–86); John Kantakouzenos, *Historiarum Libri IV*, vol. 2, bk. 3, ch. 95, pp. 582–3; Giovanni Villani, *Nuova cronica*, vol. 3, bk. 13, ch. 39, pp. 389–90; Anonimo Romano, *Cronica*, pp. 109–14; John of Winterthur, *Chronica*, pp. 252–3; *Lettere di Mercanti a Pignol Zucchello*, pp. 31–2, doc. 13. See also Lemerle, *L'émirat d'Aydin*, pp. 191–3; Setton, *Papacy and the Levant*, vol. 1, pp. 192–3.

[55] For Adramyttion see Kunstmann, 'Studien über Marino Sanudo', 811–12 (letter 7); Roddy trans., p. 296 (letter 35). For Hugh of Cyprus, see above, note 25.

[56] *Chroniques d'Amadi et de Strambaldi*, vol. 1, p. 391; Finke, *Papsttum und Untergang des Templerordens*, vol. 2, pp. 298–302, doc. 146.

[57] Marino Sanudo, 'Liber Secretorum', pp. 82–5; Lock trans., pp. 139–42. By the fourteenth century guns were being used on ships in northern Europe, but it was probably not until the War of Chioggia in 1378–81 that they were widely used in Mediterranean galley warfare, see Dotson, 'Venice, Genoa and control of the seas', p. 133; Idem, 'Everything is a compromise', p. 38; Lane, *Venice*, p. 195; Rose, *Medieval Naval Warfare*, pp. 96–7, 110–11.

archers and catapults could be massed, but weakest amidships where few defenders could be stationed because of the oarsmen. It was hoped that the wings of the advancing fleet could close around the enemy and attack them side on, crashing into the line of oars to create chaos. Thereafter, the marines on each galley could board and gain access to the weakly defended rowing benches and access gangway which ran down the enemy vessel.[58]

Another favourite tactic was manoeuvring to put the sun behind one's back and in the enemy's eyes, as Roger of Lauria and Benedetto I Zaccaria had done on several occasions. One such example comes from 1284, when Roger of Lauria defeated an Angevin fleet in the Bay of Naples. Lauria's movements began in the morning when he lured the Angevins from their base at Naples by means of a feigned retreat and withdrew eastward towards Castellamare where a reserve squadron was concealed. Once the Angevins were sufficiently far from their base, Lauria brought out his reserve squadron and turned to give battle with the rising sun at his back and in the eyes of the Angevins.[59] In the Hospitaller–Zaccaria victory over the Aydin Turks off Chios in 1319, this tactic may have also been employed. The two letters reporting the encounter to the pope, written by the captain of the Hospitaller fleet, the Grand Preceptor Albert of Schwarzburg, and Gerard of Pins, both remark that the battle commenced at sunset. As it is known that the Latin galleys sailed out from Chios Town to engage the Turks two miles from the island, and that the Turks were approaching from the east (Ephesos), then the sun could have feasibly have been setting behind the Hospitaller and Genoese fleet approaching from the west.[60] This may explain why after entering into battle the Latin galleys managed to seize four of the Turkish vessels 'at the first strike'.[61]

However, this hypothesis remains speculative and another more convincing reason for the Latin victory is given by Albert of Schwarzburg. He mentioned that eleven galleys 'of Genoese citizens' met up with the Latin fleet whilst they were waiting at anchor for the Turks. The Hospitallers initially thought that these galleys had been dispatched by the Greek emperor to assist the Turks, but after a scout was sent to identify them this was proved not to be the case. Strangely Schwarzburg specifically reported that these galleys had sailed from Genoa, which considering their arrival on the day of the battle at the precise location, seems highly unlikely.[62] In fact, presuming that these galleys had been sent for by Martino Zaccaria, who

[58]   Pryor, 'The naval battles of Roger of Lauria', pp. 193–4.
[59]   Pryor, 'The naval battles of Roger of Lauria', pp. 191–2.
[60]   Delaville le Roulx, *Hospitaliers à Rhodes*, pp. 365–6, doc. 2; Gatto, 'Martino Zaccaria', 337–9, doc. 1.
[61]   Gatto, 'Martino Zaccaria', 338, doc. 1.
[62]   Delaville le Roulx, *Hospitaliers à Rhodes*, p. 366, doc. 2: *supervenerunt XI galee Januensium intrinsecorum de Janua.*

had heard of the intentions of the Turks some weeks before, it is more plausible that this flotilla was formed by a coalition of Genoese merchant galleys operating in the region, possibly dispatched from the nearby colonies at Pera or Phokaia. It is known that vessels could sail from Pera to Chios in as little as three days if the conditions were favourable, which makes that option conceivable.[63] However, considering that this fleet arrived on the day of the battle and in exactly the right location, the most reasonable explanation is that it had sailed from nearby Phokaia and was concealed north of Chios and out of sight of the Turks, where it awaited instructions to advance. This is a similar tactic to that which Roger of Lauria used for his reserve fleet in the Bay of Naples forty years earlier.

Either way, the episode is evidence of the high level of communication that existed between the Zaccaria and the other Genoese in the Mediterranean which, combined with a shared intelligence network with the Hospitallers, proved to be a great advantage in protecting the eastern Aegean from the Turks. In the naval leagues also, efficient communication between the different powers, as was demonstrated by the Hospitaller reinforcements on Imbros, coupled with prior warning of enemy ship movements which resulted in the surprise attacks at Longos, Smyrna and Imbros, seem to have been the principal reason for the successes of the Latins. As well as this, the fame and reputation of the Latin captains should be considered. Martino Zaccaria became renowned for his military achievements over the Turks and his successes may have boosted morale and ensured discipline amongst his crews, just as they did for Roger of Lauria during the Sicilian Vespers.[64] Martino's standing was so great that in 1343 Clement VI appointed him as the captain of the papal galleys for the Crusade of Smyrna, despite concerns that he would divert the league to Chios.[65] Evidently this risk was worth taking considering the benefits that Martino's fame and reputation would bring to the fleet. From this discussion of logistics and strategies, it is therefore clear that the anti-Turkish naval coalitions were highly effective enterprises, which combined powerful and well-equipped fleets with skilled captains and crews. The tactics adopted by the galley captains, especially the element of surprise coupled with effective communication, resulted in a series of overwhelming victories. This maintained supremacy on sea and meant that maritime warfare would be the preferred method of resisting the Turks.

---

[63] Pryor, *Geography, Technology and War*, p. 98.

[64] See Mott, 'Serving in the fleet', 73–5; Pryor, 'The naval battles of Roger of Lauria', pp. 211–13.

[65] Appendix 4, doc. 5, pp. 161–2; Clement VI, *Lettres à la France*, vol. 1, docs 404 (16 September 1343), 1113–14 (18 September 1344), 1464 (1 February 1345).

5

The Papacy and the Naval Leagues

> We grant to those faithful who proceed with the flotilla or in another fashion
> in support of the Christians in the regions of Romania against the unbelievers
> [i.e. the Turks] [...] that [same] forgiveness of their sins which is granted to
> those who cross over in aid of the Holy Land, and as a reward for the just,
> we promise them an increase in their eternal salvation.
>
> > Pope Clement VI, letter decreeing crusade measures in support
> > of the naval league against the Turks, 30 September 1343.[1]

Throughout this discussion of the naval leagues and their strategies, a fundamental question in understanding how they fit into the wider crusading
movement needs to be addressed. Contrary to what is commonly thought,
the leagues were not papal-led operations from the outset, neither were they
always associated with a general crusade to the Holy Land; instead they were
initiated by the resident Latin powers of the eastern Mediterranean, largely
independent of papal control and with minimal influence from the great
powers of western Europe. As a result only some of the participants in these
campaigns received the rewards usually associated with a crusade. To understand how the leagues – and crusading against the Turks in general – fitted
into wider crusade thinking, it is first necessary to analyse their connection with other papal crusade initiatives. Once this has been undertaken
the implementation of crusading mechanisms in the Aegean theatre will be
analysed, with specific attention given to the indulgences granted for the
leagues and other campaigns against the Turks.

The Leagues in the Context of Papal Crusading Strategy

John XXII and the First Naval League

By the time of the election of John XXII in 1316, the Latin powers in the
Aegean had already formed their own initiatives against the Turks. These
soon evolved into the concept of a naval league which was adopted by the
Venetian government in the mid 1320s. The Venetians set about recruiting
other powers to the league and in the sketchy records of the negotiations

---

[1] *Documents on the Later Crusades*, pp. 78–80, doc. 22.

that followed evidence emerges of formal attempts to bring the papacy into the coalition. The first instances of this seem to have come in the late 1320s when embassies in Venice and at the papal curia discussed the idea of forming a fleet against the Turks.[2] However, despite these measures, the point of concrete papal commitment to the naval league only came in the late summer of 1333, some ten years after Marino Sanudo had first proposed a provisional flotilla and eight years after the Venetians had adopted the same strategy.

There were several reasons for the pope's reluctance to lend his support to the league. These were interconnected and centre around the position which the Byzantines occupied between the crusade priorities of the French, Angevins and papacy, on the one hand, and those of Venice on the other. First, although the Venetians, the Angevins and the papacy shared a common interest in defending Frankish territories in Greece and the western Aegean, their policies in this regard diverged markedly during the 1320s. The papacy, along with Martino Zaccaria, supported the defence of Angevin Greece from the Catalans and also the Greeks of Mistras, whilst Venice sought peace with these groups and instead focussed its attention on a maritime response to the Turks. Evidence of the papal support of the Angevins can be found in the plans of the titular Latin emperor of Constantinople, Philip of Taranto, in the early 1320s, who repeatedly attempted, but failed, to raise an army to campaign in Achaia.[3] The initiative in defending Angevin lands in Greece passed to Philip's younger brother, John of Gravina, who had been invested with the principality of Achaia in 1318.[4] John's plans reached a climax in 1325 when he managed to lead an expedition to the Morea against the Greeks and Catalans, but despite receiving the support of several Frankish lords upon his arrival in Greece, including Martino Zaccaria and

---

[2] In 1328–9 the archbishop of Thebes travelled to Avignon by way of Venice. His mission was to promote an Angevin-led union against the schismatics and infidels in Achaia, but the idea of a galley fleet against the Turks was also discussed: ASVat, *RV* 115, fols 93v–4, ep. 413 (15 Aug 1328); summary in R.-J. Loenertz, 'Athènes et Néopatras: Régestes et documents pour servir à l'histoire ecclésiastique des Duchés catalans (1311–1395)', *Archivum Fratrum Praedicatorum* 28 (1958), 5–91, at 37, doc. 34; Marino Sanudo, 'Epistolae', ed. Bongars, pp. 312–13 (letter 20), 315–16 (letter 22); Roddy trans., pp. 201–13 (letter 26), 213–17 (letter 27). In 1330 the doge wrote to the pope to secure formal papal support for a naval league: Kunstmann, 'Studien über Marino Sanudo', 779 (letter 2); Roddy trans., pp. 255–6 (letter 30); *Le deliberazioni (Senato)*, vol. 1, p. 434; Laiou, 'Marino Sanudo Torsello', 383–4.

[3] For these events, see A. Cagesse, *Roberto d'Angiò e i suoi tempi*, 2 vols (Florence, 1922–30), vol. 2, pp. 307, 316.

[4] Once Philip of Taranto became the titular Latin emperor of Constantinople in 1313, he ceded the principality of Achaia to Matilda of Hainault and her husband Louis of Burgundy. A succession struggle followed the death of Louis in 1316 and the principality was taken from Matilda and granted to John of Gravina in 1318. For these events see Topping, 'The Morea, 1311–1364', pp. 109–15; B. Berg, 'The Moreote expedition of Ferrando of Majorca in the Aragonese Chronicle of Morea', *Byzantion* 55 (1985), 69–90.

the duke of Naxos, Niccolò Sanudo, the enemy refused to meet his army in the field and he was forced to return to Italy within a year.[5] In 1331, a similar campaign was also launched, this time by the titular duke of Athens, Walter of Brienne, for which he and his followers were granted the full crusade indulgence by the pope.[6] This crusade was intended to wrest the duchy of Athens from the Catalans, but Walter was forced to return to Italy a year later because of financial problems before he could win any meaningful victories.[7] Throughout this time John XXII made repeated attempts to draw the Venetians into the Angevin-papal coalition, in 1318–20, 1324 and 1328, but Venice declined these overtures on every occasion.[8] Furthermore, in the early 1330s, despite the pope's insistence, the Republic also refused to support Walter of Brienne's crusade to the Morea, instead choosing to make peace with the Catalans.[9]

The unwillingness of the Venetians to engage with the papal-Angevin initiatives in the Morea is evidence of the wider differences in attitudes towards the Greeks at this time. This leads to the second factor, which was that Venice's plans for a Christian alliance against the Turks depended on the involvement of the Byzantine emperor and his Greek subjects. Considering that a crusade against the Greeks had formed a substantial component of papal policy in the Aegean up to this point, as discussed in Chapter 1, it comes as little surprise that the Byzantines were not yet regarded as trustworthy allies by the pope. Negotiations for church union from 1324 to 1327 had temporarily thawed relations between the Greek and Latin Churches, but after they had broken down papal policy once again reverted to one of hostility towards the Greeks. This was demonstrated by a letter of April 1330, in which John XXII wrote that Andronikos III and the Greek 'schismatics' were threatening Hospitaller Rhodes.[10] Moreover, in a letter of July 1332

---

[5]   Caggese, *Roberto d'Angiò*, vol. 2, p. 317; Housley, 'Robert the Wise and the naval league of 1334', 549.

[6]   *DOC*, doc. 150 (14 Jun 1330).

[7]   Setton, *Catalan Domination of Athens*, pp. 38–41.

[8]   The Angevin-papal appeals and Venetian refusals are found in *DOC*, doc. 89–91, 94 (1318); *Commerce et expéditions militaires de la France et de Venise au moyen âge*, ed. L. de Mas Latrie (Paris, 1880), pp. 43–4 (1319) = vol. 3 of *Mélanges historiques: Choix de documents*, 5 vols (Paris, 1873–86); *DVL*, vol. 1, docs 82–3 (1320); *Le deliberazioni (Senato)*, p. 266, bk. 5, docs 62, 66 (1320); *DOC*, doc. 122 (1324); ASVat, *RV* 115, fol. 93v (15 Aug 1328); Housley, 'Robert the Wise and the naval league of 1334', 551.

[9]   *Le deliberazioni (Senato)*, vol. 2, pp. 38–9, bk. 15, docs 126–7.

[10] John XXII, *Lettres secrètes*, vol. 4, docs 4174, 4308–10. A year later the pope awarded indulgences to those who would join a Hospitaller *passagium* to the East: ASVat, *RV* 116, fol. 218v, ep. 954; summary in John XXII, *Lettres secrètes*, vol. 4, doc. 4604 (19 June 1331). This may have been connected to the defence of Rhodes, although it seems more likely that it was issued in connection with a licence for the Hospitallers to visit the Holy Sepulchre issued a few days earlier: John XXII, *Lettres secrètes*, vol. 4, doc. 4591 (11 June 1331).

(only a year before the final papal agreement to take part in the league) the pope condemned the Venetians for harbouring and welcoming 'schismatics and enemies of God' into their lands, presumably referring to the Republic's conciliatory attitude to the Greeks and Catalans. On this occasion the pope even went as far as to state that the depredations the Venetians were suffering at the hands of the Turks were a result of divine retribution, meted out for a lack of vigilance towards these 'schismatics and heretics'.[11]

Relations with Byzantium also hint at another factor. In the late 1320s John XXII had shifted his attention increasingly towards a crusade to recover Jerusalem, promoted by the new French King, Philip VI of Valois. Philip immediately showed an enthusiasm for such a mission and from 1328 to 1333 he was granted papal support, in the form of church tithes and indulgences, for his *passagium generale* which initially was to depart before March 1334.[12] It was widely believed that the agreement of church union with the Byzantines would be greatly beneficial to a Holy Land crusade. Union would, for example, enable Latin Christians to focus all of their attention on the liberation of Jerusalem, to which it was hoped the Byzantines would also lend their assistance.[13] By the time preparations were begun for Philip VI's crusade the earlier negotiations for church union had broken down, but a few years later, on the eve of the scheduled departures of the league and the Holy Land crusade in 1332–4, negotiations for church union were once again opened with the Byzantine emperor. This was again justified on the basis that union would be beneficial to the liberation of Jerusalem, but also that it would help rid the Aegean of the Turkish threat.[14] Although Andronikos III never accepted the proposals, it seems that union was still perceived by the pope as a pre-requisite to the consignment of assistance to Byzantium and therefore of papal commitment to the league. This, along with papal preference for an Angevin or Brienne campaign in the Morea, shows that Venetian policy in regard to the Greeks was out of step with that of the papacy and helps to explain why John XXII did not commit to an initiative led by the Venetians until the very last moment.

---

[11] *AE*, vol. 24, p. 499, ch. 23.

[12] See *AE*, vol. 24, pp. 478–80, ch. 30; John XXII, *Lettres communes*, vol. 13, doc. 58207 (5 Dec 1331); John XXII, *Lettres secrètes*, vol. 4, docs 5207–5227 (26 Jul 1333); *Documents on the Later Crusades*, pp. 68–70, doc. 18; J.B. Henneman, *Royal Taxation in Fourteenth Century France: The Development of War Financing, 1322–1356* (Princeton, 1971), pp. 91–105; Tyerman, 'Philip VI and the recovery of the Holy Land', 25–52.

[13] See, for example, Marino Sanudo, 'Epistolae', ed. Bongars, pp. 290–1 (letter 2), 294–7 (letter 4), 299 (letter 7), 299–300 (letter 8), 301 (letter 9); Roddy trans. pp. 113–15 (letter 2), 116–20 (letter 3), 123–28 (letter 6), 136–45 (letter 8), 145–49 (letter 9).

[14] John XXII, *Lettres communes*, vol. 12, docs 60898–900, 61258; *AE*, vol. 24, pp. 515–16, ch. 19; Kunstmann, 'Studien über Marino Sanudo', pp. 791–9 (letter 5); 799–808 (letter 6); Roddy trans., pp. 272–81 (letter 33), pp. 281–92 (letter 34); Laiou, 'Marino Sanudo Torsello', 390.

If union negotiations and divergent attitudes towards the Greeks help to explain why the pope was reluctant to lend his support to the league, they do not necessarily explain why the papacy committed to the league when it did, especially as church union was never agreed. In order to answer this question, we need to look at an overarching requirement for papal support of the naval league: that is, the linking of it to the larger Franco-papal campaign to the Holy Land. The union negotiations of 1332–4 linked the crusade to Jerusalem with the fight against the Turks, but even before they were undertaken the Venetians had already taken care to connect the two campaigns explicitly in a way that was not dependent on reconciliation with the Greeks. This came in November 1331 when Philip VI wrote to Doge Giovanni Soranzo for logistical advice concerning his proposed crusade.[15] Soranzo took this opportunity to expand his plans for the naval league by linking it to the forthcoming French expedition; in his reply of May 1332, he provided the king with the advice he requested for the recovery of the Holy Land and also stressed the need to blockade Mamluk ports and protect the Aegean from the Turks, 'the most evil persecutors of the Christian faith'. In particular, the doge stressed that provisions would be needed from the Black Sea if the general crusade to the Holyland was to succeed. The king would therefore need to help drive the Turks and their fleets from the Aegean before the *passagium generale* could depart. The notion of a preparatory blockade on Egypt was not original in itself, but the doge's letter marks the first occasion on which it was recommended that a fleet intended for combating Turkish piracy could be used as a *passagium particulare* to pave the way for a crusade to the Holy Land. By doing this, the Venetians directly linked the Turkish expansion into the Aegean with the liberation of Jerusalem – the clearest example yet that the concept of a fleet intended to enforce the trade embargo had evolved into an anti-Turkish league.[16]

It is only after the Franco-Venetian negotiations of 1331–2 that the pope began to show a firm interest in supporting the naval league, as it could now be linked with the French *passagium generale* and incorporated into a wider, three tiered crusade. The first wave would be the naval league, followed by another *passagium particulare* (to land a provisional force of troops in Asia Minor), and then finally the *passagium generale* led by Philip of France, which was now to depart for the Holy Land in August 1336.[17] Evidently, the king and the pope recognized that the chance to participate in a league

---

[15] *DVL*, vol. 1, doc. 109.

[16] *DVL*, vol. 1, doc. 110. The month before this letter was sent, Marino Sanudo had also written to Philip VI in a similar vein, advocating that a league be formed to combat the Turks as a precursor to the main crusade, although he was less explicit about the reasons why the Turks needed to be subdued: F. Kunstmann, 'Studien über Marino Sanudo', 791–8 (letter 5); Roddy trans., pp. 272–81 (letter 33).

[17] Housley, *Avignon Papacy*, pp. 24–6.

against the Turks, for which the Venetians had already done the majority of the organization, was too good an opportunity to miss, especially when the league could prove integral to the success of a general crusade as the doge had suggested. In late August 1333, John XXII took the first active steps in assisting the Venetian league by appealing for more rulers to join the Christian alliance.[18] At the same time the pope wrote to the doge that clerical ambassadors had been dispatched to Venice to discuss the participation of the papacy in the coalition.[19] It is also at this point that John XXII urged Andronikos III to accept the union of churches and a common front against the Turks.[20] Finally, on 10 October he wrote of the Turkish threat to the archbishop of Embrun, whom he sent to negotiate the formation of a league with the doge and Robert of Naples.[21] The embassy from the papal curia arrived in Venice in December, where logistical considerations were agreed upon, and in the early months of 1334, Venetian and Hospitaller ambassadors at the papal curia finally settled the arrangements for the league.[22]

In March a contract was drawn up on behalf of John XXII which commissioned the construction and armament of four galleys in Marseille for the league. Amongst other things, each galley was to consist of between 174 and 180 oars and was to carry twenty-five marines plus retinues, scribes and other suitable officials, and adequate provisions and equipment were to be supplied. Moreover, the crews were expected to fight on land and sea and to obey every command of the pope. These galleys, which would each cost 600 florins a month to maintain, were to join four more from the king of France before sailing to the Aegean.[23] In the same month, the French knight John of Cepoy was appointed as the captain of the Franco-papal flotilla and indulgences were granted to him and those who were to accompany him overseas.[24] The papacy was now fully committed to the expedition

---

[18] John XXII, *Lettres secrètes*, vol. 4, docs 5247, 5324; John XXII, *Lettres communes*, vol. 12, doc. 60781; Theotokes, *Thespismata*, vol. 2.1, pp. 136–8, doc. 20. Philip of France joined the league in November 1333: *Commerce et expéditions*, ed. Mas Latrie, vol. 3, pp. 101–4, docs 3–4; G. Tabacco, *La casa di Francia nell'azione politica di Papa Giovanni XXII* (Rome, 1953), pp. 312–36; Tyerman, 'Philip VI and the recovery of the Holy Land', 32–7.

[19] *AE*, vol. 24, pp. 511–12, ch. 13; *DVL*, vol. 1, doc. 115; Ivanov, '*Sancta Unio*', 162.

[20] See above, note 14.

[21] *AE*, vol. 24, pp. 513–14, ch. 15.

[22] *DVL*, vol. 1, doc. 124; Theotokes, *Thespismata*, vol. 2.1, pp. 139–41, bk. 16, doc. 27; Theotokes, 'E prôte summachia', 287–8; Setton, *Papacy and the Levant*, vol. 1, pp. 181–2.

[23] *Documents on the Later Crusades*, pp. 71–4, doc. 20.

[24] Three documents announcing Cepoy's appointment as captain were dispatched on 19 May 1334: *AE*, vol. 25, p. 4, ch. 10; John XXII, *Lettres secrètes*, vol. 4, docs 5485–6; summaries in John XXII, *Lettres secrètes*, vol. 4, doc. 5484; John XXII, *Lettres communes*, vol. 13, doc. 63890. The indulgences were issued on the same day: Appendix, doc. 4, pp. 160–1; ASVat, *RA* 46, fol. 560v; *RV* 107, fol. 243r, ep. 729–30; summaries in John XXII, *Lettres communes*, vol. 13, docs 63170–1.

and had decreed spiritual rewards for the participants. However, as will be discussed in more detail later in this chapter, it should be understood that the spiritual privileges granted for the league were less than those awarded for Philip VI's crusade to the Holy Land, and probably unconnected to that mission. Nevertheless, the creation of a united naval league, at a time when most other attempts to form any kind of coherent front against the Turks had failed, was in many ways a remarkable success. It proved that by the 1330s the threat of the Turks had permeated beyond the Latin states of Romania to the courts of both France and the papacy. However, for both John XXII and Philip VI, a crusade against the Turks still ranked far below one aimed at recovering Jerusalem. Venice had after all been forced to connect the naval league to the recovery of the Holy Land in order to secure their participation. As Housley has suggested, the 1334 league constitutes the strongest evidence yet of the shift in crusade strategy from complicated and expensive plans to recover the Holy Land to expeditions organized first and foremost by the Latin powers with a vested interest in the East – in this case the merchant crusaders of Venice.[25] As a consequence, the first naval league was a Venetian project until just a few months before it sailed to the Aegean. John XXII had certainly not agreed to contribute galleys, nor had he granted any papal privileges for the project before this time, both of which make clear that his role in planning the league has traditionally been overstated.[26]

The Reduction of Papal Involvement under Benedict XII

Benedict XII was elected pope on 8 January 1335, only a few months after the victory of the league at Adramyttion. Initially, the new pope gave the crusade plans he had inherited his full support. He wrote to various Latin rulers about the equipping of galleys for the naval league, granted indulgences to the new papal captain Hugh Quiéret and even ordered the construction of four papal galleys in Marseille.[27] These galleys, to be accompanied by five provided by the French, were to set out in May and serve

---

[25] Housley, *Avignon Papacy*, p. 25; Housley, 'The Franco–papal crusade negotiations', 184.

[26] Examples of the overstated influence of the papacy in these years include: Nicol, *Last Centuries*, p. 177, who implied that the initiative for organizing the league fell to the pope after Venice's initial proposals of 1327. This argument has been followed by Geanakoplos, who commented that the pope's role before 1334 had been 'decisive behind the scenes during earlier negotiations', and Housley, who wrote that Venice had prepared the league 'under the papal aegis' in 1330–1: Geanakoplos, 'Byzantium and the Crusades', p. 51; Housley, 'Robert the Wise and the naval league of 1334', 551. A revised sequence of events is given by Ivanov, '*Sancta Unio*', esp. 162–7.

[27] These indulgences were identical to those granted to John of Cepoy in the previous year: ASVat, *RV* 119, fols 132–3, ep. 343–8 (20 April 1335); summaries in Benedict XII, *Lettres communes*, vol. 1, docs 2247–50, 2253. For the galleys, see Benedict XII, *Lettres à la France*, docs 28, 40, 54; Benedict XII, *Lettres communes*, vol. 1, doc. 2467.

in the Aegean for five months. Benedict also lent support to the general passage being organized by Philip VI to the Holy Land by confirming his predecessor's bulls relating to the crusade, including the continuation of the clerical tenth for the expedition.[28]

After this brief flurry of activity, however, a number of external factors dampened Benedict's enthusiasm for the crusade and prevented a naval league, or any other campaign to the East, from materializing. The most serious of these were the escalation of the conflict between France and England, marking the beginning of the Hundred Years' War, and the difficulties afflicting the financial institutions of Europe, which would eventually lead to the collapse of the Italian banking houses in the 1340s. In the case of the latter, this had a particularly detrimental effect on the relationship between the Hospitallers and the papacy. The Order had amassed massive debts during its seizure of Rhodes, but it had returned to solvency in around 1335 after making repeated payments to the Florentine banking houses. After this point it even amassed a credit with the banks, who until at least 1339 also acted as the official bankers to the papacy. Benedict XII was aware of the difficulties the banking houses were experiencing in the 1330s, and was unwilling to jeopardize their precarious position by allowing the Hospitallers to expend the credit they had amassed on a prolonged campaign against the Turks.[29]

The outbreak of war with England resulted in the French galleys, which had been equipped for use against the Turks, being diverted to the English Channel in early 1336, which scuppered the plans for a renewed naval league in the Aegean.[30] At this point, the preparations for Philip VI's general passage to the Holy Land also began to break down because of financial problems and the emerging Anglo-French war. For the papacy and the French Crown, this was a repeat of the same old story; King Philip required security with England and sufficient church finance before fully committing to a general passage, but Benedict was unwilling to allow the crusade tenth to be used for purposes not directly linked with the crusade, especially when Europe was in such a state of disorder. Even if the French considered their own security as an integral prerequisite for the general passage, the papacy had

---

[28] Housley, *Avignon Papacy*, pp. 27–9; Tyerman, 'Philip VI and the recovery of the Holy Land', 37–8.

[29] See Carr, 'The Hospitallers of Rhodes', pp. 172–3; A.T. Luttrell, 'The Hospitallers and their Florentine bankers: 1306–1346', in *Karrissime Gotifride: Historical Essays Presented to Professor Godfrey Wettinger on his Seventieth Birthday*, ed. P. Xuereb (Msida, 1999), pp. 17–24, at pp. 21–2 (repr. in Idem, *Studies on the Hospitallers after 1306*, Variorum Reprints (Aldershot, 2007), item VI); E.S. Hunt, *The Medieval Super Companies: A Study of the Peruzzi Company of Florence* (Cambridge, 1994), pp. 134–9, 234–5.

[30] See de la Roncière, *Histoire de la Marine Française*, vol. 1, pp. 389–91; Depréz, *Les préliminaires de la guerre de cent ans*, p. 127; Tyerman, 'Philip VI and the recovery of the Holy Land', 47; Zachariadou, *Trade and Crusade*, p. 34.

refused to grant church tenths for the defence of France.[31] In March 1336, Benedict wrote to the French king that the Holy Land crusade had been cancelled.[32] Benedict, unlike his predecessor, was concerned with church reform and unity rather than the suppression of the infidel, a factor which characterized his policies in the eastern Mediterranean.[33] For example, his primary initiatives in the region concerned the combating of the Catalan 'schismatics', and bringing the Greeks and Armenians back into the fold of Rome, rather than resisting the Turks in the Aegean, an area to which he gave comparatively little attention.[34]

Despite these difficulties and the cancellation of the crusade plans, this period did not mark the end of appeals from the Latin rulers in the East for papal assistance in reassembling the naval league. In 1336, for example, the Knights Hospitallers and the Venetians sent ambassadors to the papal curia to ask for support in forming an allied fleet in the Aegean, but these overtures were rejected by the pope. The Hospitallers and Venetians did still manage to assemble a small fleet at Crete in the summer of that year, but after failing to receive any papal support they undertook no concerted action in the Aegean.[35] In fact, this response was to be characteristic of Benedict's pontificate, as is demonstrated by his unwillingness to aid Hugh of Cyprus, the most active of the eastern rulers in resisting the Turks at this time. According to a sixteenth-century continuation of the *Liber Pontificalis*, in 1336 and again in 1337, Hugh sent fleets of galleys against the Karaman Turks, defeating them on both occasions and even managing to kill a prominent Turkish captain.[36] Another victory (or possibly the same one) was reported in a papal letter of February 1338, where Hugh was praised for his

---

[31] For this in general see H. Jenkins, 'Papal Efforts for Peace under Benedict XII: 1334–1342' (Unpublished PhD thesis, University of Pennsylvania, 1933), pp. 5–25, 34–5.

[32] Benedict XII, *Lettres autres que la France*, doc. 786; *AE*, vol. 25, p. 78, ch. 44. Tyerman, 'Philip VI and the recovery of the Holy Land', 44–7; Housley, *Avignon Papacy*, pp. 29, 180–1; Jenkins, *Papal Efforts for Peace*, pp. 23–5; Depréz, *Les préliminaires de la guerre de cent ans*, pp. 23–4, 410–13.

[33] See F. Giunta, 'Benedetto XII e la crociata', *Anuario de estudios medievales* 3 (1966), 215–34; Housley, *Avignon Papacy*, pp. 27–31; Luttrell, 'The Hospitallers and their Florentine bankers', pp. 21–2.

[34] For Benedict's policies in regard to the Greeks, Catalans and Armenians see Gill, *Byzantium and the Papacy*, pp. 196–9; Geanakoplos, 'Byzantium and the Crusades', pp. 53–7; Setton, *Catalan Domination of Athens*, pp. 42–7.

[35] ASVen, *Deliberazioni Misti del Senato* 17, fol. 60v (8 Jun 1336); *Venezia-senato: deliberazioni miste*, ed. F.-X. Leduc *et al.*, 20 vols (Venice, 2004 – ongoing), vol. 4 (*Registre XVII, 1335–1339*), pp. 250–2, docs. 664–7; A.T. Luttrell, 'Venice and the Knights Hospitallers of Rhodes in the fourteenth century', *Papers of the British School at Rome* 13 (1958), 195–212, at 203 (repr. in Idem, *The Hospitallers in Cyprus, Rhodes, Greece, and the West, 1291–1440: Collected Studies*, Variorum Reprints (Aldershot, 1978), V).

[36] *Le Liber Pontificalis*, vol. 2, p. 527; Coureas, *The Latin Church in Cyprus: 1313–1378*, p. 100.

'glorious victory against the Turks, the blasphemers of the Christian name'.[37] A few years later, the travel writer Ludolf of Sudheim even reported that many of the coastal towns of southern Asia Minor were paying tribute to him.[38] However, despite Hugh's actions, papal support for Cyprus was not forthcoming, which led the king in 1341 to take the initiative of dispatching an ambassador, the bishop of Limassol, Lamberto Baldwin della Cecca, to Rhodes and Venice in order to establish a new coalition and to put pressure on the pope for his support.[39] From the correspondence of Lamberto it is apparent that the Hospitallers had also (unsuccessfully) appealed to the pope repeatedly for assistance against the Turks in these later years and that the Venetians were also willing to add their weight to a coalition and to make petitions at the papal curia.[40]

In the end these appeals to the pope came too late, as in April 1342, before any action could be taken, Benedict XII died, leaving his response to the Cypriot embassy unknown. Nevertheless, the pope's unwillingness to contribute to any revival of the league had resulted in the resident Latin powers taking the initiative for themselves. Therefore, because Benedict's pontificate marked the greatest disassociation between the papacy and the plans to protect the Latin East during this period, it became the time when the organization and the initiation of crusades was further transferred to the merchant crusaders, who formed strategies increasingly independent of the papacy.

Clement VI and the Crusade of Smyrna

It is ironic that the detachment of the papacy from the defence of the Latin East under Benedict XII actually contributed to the swift formation of a new naval league only a year after his death in 1342. This occurred when the new pope, Clement VI, adopted the plans first instigated by Hugh of

---

[37] Benedict XII, *Lettres autres que la France*, doc. 1673; *AE*, vol. 25, p. 140, ch. 72; Coureas, *The Latin Church in Cyprus: 1313–1378*, p. 100; Hill, *A History of Cyprus*, vol. 2, p. 299.

[38] Ludolf of Sudheim, 'De itinere Terre Sancte', p. 337; Stewart trans., p. 44. It has been claimed that a report was written in 1340 to one of Benedict's cardinals by Martino Zaccaria which lists sixteen galleys serving overseas, eight of which were patrolling the waters of Cyprus. However, this document – copied into an appendix of the registers of Benedict XII – was in fact written by Manuel Zaccaria during the Apostolic vacancy in 1292–4: see Ch. 3, note 9; ASVat, *RA* 54, fols 467v–468; summary in Benedict XII, *Lettres communes*, vol. 2, doc. 8378; Richard, 'Le royaume de Chypre et l'embargo', p. 123; cf. Coureas, *The Latin Church in Cyprus: 1313–1378*, p. 100.

[39] The letter is published in L. de Mas Latrie, *Histoire de l'île de Chypre*, vol. 2, pp. 180–1; summary in *I libri commemoriali della Republica di Venezia regesti*, ed. R. Predelli, 4 vols (Venice, 1876–83), vol. 2, doc. 563.

[40] The letter is published in G. Fedalto, *La chiesa latina in Oriente*, 3 vols (Verona, 1973–8), vol. 3, p. 51; Coureas, *The Latin Church in Cyprus: 1313–1378*, pp. 100–1; Edbury, *The Kingdom of Cyprus*, p. 158.

Cyprus for a league with the Hospitallers and Venice. In this sense, Clement's participation in the 1343 league bears a close resemblance to that of John XXII ten years earlier, in that much of the groundwork had already been undertaken. However, from the very outset, Clement's involvement in the league was far greater than that of his predecessor, especially in terms of finance, organization, level of control asserted over the fleet and privileges granted to the participants.

Clement's commitment to the league is not surprising considering his dedication to crusading, evidence of which can be found in his earlier life when, as archbishop of Rouen, he had preached a sermon in Paris in 1332 after which King Philip VI had taken the cross for his aborted crusade to the Holy Land. Moreover, the pope's skills as a diplomat undoubtedly enabled him to progress negotiations for the expedition quickly, ultimately allowing him to succeed in launching a successful crusade to the East where many others had failed.[41] This is demonstrated in the earliest months of his pontificate, when Clement took measures to secure Venetian participation in the league and also wrote letters of encouragement to the other prospective members, reminding them of the threat posed by the Turks and the necessity for naval action against them.[42] The pope also took steps to ensure that he maintained greater control over the league than John XXII had by appointing a papal legate, the patriarch of Constantinople, Henry of Asti, as the head of the fleet; a measure not taken in the league of 1334.[43] To further ensure papal authority, instructions were sent to the various ecclesiastical and lay authorities involved in the enterprise, including the captains and patrons of the galleys, ordering them to accept Henry's authority under penalty of ecclesiastic censure.[44] At this point, the old papal favourite Martino Zaccaria was appointed as captain of the papal galleys for the league.[45] To ensure the success of the expedition the pope also made attempts to encourage peace within Christendom before the fleet set out. The government of Genoa was asked to cease hostilities against King Hugh of Cyprus, who was apparently willing to make amends for past injustices in the interests of the faith.[46]

---

[41] For more on Clement's early career and character, see Wood, *Clement VI*, esp. pp. 1–18; Mollat, *The Popes at Avignon*, pp. 37–42; Housley, *Avignon Papacy*, pp. 121–2.

[42] ASVat, *RV* 157, fols 1v–3v, ep. 19–25; *RV* 62, fols 48–50v; summaries in Clement VI, *Lettres à la France*, vol. 1, docs 332, 333–8, 341, 414–17; Theotokes, *Thespismata*, vol. 2.1, pp. 216–19, bk. 20, doc. 9; Thiriet, *Sénat*, vol. 1, doc. 142; *I libri commemoriali*, vol. 2, p. 117, bk. 4, doc. 18; Loenertz, *Les Ghisi*, pp. 162–3, 306–7; Demurger, 'Le pape Clément VI et l'Orient', 208–9.

[43] *DOC*, doc. 181; summary in Clement VI, *Lettres à la France*, vol. 1, doc. 340.

[44] See the summaries in Clement VI, *Lettres à la France*, vol. 1, docs 340, 388–90, 404–13 and also J. Muldoon, 'The Avignon Papacy and the frontiers of Christendom: The evidence of Vatican Register 62', *Archivium Historiae Pontificiae* 17 (1979), 125–95, at 164–6.

[45] Appendix 4, doc. 5, pp. 161–2; Clement VI, *Lettres à la France*, vol. 1, docs 368, 404–5.

[46] Clement VI, *Lettres à la France*, vol. 1, doc. 360.

Henry of Asti was instructed to attempt to pacify relations between the Catalans of Athens and Walter of Brienne, to ensure peace in Greece.[47] The Byzantines were repeatedly called on to put an end to the church schism and help aid the league.[48] Above all, the kings of France and England were urged to respect the recently signed Truce of Malestroit and stem the rising tide of war which threatened to engulf northern Europe.[49]

When the fleet was active in the Aegean, Clement continued in his attempts to maintain authority over its actions, evidence of which exists in the large number of papal letters dispatched from Avignon to the papal legate and the other members of the league. For example, he wrote to Henry of Asti on several occasions ordering him to ensure that the league was not diverted from action against the Turks, especially by Martino Zaccaria whom he suspected of attempting to recover his old domain of Chios.[50] After the death of the crusade leaders, including Martino Zaccaria and Henry of Asti in January 1345, the pope was also quick to appoint new officials for the league, as well as to console the crusaders who remained at Smyrna.[51] Clement VI's involvement increased even further during the campaign of Humbert of Viennois to Romania when he advised the dauphin on many strategic matters, including the negotiations with the Byzantines over the use of Chios as a base of operations.[52] Even during the final years of the Smyrna campaign, when the crusaders sought a truce with the Aydin-oglus, the pope continued to maintain close control over what was to be agreed.[53]

In terms of finance, Clement also committed more church money to the league than any of his predecessors. In 1343 and 1345 he levied a tithe on ecclesiastical benefices in over sixty dioceses in Europe and the East for the league against the Turks.[54] This was greater than any crusade tithe levied since the Vienne tenth of 1312 and constituted the first to be levied especially for a crusade against the Turks. The pope also went to great lengths raising money through other means, such as by allowing spiritual privileges to be made available in exchange for payment. In particular Clement offered a plenary indulgence to all who would make a financial contribution to the expedition equal to that which they would have spent if they had campaigned for one year.[55] In terms of contribution, according to Housley, the money

---

[47] *DOC*, doc. 182–3; summary in Clement VI, *Lettres à la France*, vol. 1, doc. 465.

[48] Clement VI, *Lettres à la France*, vol. 1, docs 466–71, 490–3, 522–3, 547.

[49] Clement VI, *Lettres à la France*, vol. 1, docs 448–52; Setton, *Papacy and the Levant*, vol. 1, p. 189; Demurger, 'Le pape Clément VI et l'Orient', 211.

[50] Clement VI, *Lettres à la France*, vol. 1, docs 405, 1113–14, 1464.

[51] Clement VI, *Lettres à la France*, vol. 1, docs 1570, 1582, 1704.

[52] Carr, 'Humbert of Viennois and the Crusade of Smyrna', 237–51.

[53] Housley, *Avignon Papacy*, pp. 253–8.

[54] Clement VI, *Lettres à la France*, vol. 1, docs 368–70, 464, 559, vol. 2, docs 1855–6, 2203–6.

[55] *Documents on the Later Crusades*, pp. 78–80, doc. 22.

Clement spent on the maintenance of the papal galleys for the expedition represented 'the most substantial papal contribution to the defence of the Christian East' for the entire period of the Avignon Papacy.[56] The specific amount spent on the Smyrna expedition was probably in the region of 110,000–150,000 florins which, although considerably less than the amount spent on the pope's Italian wars, still constituted a significant proportion of the overall papal budget.[57] In fact, during the latter years of the Crusade, Clement claimed that financial support from the Church could no longer be relied upon because the 'tithes and other subsidies' could not be raised.[58]

The pope also decreed the most generous spiritual rewards yet for a campaign against the Turks, the details and effects of which will be discussed later in this chapter, and he made compromises which his predecessors had been unwilling to make in the interests of the Crusade. In June 1346, at Humbert's request, the pope agreed to suspend the sentences of excommunication and interdict imposed on the Catalan Company for three years in the hope that they too would contribute to the aid of the crusaders at Smyrna.[59] This is in stark contrast to Benedict XII, who obstinately refused to incorporate the Catalan Company into any plan for the defence of the Latin East, and in 1339 even summoned Archbishop Isnard of Thebes to Avignon to stand trial for wrongfully relaxing the ban of excommunication.[60] Clement was also not ignorant of the restrictions on trade caused by the Crusade of Smyrna and the aggressive Tartar policies in the Black Sea. These were seriously compromising the ability of the Venetians and others to commit to the league, so throughout the duration of the campaign he granted the Republic and other crusaders trade licences allowing them to trade with Mamluk lands, a measure which his predecessors had been reluctant to take.[61] Bearing this in mind it is reasonable to conclude that Clement did not envisage the Smyrna crusade as forming part of a wider strategy to conquer Jerusalem, as John XXII considered the first naval league. In fact Clement only once – in 1348 – mentioned the possibility of recovering the Holy Land at the time of the Smyrna expedition, but even on this occasion there is little evidence to suggest that the campaign was seriously considered

[56] Housley, *Avignon Papacy*, pp. 138, 196–8. See also Demurger, 'Le pape Clément VI et l'Orient', 210–11; Luttrell, 'The Hospitallers and their Florentine bankers', pp. 21–2.
[57] Housley, *Avignon Papacy*, pp. 301–2; cf. Setton, *Papacy and the Levant*, vol. 1, pp. 184–7.
[58] Clement VI, *Lettres à la France*, vol. 2, doc. 2957; Clement VI, *Lettres autres que la France*, docs 2024, 2060.
[59] Clement VI, *Lettres à la France*, vol. 2, docs 2580–95; *DOC*, docs 188–9; Setton, *Papacy and the Levant*, vol. 1, pp. 205–6; Housley, *Avignon Papacy*, pp. 255–6.
[60] See Setton, *The Catalan Domination of Athens*, pp. 45–6.
[61] These trade licences are discussed in more detail in Chapter 6, pp. 132–7.

as forming part of a preliminary crusade to Jerusalem, or that, crucially, contemporaries ever viewed it in that manner.[62]

The position of the leagues in the wider context of papal crusading strategy was therefore a complicated and sometimes ambiguous one. For the league of 1333–4, it is clear that the campaign was first and foremost a Venetian initiative to reduce Turkish piracy in the Aegean. It is only after it was suggested as a *passagium particulare* for a general crusade to the Holy Land that it began to assume any of the characteristics of a crusade, and even then it clearly ranked below an expedition to liberate Jerusalem. The second league was, however, a different matter altogether. It was regarded as an expedition largely separate from attempts to liberate the Holy Land, but still enjoyed greater papal involvement than any of the previous Aegean campaigns. Nevertheless, the leagues were ultimately a product of the Latin powers of the East and the new breed of merchant crusader who made up their numbers.

Crusade Mechanisms in the Aegean Theatre

Now that the level of papal involvement in the naval leagues has been outlined, it is possible to undertake a detailed analysis of the crusade mechanisms allocated for them. These can subsequently be compared with those decreed for other campaigns in the Aegean as well as elsewhere. These mechanisms included the papal proclamation of an expedition and the preaching of the cross, the granting of indulgences and other privileges to participants, the taking of the cross and the crusade vow by recruits, and the raising of funds through tithes, donations and the redemption of vows.[63] Most of these mechanisms have been touched on already and in many senses reflect the level of papal involvement in the leagues, as outlined above. However, the mechanisms differed considerably from campaign to campaign and benefit from a more thorough analysis. Indulgences, for example, were not always the same; on some occasions participants were awarded the 'full' plenary indulgence given to crusaders for the Holy Land, but sometimes only lesser spiritual privileges were allocated, such as a plenary indulgence in the case of death on campaign, or for a specific duration of service (see the examples in Appendix). In addition, the status of the recipients was not always equal or clearly defined; for some campaigns it was stipulated that all contributors would benefit from papal benefits, but for others only

---

[62] See Clement VI, *Lettres autres que la France*, doc. 1605; Housley, *Avignon Papacy*, p. 32; cf. Demurger, 'Le pape Clément VI et l'Orient', 207–14, esp. 212–14; Clement VI, *Lettres à la France*, vol. 1, doc. 914.

[63] For more on crusade mechanisms, see J.S.C. Riley-Smith, *What Were the Crusades?*, 4th edition (Basingstoke, 2009), pp. 27–48, 53–69.

specific individuals or contingents were singled out. Finally, some of these privileges were issued on petition by those who were fighting or seeking to recruit crusaders, whereas some were granted at the behest of the papacy. Thus, when analysed in detail these mechanisms reveal the subtle variations between the leagues and other initiatives against the Turks, as well as the spiritual priorities and concerns of the crusaders who participated in them.

Of these mechanisms the indulgence is an especially revealing indicator. It was the most important privilege for participants, in that it was widely understood to be the complete cleansing of sin which guaranteed the crusader access to heaven.[64] By the end of the twelfth century a plenary indulgence (full remission of sins) was granted to crusaders going to the Holy Land and those who paid for others to go in their place. Indulgences were also granted for fighting in other theatres, such as against the Moors in Iberia, heretics in southern France, or pagans in the Baltic. In the Aegean, the crusade indulgence was first granted in 1205 by Innocent III to those who fought in support of the Latin empire, and then more widely by his successor Honorius III who extended spiritual privileges as the position of the Latins in Romania became increasingly imperilled. Once Constantinople was recovered by the Byzantines in 1261, plenary indulgences were then granted to those who would fight against the Greeks in order to restore the Latin empire.[65] This occurred in 1304 and 1306, when indulgences were granted by Benedict XI and Clement V to those who would support Charles of Valois in his planned expedition to Constantinople, discussed in Chapter 1. In 1312 similar indulgences were extended to his son-in-law Philip of Taranto for his mission to Greece, planned in conjunction with Philip VI's crusade to the Holy Land. A few years earlier, in 1308, Clement had also granted indulgences for the Hospitaller *passagium* to the East, but Rhodes and the Greeks were not designated as the target of that mission.[66] By the 1320s indulgences began to be issued for fighting against the Turks, first by John XXII in November 1322 in the principality of Achaia, and then a month later for the defence of Cilician Armenia and Cyprus. In 1323 and 1325, indulgences were extended to those fighting with the Zaccaria for the defence of Chios and the neighbouring lands, and they were also granted for the first naval league in 1334 and for the aborted follow-up campaign a year

---

[64] The indulgence and other privileges have been summarized by Chrissis, 'New frontiers', pp. 21–3. For the crusade indulgence in general, see J.A. Brundage, *Medieval Canon Law and the Crusader* (Madison, 1969), pp. 145–53; M. Purcell, *Papal Crusading Policy: The Chief Instruments of Papal Crusading Policy and Crusade to the Holy Land from the Final Loss of Jerusalem to the Fall of Acre: 1244–1291* (Leiden, 1975), pp. 52–98. On indulgences issued during the Avignon period, see Housley, *Avignon Papacy*, pp. 124–58.

[65] For more on the implementation of indulgences in Romania, see Chrissis, 'New frontiers', pp. 22–33; Chrissis, *Crusading in Frankish Greece, passim*.

[66] See Clement V, *Regestum*, vol. 3, docs. 2988–90. For more on the preaching of the Hospitaller *passagium*, see Georgiou, 'Propagating the Hospitallers', *passagium*', pp. 53–63.

later. Finally in 1343 Clement VI issued indulgences for his great expedition which would capture the harbour-fortress of Smyrna a year later.[67]

Indulgences *in articulo mortis*, 1322–1334

To look specifically at the conditions attached to these indulgences and the other mechanisms associated with these campaigns, it is worth noting that the planned crusades to Greece and Constantinople in 1304–6 and 1312 followed a long tradition of crusading against the Greeks and were themselves intended to help pave the way for a general passage to the Holy Land.[68] Because of this, full crusade preaching was decreed, including the taking of the cross by participants, and plenary indulgences equal to those granted for crusaders going to the Holy Land were issued. This contrasts with the status of the earliest papal-endorsed actions against the Turks, authorized by John XXII. For these there was no preaching of the cross or the taking of vows by recruits and full remission of sins was only awarded to those who would die in 'war or battle' or of wounds received thereafter and not solely for participation. These are indulgences granted *in articulo mortis*.

It should also be highlighted here that indulgences *in articulo mortis* were all awarded on petition, which meant that the recipients (or their representatives) had visited the papal chancery to make a successful supplication, usually in the presence of the pope. Because of this, these privileges should be seen as representing the initiatives of the recipients, rather than the papacy. As such, when extracts of the original petitions survive, they can be extremely useful in revealing how merchant crusaders projected their own motivations to the pope. As Housley has suggested, indulgences *in articulo mortis* had become the standard papal response to a situation which required some spiritual reward for military service, but could not be afforded full-scale crusade preaching; either because it would not benefit from such a measure, or because the Church could not allow for the necessary expense or organization. As a result, the papal curia was far more liberal in its granting of indulgences *in articulo mortis* than in preaching a general crusade. These indulgences were also less complicated for the recipient; it is unlikely that any took the cross, since the legal framework of the vow would be hard to implement. Instead the soldier would be granted the indulgence at the point of death, after a priest had heard his confession.[69]

The first instances of indulgences *in articulo mortis* being decreed for fighting against the Turks came in 1322 when they were awarded to 'all

---

[67] These indulgences are summarized in Appendix, pp. 149–52.

[68] *Le registre de Benoît XI*, doc. 1007 (20 Jun 1304); Clement V, *Regestum*, vol. 1, doc. 247 (14 Jan 1306); Clement V, *Regestum*, vol. 7, doc. 7893 (7 May 1312). For more on this, see Chapter 1, pp. 27–31.

[69] Housley, *Avignon Papacy*, pp. 112–13, 132–3.

of the faithful of Christ located throughout the principality of Achaia'.[70] These were, however, not granted for fighting exclusively against the Turks, but also for combating 'the schismatic Greeks, the Bulgars, the Alans [...] and other diverse nations of infidels'. The exact identity of the 'faithful' in Achaia is unfortunately unclear. It is possible that they were Angevin vassals who had sought the privileges for the ongoing campaigns in the region, such as those planned by Philip of Taranto and John of Gravina. However, the absence of the Catalan Company from this bull of indulgence makes this far from certain: the Catalans were the primary threat to Angevin interests at this time and it seems unlikely that they would have been omitted from the indulgence if it was in any way connected to them.[71] Still, these indulgences are illustrative in another manner. They demonstrate that although some residents in Achaia were concerned with the threat posed by the Turks, the need to defend the region from the Greeks, Bulgars and others was regarded as being equally important.

A month later John XXII granted plenary indulgences 'as for the Holy Land' to those who fought in aid of the kingdoms of Cyprus and Armenia against the Mamluks and 'other infidels', which included the Tartars and possibly the Karaman Turks, but it was not for another year that he would decree spiritual privileges for fighting specifically against the maritime beyliks in the Aegean.[72] On this occasion, indulgences for three years were allocated to Martino Zaccaria and those who served under him (re-issued in 1325).[73] Like the Achaia indulgences these were awarded *in articulo mortis* and were not accompanied by full crusade preaching. But in contrast to the earlier indulgences, on this occasion the pope was far more specific in identifying the intended recipients and their target. As the letter reads, fighters were to be recruited specifically from the Aegean and Black Sea regions ('all those faithful to Christ who could be found from the island of Crete all the way to the state of Caffa') and they were to serve Martino Zaccaria against the 'Turks and other infidels' on Chios and the lands nearby (it is unclear who these 'other infidels' were). In addition, the pope also awarded Martino protection against wayward Christians and potential rivals. This is

---

[70] Appendix 4, doc. 2, pp. 158–9; ASVat, *RA* 18, fol. 152v, ep. 209; *RV* 74, fol. 93v, ep. 209 (20 Dec 1322); summary in John XXII, *Lettres communes*, vol. 4, doc. 16672.

[71] Cf. the comments of Housley, 'Angevin Naples and the defence of the Latin East', 549, n. 6.

[72] The indulgences were awarded to those 'who go in aid and succour of the kingdoms of Armenia and Cyprus against the [Mamluk] Sultan and other infidels'. The 'other infidels' referred certainly to the Tartars, who are mentioned often in the bulls, but possibly also to the emir of Karaman (*Haramanus Turcomanorum*) referred to in one of the documents: John XXII, *Lettres secrètes*, vol. 2, docs. 1571–3, the reference to Karaman is in doc. 1572, col. 208.

[73] Appendix 4, doc. 3, pp. 159–60; Gatto, 'Martino Zaccaria', 344–5, doc. 5 (20 Feb 1323); ASVat, *RA* 22, fol. 450v; *RV* 78, ep. 882 (28 Apr 1325); summaries in John XXII, *Lettres communes*, vol. 4, doc. 16977, vol. 5, doc. 22117.

seen in the final clause of the letter, which decreed that anyone who formed
an 'alliance, association or coalition' with the Turks and attacked Martino
Zaccaria, his possessions, or any of those who were fighting for him, would
incur sentence of excommunication. The specificity of these conditions is
striking and mirrors both the importance of the concession, which marks
the first instance of crusading privileges being allocated specifically against
the Turks, and the high standing of the recipient at this time.

These papal letters are consequently very important for establishing how
Martino Zaccaria projected his own motivations to the papacy. It is sometimes claimed that merchants were devoid of pious motivations and that
they used crusading merely as a veneer to exploit economic advantage.[74]
This undoubtedly has an element of truth to it. After all, by defending
the Christians of the Aegean, Martin Zaccaria was also protecting his own
interests in the region, be they the mastic farms on Chios, the alum mines
at Phokaia, or the trade routes which his industry relied upon. Nevertheless,
the pope was evidently convinced that his actions were primarily motivated
by the desire to defend Christians from the Turks, as is represented in the
wording of the original petition. This saw the subtle blending of crusade
rhetoric with personal protectionism: Martino made much of the numerous
victories he had won over the Turks (presumably referring to events around
1319), that he was paying for his army from his own funds, and that he
was maintaining his forces specifically in order to hold back the Turkish
advances. Finally Martino stressed his concern over the spiritual wellbeing
of his followers and the importance of the indulgence in this regard.

In comparison, the status of the indulgences granted for the first naval
league in May 1334 to John of Cepoy are more ambiguous.[75] This confusion arises from the planned general passage to the Holy Land to be led
by Philip VI of France, for which the preaching of the cross was decreed
and full plenary indulgences were granted in 1331 and again in July 1333.[76]
As was shown earlier, the naval league only became connected to Philip's
passagium in the late summer and the winter of 1333–4, when the French
and the papacy formally agreed to contribute galleys and thus designate
it as a *passagium particulare*. This fact makes the status of the indulgences
issued earlier unclear: did participants in the naval league receive the same
indulgences as those going on the Holy Land crusade? Or could the Holy
Land indulgences be commuted to fighting the Turks in the Aegean? One
would imagine that both would have been likely, considering the obvious
benefits to the *passagium particulare* that this would bring, but in fact the

---

[74] See Introduction, p. 5, for more on this.

[75] See above, note 24; Appendix 4, doc. 4, pp. 160–1; ASVat, *RA* 46, fol. 560v; *RV* 107,
fol. 243r, ep. 729–30 (19 May 1334); summaries in John XXII, *Lettres communes*, vol. 13, docs
63170–1.

[76] See above, note 12 and Appendix.

sources suggest that neither was possible. First, the indulgences issued for Philip's Holy Land crusade make no mention of the Turks whatsoever and should not be considered as connected to the league, because they were granted before the two campaigns were combined.[77] Secondly, the indulgences issued to John of Cepoy were of a lesser kind: they were not accompanied by preaching or the taking of the cross, and were granted *in articulo mortis* for fighting specifically against the Turks in Romania, suggesting that those granted for the Holy Land crusade were not valid for the participants of the league.[78] This is extremely interesting as hitherto the privileges for Philip VI's *passagium* have been conflated with those of the naval league, which in fact, was still of a lesser status than the crusade to the Holy Land.[79]

To add to this rather confusing appearance of parallel (but separate) spiritual privileges, the documents granting the indulgences to Cepoy do not make it clear whether they applied to all of the members of the league or just those of the French and papal contingents who were to accompany him overseas. At some point Cepoy may have had authority over the entire league, but this is not sufficient to suggest that those members of the Venetian, Hospitaller and Cypriot contingents already serving in the Aegean would have been retrospectively granted any spiritual rewards.[80] Either way, it should be realized that Cepoy and his followers were awarded less significant privileges for their participation in the league. Indeed, the indulgences were not as generous as many others granted by John XXII in these years, including those issued 'as for the Holy Land' to both Philip VI for his proposed crusade against the Moors in 1326 and to Walter of Brienne for his campaign to liberate the duchy of Athens from the Catalans in 1330.[81] The preference given to the French king is not surprising considering his prominence in the crusading plans of these years, but the crusade preached on behalf of Walter of Brienne is further indication that the Angevin cause in

---

[77] See the following papal bulls: ASVat, *RA* 44, fols 73–136; *RV* 104, fols 3–34, ep. 7–26; John XXII, *Lettres secrètes*, vol. 4, docs 5207–27; summaries in John XXII, *Lettres communes*, vol. 12, docs 61202–60. Contemporaries also do not seem to have linked the indulgences for the Holy Land crusade to the naval league, for example: *Documents on the Later Crusades*, pp. 67–8, 70–1, docs. 17, 19; William of Nangis, *Chronique latine de Guillaume de Nangis*, vol. 2, pp. 130–5.

[78] To further complicate matters, it seems that the indulgences for the Holy Land *passagium* were also to be preached to the Byzantines if they accepted union, as is indicated in a papal letter of July 1334: Gill, *Byzantium and the Papacy*, pp. 195–6.

[79] Cf. the comments of Coureas, *The Latin Church in Cyprus: 1313–1378*, pp. 97–8 and Zachariadou, *Trade and Crusade*, pp. 30–1.

[80] For Cepoy's status during the campaign, see *AE*, vol. 25, p. 4 (ch. 9); John XXII, *Lettres secrètes*, vol. 4, doc. 5247; Housley, *Avignon Papacy*, p. 251.

[81] John XXII, *Lettres secrètes*, vol. 3, doc. 2739 (14 March 1326); *DOC*, doc. 150 (14 June 1330). Walter's crusade was preached in Southern Italy and Greece: *Documents on the Later Crusades*, pp. 63–4, doc. 15.

Greece still took precedence over a crusade against the Turks. This therefore confirms that, even in terms of spiritual concessions, John XXII's support of the naval league was less than that of other operations. In fact, in spiritual terms, the papal privileges granted for the naval league were no different from those granted in other areas of Greece and the Aegean during the 1320s. The real change in the stance of the pope towards the league was that he agreed to contribute and finance four galleys from the papal camera – a commitment which suggests that this campaign against the Turks was regarded as more important than those of previous years, even if this was not reflected by the spiritual privileges.

As would be expected, indulgences *in articulo mortis* were commonly sought by harassed local authorities in theatres where specialized fighters were already active, such as for armed defence against *routiers* in France or Italy.[82] Does this therefore suggest that the pope did not consider that full-scale crusade preaching was necessary to attract specialist recruitment in the Aegean theatre, or just that it was too difficult or costly for the Church to implement? As seen in the previous chapter, both the naval league and the forces fighting for the Zaccaria were made up primarily of maritime personnel, such as sailors and oarsmen, along with some professional soldiers. The recruitment of maritime participants had certainly been an issue with full crusade preaching in the past. In 1213, for example, Innocent III had sought to demand maritime assistance in the crusading bull *Quia Maior*.[83] Whereas Clement V had taken measures to encourage specialized maritime participation for the Hospitaller *passagium* in 1308 by specifically stating that sailors, rowers, commanders and other crewmen were to be awarded indulgences.[84] Clement VI may have also have been referring specifically to sailors and other maritime participants when he decreed that indulgences were to be awarded to 'all those who proceed with the flotilla, or in another fashion […] by land or by sea' in 1343.[85]

For indulgences granted *in articulo mortis*, it is unfortunately extremely hard to determine the exact numbers of recipients, or indeed how many requests were made for these privileges at the papal curia.[86] Nevertheless, contemporary sources suggest that the numbers fighting for the Zaccaria were high. Indeed, according to William of Adam, who wrote his trea-

---

[82] See N. Housley, 'The mercenary companies, the papacy and the crusades, 1356–1378', *Traditio* 38 (1982), 253–80, at 260–1, 264 (repr. in Idem, *Crusading and Warfare in Medieval and Renaissance Europe*, Variorum Reprints (Aldershot, 2001), XV).

[83] *The Crusades: Idea and Reality, 1095–1274*, ed. and trans. L. Riley-Smith and J.S.C. Riley-Smith (London, 1981), p. 122, doc. 26.

[84] Clement V, *Regestum*, vol. 3, doc. 2988; Housley, *Avignon Papacy*, p. 137, n. 70.

[85] *Documents on the Later Crusades*, p. 80, doc. 22.

[86] Housley, *Avignon Papacy*, p. 113. Some examples of the indulgences can be seen in Appendix 1, pp. 149–52.

tise sometime between 1316 and 1318, they held one thousand infantry, one hundred horsemen and two fully-armed galleys on Chios.[87] These numbers should not necessarily be taken at face value, but other contemporaries, such as the anonymous *Directorium ad Passagium Faciendum*, written in 1331–2, confirm that Martino Zaccaria had significant military forces at his disposal.[88] To add to this it seems that, despite its many difficulties, the first naval league did not appear to have suffered from any serious recruitment problems. Indeed, attracting soldiers for a *passagium particulare* may have been relatively easy, as is indicated by a Cypriot report of 1323 which stated that the response to a *passagium particulare* would be so high that it might turn into a general passage.[89] This is not to say that the smaller campaigns waged against the Turks were met with the same level of popular enthusiasm as those preached for the Holy Land. Two popular crusades of the early fourteenth century, the 'Crusade of the Poor' of 1309 and the *Pastoureaux* or 'Shepherds' Crusade' of 1320, are examples of the uncontrollable passions which were aroused when people thought that a general passage might materialize.[90] But it is possible that full-scale crusade preaching was not deemed by John XXII as being suitable, or necessary, for the recruitment of the personnel needed for a primarily maritime campaign against the Turks in the Aegean, which for the majority of his pontificate was of a lower status than other crusading initiatives.[91]

Privileges for the Crusade of Smyrna

Clement VI, in contrast to his predecessor, granted privileges for the second naval league that were more generous than any awarded in the past. He decreed full-scale crusade preaching for the campaign on 30 September 1343 in the bull *Insurgentibus contra fidem*, dispatched to the clergy of Italy, Germany, Central and Eastern Europe and Romania.[92] The bull instructed the prelates to begin publicly preaching the word of the cross to the faithful

---

[87] William of Adam, *How To Defeat the Saracens*, pp. 49–51.

[88] 'Directorium ad Passagium Faciendum', vol. 2, p. 457. Also see Carr, 'Trade or crusade?', pp. 128–9.

[89] John XXII, *Lettres secrètes*, vol. 2, doc. 1690; N. Housley, 'Costing the crusade: budgeting for crusading activity in the fourteenth century', in *The Experience of Crusading*, ed. M. Bull and N. Housley, 2 vols (Cambridge, 2003), pp. 45–58, at p. 56.

[90] On these popular crusades, see Schein, *Fideles Crucis*, pp. 233–8; Housley, *Avignon Papacy*, pp. 22, 144–6, 148–9; M. Barber, 'The *Pastoureaux* of 1320', *Journal of Ecclesiastical History* 32 (1981), 143–66; Guard, *Chivalry, Kingship and Crusade*, pp. 137–9.

[91] Housley, 'Costing the crusade', pp. 56–7.

[92] *Documents on the Later Crusades*, pp. 78–80, doc. 22; Housley, *Avignon Papacy*, pp. 144–8. Many crusaders from England also responded to the preaching in 1343–4, even though it was not extended to England until the following year. Participants often travelled to the East via Avignon, where they petitioned for safe conducts and indulgences: Guard, *Chivalry, Kingship and Crusade*, pp. 33–6.

in their individual cities and dioceses, with the sign of the cross to be given to all who wished to receive it, in order that they could 'rise up manfully against the unbelievers'. To pay for the fleet, tenths of church revenues and incomes were to be granted as well as certain other subsidies. But since the matter entailed 'extraordinary expenditure', even greater assistance was required, which it was hoped would take the form of charitable help from the faithful.

Indulgences and remission of sins were granted to those who wished to participate or contribute in another way. Those who accompanied the fleet in person at their own expense and who remained on campaign for one year were to receive full remission of sins 'as for the Holy Land', which included an additional increase of heavenly reward (*salutis eterne augmentum*). Those who died whilst on campaign, or afterwards from wounds received on the campaign, would also receive the same indulgence. In an attempt to attract specific recruitment and to raise money for the expedition, the pope also specified that a similar but slightly lesser privilege was granted to those faithful who contributed to the expedition but who could not take part in person. This referred specifically to those who sent suitable soldiers at their own expense, in accordance to their means, those who took part at another's expense, and those who offered as much from their own goods as they would have spent on campaign for one year. Recipients of this indulgence were promised the same remission of sins (*concedimus eandem veniam peccatorum*), but without the *salutis eterne augmentum* clause relating to an increase in their heavenly reward.[93] Chests were also to be placed in churches and proceeds collected by papal agents.

During the second wave of the crusade, led by Humbert of Viennois, Clement continued to show full support for the expedition, extending the preaching campaign to such a level that it resulted in one of the greatest outbursts of popular enthusiasm seen in the fourteenth century. In July 1345 indulgences were decreed for Humbert's crusade and the pope ordered Franciscan, Augustinian, Dominican and Carmelite friars to undertake preaching, which was also extended to England.[94] To further bolster recruit-ment, Clement wrote to the archbishop of Smyrna in 1346 granting him the power to commute vows, except those of religion and chastity, to partic-ipation in the Smyrna expedition; the first such example of vows being

---

[93] The exchange of indulgences for money was last introduced by Clement V for the Hospitaller *passagium* of 1308–9, although in that instance a scale of lesser indulgences was established with a specific sum to be paid for each, see Housley, *Avignon Papacy*, pp. 135–9.
[94] Clement VI, *Lettres à la France*, vol. 2, docs 1855–6; W.E. Lunt, *Financial Relations of the Papacy with England to 1327–1534*, 2 vols (Cambridge, MA, 1939), vol. 2, pp. 531–2. On the participation of English crusaders in the Smyrna campaigns, see Guard, *Chivalry, Kingship and Crusade*, pp. 33–8.

commuted for a crusade against the Turks.[95] The response to this preaching campaign was, according to contemporaries, exceptionally high. This was no doubt aided by the appearance of "miracle stories" which circulated in the west during the summer of 1345.

One such story can be found in a letter purporting to be written by Hugh IV of Cyprus to Queen Joanna of Sicily, which circulated in parts of Italy and France. The letter described an exaggerated victory of 200,000 *crucesignati* over a force of 1,200,000 Turks on a plain between Smyrna and Ephesos in June 1345. During the encounter the Christians were on the brink of defeat until the figure of John the Baptist appeared above the army. He assured the crusaders of divine assistance and the promise of 'eternal life' to those who died, after which they arose as if they had never done battle and attacked the Turks again and again, eventually killing 70,000 of them and winning the battle.[96] The emphasis this story gives to the promise of eternal reward suggests that it was used as a recruitment aid for preachers, a factor which may have prompted contemporaries to comment on the generous privileges awarded by the pope at this time.[97]

Another miracle, reported by a Pistoian chronicler, recounts the appearance of the Virgin in a small church at L'Aquila in Abruzzo. The Virgin appeared above the church altar carrying the infant Christ, holding a cross in his hand. On hearing this, all of the townsfolk flocked to the church, where the Virgin remained until the third hour, more resplendent and beautiful than the sun. According to the chronicler, all of the children born that day in L'Aquila had the imprint of the cross on their right shoulder.[98] The chronicler mentioned that because of this miracle 'many *Aquilani* and others from the countryside took the cross and went to fight against the infidels'.[99] Indeed, many other contemporaries attest to the large numbers of Italians taking the cross for the second wave of the Smyrna expedition. The Florentine Giovanni Villani wrote that 400 men from Florence, 350 from Siena, and many others from Tuscany and Lombardy departed for the East.[100] A chronicler from Bologna commented that three groups set out from his city between October 1345 and April 1346, the first two consisting

---

[95]   ASVat, *RV* 169, fol. 3v ep. 10 (6 May 1346); summary in Clement VI, *Lettres autres que la France*, doc. 980.

[96]   Letter published in Jorga, 'Une lettre apocryphe sur la bataille de Smyrne', 28–31. It is discussed in detail by Setton, *Papacy and the Levant*, vol. I, pp. 201–2; Gay, *Clément VI*, pp. 66–7; Jorga, *Philippe de Mézières*, pp. 51–6. The chronicler of Pistoia recounted the same battle, probably after having read the letter or heard it read to him: *Storie pistoresi (1300–1348)*, pp. 215–16.

[97]   For example, Giovanni Villani, vol. 2, bk. 13, ch. 39, pp. 390–1; 'Cronica di Bologna', col. 393; Setton, *Papacy and the Levant*, vol. I, p. 202.

[98]   *Storie pistoresi*, p. 214.

[99]   *Storie pistoresi*, p. 214.

[100]   Giovanni Villani, vol. 3, bk. 13, ch. 39, pp. 390–1.

of forty men, the last of over one hundred.[101] The necrology of the convent of Santa Maria Novella at Florence also named six Dominicans who took the cross for the crusade.[102] In addition to this, many participants from northern Europe travelled through northern Italy en route to the East and are attested to in the fighting at Smyrna.[103] The enthusiasm surrounding the crusade is encapsulated by the somewhat overblown comments of the Anonimo Romano who stated that there was not a city, town or state in the whole of Christendom from which innumerable men did not flock to take the cross.[104]

As Housley has suggested, Clement VI approved of the popular enthusiasm shown towards the crusade and the miracle stories which helped to inspire it. On 21 July, he wrote in a letter to Edward III of England that 'it is clear from amazing miracles that the mercy of divine goodness is working in various lands in favour of the said task'. The pope went on to describe the appearance of 'shining crosses' in very many lands, which had given health benefits to those who were 'burdened with ailments'. Moreover, he claimed that an 'innumerable multitude' of nobles and powerful people, especially from Italy, were preparing to go on crusade against the Turks 'to avenge the injuries of the crucified Redeemer'.[105] The Smyrna campaign thus inspired an outburst of widespread popular enthusiasm on a similar scale to that shown for the 'Crusade of the Poor' in 1309 and the *Pastoureaux* in 1320. In the end, the arrival of so many crusaders at Smyrna – especially with the army of Humbert of Viennois – ended in disaster as overcrowding combined with the heat of the summer and a lack of provisions caused disease to break out.[106] Nevertheless, the measures Clement took to foster enthusiasm for this crusade were successful and the high level of response can in part be attributed to him.

---

[101] 'Cronica di Bologna', cols 393–4, 399.

[102] *Necrologio di S. Maria Novella: testo integrale dall'inizio (MCCXXXV) al MDIV*, ed. S. Orlandi, 2 vols (Florence, 1955), vol. 1, docs 377, 344, 371, 376, 389, 443, pp. 70–100; M.D. Papi, 'Santa Maria Novella di Firenze e l'*Outremer* domenicano', *Toscana e Terrasanta nel Medioevo*, ed. F. Cardini (Florence, 1982), pp. 87–101, at pp. 99–100.

[103] See Guard, *Chivalry, Kingship and Crusade*, pp. 33–8; Carr, 'Crossing boundaries', 117; ASVat, *RS* 7, fol. 79v (30 Nov 1344); *RS* 23, f. 49r (8 July 1351); *Calendar of Entries in the Papal Registers Relating to Great Britain and Ireland: Petitions to the Pope (1342–1419)*, ed. W.H. Bliss et al., 20 vols. (Dublin, 1896–, in progress), vol. 3, pp. 186, 213.

[104] Anonimo Romano, *Cronica*, p. 115.

[105] Clement VI, *Lettres à la France*, vol. 2, doc. 1844, p. 26; Housley, *Avignon Papacy*, pp. 146–7.

[106] See Carr, 'Humbert of Viennois and the Crusade of Smyrna', 246 and the Anonimo Romano, *Cronica*, pp. 16–17, who claimed that there were over 15,000 men at Smyrna before Humbert's arrival. This is undoubtedly an inflated number, but nevertheless is suggestive of the overcrowding in the city.

Papal support for the Crusade of Smyrna therefore contrasts starkly with the mechanisms allocated by John XXII to those fighting the Turks during the 1320s and 1330s. In many ways this was a reflection of how the two popes viewed a crusade against the Turks. During the pontificate of John XXII military action against the Turks was organized and initiated by the resident powers in the Aegean, to whom the pope awarded indulgences, but did not initiate full crusade preaching. Even for the naval league in 1333–4, for which the papacy contributed four galleys, the organization of the campaign was predominantly in the hands of the Venetians. The pope only lent his support in the final months and seemingly only once the Venetians had demonstrated how a fleet for use in the Aegean could be linked to a greater crusade to the Holy Land. Clement VI also responded to initiatives already undertaken by the local maritime powers in the Aegean, but unlike John XXII he took up the mantle of control and committed the full arsenal of crusading mechanisms to the cause, including preaching, church tithes, and the full crusade indulgence 'as per the Holy Land'. The dramatic response to the Crusade of Smyrna, not just from the maritime powers but also from those who had little or no connection to the Aegean, demonstrated that when a crusade against the Turks was awarded full papal support it could attract substantial enthusiasm on a level comparable to other crusading initiatives of the period.

6

Cross-Cultural Trade in the Aegean and Economic Mechanisms for Merchant Crusaders

For the undertaking in defence of the Faithful in overseas lands cruelly harassed by the Turks and other Infidels [...] we grant you licence to send one galley, together with merchandise and sailors, to Alexandria and other overseas regions and lands held by the Sultan of Babylon.

Pope Clement VI, letter to Garin of Châteauneuf,
Hospitaller prior of Navarre, 3 May 1345.[1]

Naval power from the Latins in the East, at times with assistance from the French Crown and the papacy, came to form the forefront of crusading against the Turks in the Aegean, culminating in the naval leagues of the 1330s and 1340s. But the merchants and mariners who made up the Aegean fleets were not just motivated by a desire to defend the faith from the infidel; their interests were also inseparably intertwined with the web of cross-cultural commerce in the eastern Mediterranean. This often resulted in a dilemma for the participating merchant states, as they attempted to balance peaceful commercial relations in the East with the need to defend their lands from Muslim aggression, and the inevitable disruption to trade that this caused.[2] The commercial priorities of these merchant crusaders were far removed from those of the traditional crusading powers of western Europe and consequently posed new problems for the Church, which had to re-orient its policies to accommodate the new political-economic situation in the Aegean region, whilst not being seen to be completely relaxing its policy towards trading with infidel. As a result of this, trade licences, such as that granted to Garin of Châteauneuf above became a prominent feature of papal crusading policy.

---

[1]   ASVat, *RV* 138, fols. 268v–269r, ep. 524.
[2]   For an overview of the effects of warfare on commerce, see J. Preiser-Kapeller, 'Liquid frontiers', esp. pp. 121–30.

Initial Conflicts between Commerce and Crusade in the Aegean

During the first half of the fourteenth century successive popes promulgated a 'total embargo', which theoretically forbade trade with the entire Muslim world. This prohibition was then reiterated by the authorities of the maritime republics, who provided detailed lists of the penalties for those who broke the papal decrees, even though in reality these reiterations were not always carried out in full. The trade ban had a mixed impact on Mediterranean commerce: it did not result in the complete isolation of Muslim lands from Latin merchants, as many private individuals still broke the embargo, but it was sufficient to force the re-direction of much Christian trade from Egypt to lands further north; a factor which was accentuated by the loss of the Holy Land and the expansion of Latin colonies in the Aegean and the Black Sea.[3] Because of this, when a more aggressive military policy was adopted by the Latin states against the Turks, the papal embargo had the unforeseen consequence of cutting off a vital source of revenue needed to fund crusading activities in the Aegean by restricting trade with Mamluk lands.

The Zaccaria

The dilemma this posed to Latin merchant crusaders is most clearly represented by the Genoese Zaccaria family, whose fortunes were intrinsically linked with the defence of their lands from the Anatolian Turks and the export of goods to northern Europe and the Mamluk sultanate. The Zaccaria specialized in two main commodities. The first of these was alum, which was extremely valuable and had a number of uses: it was the most effective fabric mordant (fixative for dyes) known at the time, an important product for preparing and softening leather, and it was considered to be an effective styptic as well as having numerous other medicinal benefits.[4] The Phokaia mines under the control of the Zaccaria were the most productive of the time and produced alum of an extremely high quality, only bettered by that of Karahissar (Koloneia) in north-eastern Anatolia.[5] Importantly for the Zaccaria, although the Phokaia mines were situated in *Turchia* just north of Smyrna, the Turks do not seem to have played any part in the extraction of the chemical or its shipment: the Zaccaria employed Greek miners (some

[3] These points are discussed in detail by Stantchev, *Spiritual Rationality*, esp. pp. 117–62.
[4] For more on alum, see C.S. Singer, *The Earliest Chemical Industry: An Essay in the Historical Relations of Economics and Technology Illustrated from the Alum Trade* (London, 1948), esp. pp. 79–135; Balard, *La Romanie génoise*, pp. 769–81; D. Jacoby, 'Production et commerce de l'alun oriental en Méditerranée, XIe–XVe siècles', in *L'alun de Méditerranée*, ed. P. Borgard, J.-P. Brun and M. Picon (Naples, 2005), pp. 219–67.
[5] Francesco Balducci Pegolotti, *La Pratica Della Mercatura*, pp. 367–70; Lopez and Raymond, *Medieval Trade in the Mediterranean World*, pp. 353–5, doc. 176.

3,000 by 1305),[6] and exported the commodity to the textile industries of northern Europe.[7] For this reason, when the Zaccaria resorted to military action against the Turks from 1319 onwards, the trade in alum does not appear to have been adversely affected.

However, this was not the case for the other main commodity that the family specialized in; the unique Chiote product of mastic gum.[8] Mastic was highly valued as an aromatic chewing gum and for its medicinal properties. It was popular in Europe, but even more so in the Islamic world, especially Mamluk Egypt.[9] By the time the Zaccaria had engaged in concerted military operations against the Aydin Turks in 1319 several factors had effectively cut off the mastic trade at a time when the revenue was needed most, as is illustrated by a petition of the brothers Martino and Benedetto II Zaccaria to Pope John XXII in 1320. According to them, the conflict with the Turks and civil war in Genoa had prevented Christian merchants from exporting mastic from Chios to the West. This left the Saracens as the only ones shipping the product from the island, as Christian merchants were forbidden from visiting Mamluk lands. The brothers claimed that the loss of revenue caused by these obstructions had forced them to release soldiers from their employ, which in turn was compromising their ability to resist the Turks; a factor which gravely imperilled both the Christians on Chios and on the neighbouring islands. The pope was evidently moved by the Zaccaria appeals and in response issued the brothers with a special licence (*licentiam*) to generate money for their operations against the Turks. This 'trade licence' allowed the family unrestricted right to ship mastic to the lands of the Mamluk sultan for a period of two years and to bring back other merchandise, except explicitly forbidden goods (i.e. war materials and slaves), on their same ships without incurring any of the penalties usually imposed for

---

[6]   Ramon Muntaner, *The Catalan Expedition to the East*, pp. 127–8.

[7]   See Lopez and Raymond, *Medieval Trade*, pp. 219–20, doc. 108 (8 Jul 1268); *Les relations commerciales entre Gênes*, ed. Doehaerd, vol. 3, docs 1356–7 (12 May 1278), 1530 (29 Oct 1298); Archivio di Stato di Genoa, Notai Antichi, Not. Andreolus de Laneris, vol. 1, fols 37v–38r, 40r–v (29–30 Oct 1298).

[8]   Mastic was a gum extracted from the *Pistacia lentiscus* tree, which although native to the Mediterranean, only produces high-grade gum on Chios. For more on mastic production, see P. Freedman, 'Mastic: A Mediterranean luxury product', *Mediterranean Historical Review* 26 (2011), 99–113; C. Belles, *Mastiha Island*, trans. C. Sachtouri (Athens, 2005), pp. 29–95, 245–83; J. Perikos, *The Chios Gum Mastic* (Athens, 1993), pp. 13–21.

[9]   Sanudo claimed that the import tax levied on the product generated much revenue for the sultan: Marino Sanudo, 'Liber Secretorum', pp. 24–5, 33, 46; Lock trans., pp. 53, 66, 85. See also the comments by Ludolph of Sudheim, *Description of the Holy Land, and of the Way Thither*, p. 29; William of Boldensele, 'Des Edelherrn Wilhelm von Boldensele Reise nach dem gelobten Lande', p. 32. This is discussed by Carr, 'Trade or crusade?', pp. 119–20; Freedman, 'Mastic', 102, 105.

breaking the trade embargo.[10] It was renewed for four years in 1322 and for a further three years in 1325.[11]

It is unfortunate that the lack of notarial documents relating to Chios under the first Genoese occupation means that determining the effectiveness of the mastic licence is extremely difficult. With the exception of sporadic mastic shipments, such as one to Liguria in 1327, evidence of exports from the island during the 1320s is scarce.[12] This is especially the case for exports to Mamluk lands, which despite being mentioned in the Cairo Geniza do not exist for this particular period.[13] Nevertheless, various sources provide glimpses of the wealth and prosperity of Chios in the 1320s, which could plausibly have been a result of the papal privileges. It has been claimed that the high quality of gold and silver coinage struck on the island is a reflection of the high level of economic prosperity, which was a direct result of the steady inflow of Byzantine and Italian money from the sale of mastic.[14] This seems likely considering the comments of the contemporary Turkish *Manaqeb al-ʿarefin*, which stated that in the late 1320s the forces of Umur of Aydin carried away 'more mastic than can be described' from Chios (*Saqez Adasi*).[15] Another source, John Kantakouzenos, who was present during the conquest of the island by the Byzantine emperor in 1329, claimed that the annual income of Martino Zaccaria had reached 120,000 *hyperpyra*; a huge sum which equates to roughly one-fifth of the annual imperial revenue under Andronikos III.[16] Contemporaries also commented on the large forces which the family were able to maintain in the defence of their island which

[10] The document is in printed in Appendix 4, doc. 1, pp. 157–8. See also Carr 'Trade or Crusade?', pp. 125–6.

[11] ASVat, *RA* 17, fols 242–242v; *RV* 73, ep. 1071 (25 Jun 1322); *RA* 23, fol. 143; *RV* 79, ep. 1449 (29 Jan 1325); summaries in John XXII, *Lettres communes*, vol. 4, doc. 15644, vol. 5, doc. 21494. In the 1340s more licences were granted to permit mastic shipments to Egypt, but by then the Zaccaria had lost control of Chios and there is no evidence that these later mastic licences were connected with the war against the Turks: ASVat, *RS* 9, fol. 168r (3 Sep 1345), *RS* 18, fols. 39v, 42r (18–19 Nov 1348); summaries in Carr, 'Crossing boundaries', docs 13, 38–9.

[12] *Les relations commerciales entre Gênes, la Belgique et l'Outremont: d'après les archives notariales génoises (1320–1400)*, ed. L. Liagre-de Sturler, 2 vols (Brussels, 1969), vol. 1, doc. 46.

[13] Some earlier examples are preserved in the letters of Jewish merchants: S.D. Goitein, *Letters of Medieval Jewish Traders* (Princeton, 1979), pp. 99, 131, 133, 196.

[14] This point is made by Metcalf, *Coinage of the Crusades and the Latin East*, pp. 289–91. Also see Mazarakis, 'The Chios mint during the rule of the Zaccaria family', 43–52; G. Lunardi, *Le monete delle colonie Genovesi* (Genoa, 1980), pp. 179–88; G. Schlumberger, *Numismatique de l'orient Latin*, vol. 2, pp. 413–15.

[15] Shams al-Din Ahmad-e Aflaki, *The Feats of the Knowers of God (Manaqeb al-ʿarefin)*, trans. J. O'Kane (Leiden, 2002), p. 665.

[16] John Kantakouzenos, *Ioannis Cantacuzeni eximperatoris Historiarum libri IV*, vol. 1, bk. 2, ch. 10, 12, pp. 371, 379–80; Carr, 'Trade or crusade?', p. 128.

makes it likely that the mastic licences achieved their objective of helping the Zaccaria finance their war against the Turks.[17]

The process of granting licences to reduce the total embargo to a selective one, by allowing trade with Muslims – always in non-prohibited merchandise – was not a new development in itself.[18] As early as 1198 Innocent III had granted the Republic of Venice temporary permission to trade in 'clean' merchandise with Egypt in order to persuade the doge to participate in a forthcoming crusade.[19] Similarly, only a year before the fall of Acre – when Egypt had become the primary focus of papal trade sanctions – news of a truce had persuaded Nicholas IV to allow Christian merchants to transport victuals and other non war materials between Egypt and the Holy Land as long as the truce lasted.[20] However, the Zaccaria licence was different. It marked the first occasion when a trade concession was awarded specifically in order to facilitate military action against the Turks, or *contra Turchos* as it will be referred to here. This formed the first part of a wider policy introduced by John XXII of using trade licences to shift the focus of anti-Muslim military endeavours in the Mediterranean; one which would gradually be expanded to include the conflict with Muslims in Granada from the late 1320s, and would eventually come to form an integral part of papal-merchant strategy against the Turks in the 1340s (see Appendices 2 and 3).[21]

Venice

The Venetians were also the recipients of trade licences granted *contra Turchos*, but their situation in the Aegean was more complex than that of the Zaccaria, which meant that initial negotiations with the papacy proved to be less fruitful. Venetian commercial links with the Muslim rulers of western Anatolia were an extension of formal commercial relations begun with the Seljuks in the early thirteenth century. These increased after the Seljuk domain collapsed during the Mongol invasion of 1243, when merchants began regularly to frequent the port of Makre in the lands of Menteshe.

---

[17] See Carr, 'Trade or crusade?', pp. 128–9.

[18] See the examples from the late twelfth and thirteenth centuries given by Stantchev, *Spiritual Rationality*, esp. pp. 41–87.

[19] A.J. Andrea, *Contemporary Sources for the Fourth Crusade: Revised Edition* (Leiden, 2008), pp. 23–4 (3 Dec 1198).

[20] Nicholas IV, *Les registres de Nicolas IV: Recueil des bulles de ce pape*, ed. M.E. Langlois, 2 vols (Paris, 1905), vol. I, doc. 4403 (21 Oct 1290); Stantchev, *Spiritual Rationality*, p. 121.

[21] John XXII granted licences allowing Christian rulers to send ships to Mamluk Egypt in order to recoup losses incurred in fighting Muslims in Iberia: J. Trenchs-Odena, '"De Alexandrinis" (El comercio prohibido con los Musulmanes y el papado de Avinon durante la primera mitad del siglo XIV)', *Anuario de estudios medievales* 10 (1980), 237–320, at 269–70, docs 4 (7 Oct 1328), 6 (1 Feb 1331), 7 (12 Jul 1331). He also granted a licence to Walter of Brienne, permitting him to send two cogs to Alexandria: ASVat, *RV* 98, fol. 216v, doc. 475; summary in John XXII, *Communes*, vol. 10, doc. 52188 (5 Jan 1331).

By the early years of the fourteenth century, the deeds of Candian notaries and rulings of the Venetian Senate show that Cretans were operating on the Turkish mainland and were regularly importing commodities such as soap, horses and slaves to their island, as well as grain and other foodstuffs which were of extreme importance to the Aegean colonies and to Venice itself.[22] Although documents relating to the official commercial relations with the Turks remain scarce during this early period, it seems likely that the good relations between Crete and Menteshe resulted in a formal treaty being made between the two sides sometime before 1318.[23]

During these years the Venetians appealed to the papacy for permission to trade with the Mamluks, but unlike the Zaccaria they could not cite war with the Turks as a legitimate reason for needing this concession. Instead, Venetian appeals centred around the argument that the prosperity of the Republic was derived from overseas trade and not from land, fields, vineyards or other possessions, as was the case with most other states. This was an argument first put forward in the Venetian licence of 1198 and formed a basis of subsequent petitions thereafter.[24] A supplication for a papal licence based on this rationale was discussed by the Venetian Senate in October 1317, where it was deemed a reasonable request by the papal legate who suggested that an envoy be sent to the pope.[25] In early 1319 the matter was raised again and the Senate authorized 5,000 florins to be sent to ambassadors at the papal curia to purchase a licence.[26] However, no papal records suggest that the Venetian petition was granted and in early 1323 the Senate and the authorities on Crete re-iterated the papal decrees that no Venetian 'dare go to Alexandria or to other lands subjected to the Sultan with any things or goods or send to said lands anything in any way'.[27] What followed was a period of strict embargo whereby state-sponsored trade with Egypt was halted until 1344.[28] During this time Venetian galleys going eastward were organized into just two official convoys: one to Cilician Armenia and Cyprus, or just Cyprus, and the other, called 'galleys of Romania', to Constantinople and the Black Sea.[29]

---

[22] For more information on this, see Zachariadou, *Trade and Crusade*, pp. 163–5.

[23] Zachariadou, *Trade and Crusade*, pp. 3–7, 18.

[24] See above, note 19, and Stantchev, *Spiritual Rationality*, pp. 55–8.

[25] *I libri commemoriali*, vol. 1, pp. 183–4, docs 64–5 (3, 5 Oct 1317).

[26] *Le deliberazioni (Senato)*, vol. 1, pp. 201, 207, docs 277, 353 (Feb–May 1319). See also Stantchev, *Spiritual Rationality*, p. 136.

[27] *Duca di Candia: Bandi (1313–1329)*, ed. P. Ratti Vidulich (Venice, 1965), pp. 129–30, doc. 342 (15 Apr 1323) quotation from Stantchev, *Spiritual Rationality*, p. 138. The order was originally made by the Senate on 18 January 1323: *Le deliberazioni (Senato)*, vol. 1, p. 265, doc. 239.

[28] For a detailed discussion of reasons behind this, see Stantchev, *Spiritual Rationality*, pp. 133–45; Ashtor, *Levant Trade*, pp. 44–63; cf. Ortalli, 'Venice and papal bans on trade', 242–58.

[29] F.C. Lane, 'The Venetian galleys to Alexandria, 1344', in Idem, *Studies in Venetian Social and Economic History*, Variorum Reprints (London, 1987), XIII, pp. 431–3, at p. 431.

This restriction of the Republic's official trade with Egypt coincided with the start of Turkish-Catalan raids against the islands of the western Aegean and mainland Greece, which increasingly compromised trade with Anatolia. From this point onwards the Venetian authorities had to strike a difficult balance between the facilitation of local trade with the beyliks on the one hand, and the enforcement of the papal embargo and military action against the Turks on the other. At first, the authorities on Crete resorted to a policy of appeasement with the Turks and Catalans in order to safeguard regular shipments from Anatolia. This resulted in a series of temporary truces which seem to have allowed some local trade with Menteshe.[30] But by the mid 1320s it became apparent that the Aydin Turks were posing the main threat to Venetian possessions. This allowed the Cretan authorities to cement their ties with Menteshe further, forming a new treaty with Emir Orkhan in 1331.[31] However, the re-opening of trade with Menteshe compelled the Senate to impose an embargo on trade in Turkey a year later.[32] This action further compromised the shipment of necessary provisions to Venetian territories, which was a significant problem considering the imminent arrival of the forces of the first naval league in the Aegean. Consequently, in late 1333, a Cretan embassy was sent to Venice to request permission to negotiate another agreement with Orkhan of Menteshe so that horses, animals and corn might be secured from his territories. The Senate accepted the Cretan proposal and also declared that the previous prohibition imposed on trade in Turkey only applied to Venetian subjects and not to foreigners employed by the Venetians. This ruling therefore allowed the duke of Crete to import goods from the Turks through the use non-Venetian intermediaries.[33]

After the victories of the naval league, a new prohibition was introduced on trade in *Turchia* by the Senate in 1335.[34] However, by this time the financial burden of maintaining galleys in the Aegean for almost two years was beginning to be felt by the Republic. Perhaps as a response to this, the Senate granted the Venetian captain of the league permission to transport passengers within the Aegean, probably to subsidize the expense of maintaining the galleys.[35] In 1336 the *Serenissima* also issued new orders which

---

[30] See Zachariadou, *Trade and Crusade*, pp. 13–16, 18.

[31] Full text in Zachariadou, *Trade and Crusade*, pp. 187–9, doc. 1331M, discussed at pp. 18–20.

[32] Zachariadou, *Trade and Crusade*, pp. 20, 28 (Jun 1332).

[33] For these negotiations, see Theotokes, *Thespismata*, vol. 2.1, pp. 130–3, doc. 14 (16 Nov 1333); Thiriet, *Sénat*, vol. 1, doc. 38; Zachariadou, *Trade and Crusade*, p. 28.

[34] Theotokes, *Thespismata*, vol. 2.1, p. 160, doc. 6 (20 Jun 1335).

[35] Theotokes, *Thespismata*, vol. 2.1, p. 159, doc. 1 (6 March 1335); Zachariadou, *Trade and Crusade*, p. 34. The galleys were initially expected to partially subsidise themselves through the transport of merchandise on their outward journey: *Documents on the Later Crusades*, p. 73, doc. 20, but in May 1334 John XXII ruled that no goods were to be carried as they

specifically instructed the captain of the league to capture as many Turkish ships as possible, again probably to alleviate the expense of the galleys, this time through prize money and confiscated cargoes.[36] Once the league had disbanded the Cretans sought another treaty with the Turks, this time with Aydin as well as Menteshe, in 1337.[37] These treaties provide a good insight into the concerns of the Republic at this time. As Venice and Menteshe had held commercial agreements before 1337, the clauses of this treaty were mostly concerned with amending the trading rights of Venetians in the emirate, such as the restoration of weights and measures, the securing of tax privileges, and an order that the Turks cease the construction of dwellings in the district allocated to the Venetians. There was also one clause which provides a good example of the importance of grain imports from *Turchia*. This specifically stipulated that the *shinik* – a measure commonly used for cereals – be restored to its previous status.[38] Unlike the agreement made with Menteshe, the treaty concluded with Aydin was the first to be made between the two parties. The majority of the clauses of the treaty therefore refer to settling the conditions necessary for commercial exchange, such as the fixing of customs duties, the establishment of a consul in Theologo (Ephesos) and the granting of an area for Venetian merchants. As well as this the treaties provided a good opportunity for the Venetians to gain a foothold in the alum trade – previously dominated by the Genoese – by allowing them access to one of the most productive alum mines of the period, that of Kutahya in the landlocked emirate of Germiyan.[39] The Venetians were able to do this by forcing Menteshe and Aydin to abolish the *appalto* (a state monopoly) on alum shipments from Kutahya to their ports of Ephesos and Balat, from where it could be shipped by Venetians to the West.[40] By securing the best possible trade agreements with the Anatolian Turks the Republic had therefore succeeded in securing preferential trade in

---

might hold up progress: John XXII, *Lettres secrètes*, vol. 4, doc. 5495 (30 May 1334); Housley, 'Costing the crusade', p. 47.

[36] Theotokes, *Thespismata*, vol. 2.1, p. 168, doc. 21 (15 Feb 1336). Naval forces were often expected to partially pay for themselves through the capture of enemy ships: Guilmartin, *Gunpowder and Galleys*, p. 60.

[37] Zachariadou, *Trade and Crusade*, pp. 34–7, 190–200, docs 1337A, 1337M.

[38] Zachariadou, *Trade and Crusade*, doc. 1337M, p. 198 (clause 23).

[39] According to Pegolotti, Kutahya produced around 12,000 *cantara* of alum per year, compared with 14,000 from Phokaia: Francesco Balducci Pegolotti, *La Pratica Della Mercatura*, pp. 367–70; Lopez and Raymond, *Medieval Trade*, pp. 353–5, doc. 176.

[40] See Zachariadou, *Trade and Crusade*, doc. 1337A, p. 192 (clause 12), doc. 1337M, p. 199 (clause 28); Jacoby, 'Production et commerce de l'alun', 246; Fleet, *European and Islamic Trade*, pp. 26, 77–8, 89–90. An *appalto* was a common form of monopolistic concession in the late medieval Mediterranean, see C.F. Wright, 'Florentine alum mining in the Hospitaller islands: the *appalto* of 1442', *Journal of Medieval History* 32 (2010), 175–91.

a market which had hitherto been dominated by their fiercest commercial rival.

Economic Crises during the Crusade of Smyrna

The Closure of Eastern Markets

Despite the ability of the Venetians to secure some commercial agreements with the Turks, the instability of trade in the Aegean region led Venetian representatives at the papal curia to launch fresh appeals for permission to trade in Egypt, in 1327–8 and again in 1337.[41] These appeals reiterated the arguments made in earlier supplications but again seem to have fallen on deaf ears. However, by the 1340s, when the crusade against the Turks coincided with the widespread breakdown of trade in the eastern Mediterranean and the Black Sea, supplicants at the curia – including the Venetians – began to cite their commitment to the crusade and the economic pressure that this entailed as a justification for receiving licences. Consequently the pontificate of Clement VI resulted in a dramatic increase in the awarding of trade licences, especially those granted *contra Turchos*.

The change in policy must be understood in relation to the economic background in the Mediterranean at the end of the 1330s and beginning of the 1340s. Venetian trade in Anatolia was presumably stable in the years immediately after the treaties of 1337, but by the summer of 1339 Turkish raids resumed and began to impede trade in the Aegean region once again.[42] To add to this, in 1337 the Armenian port of Lajazzo had been captured by the Mamluks, further restricting the opportunities for lawful trade for Latin merchants.[43] More problems arose a year later when the Senate passed a law prohibiting its merchants from trading with the Mongol Ilkhanate, and forbade them from purchasing Ilkhanate goods in any other lands, including the markets of Constantinople, Tana and Cyprus. The prohibition was to be proclaimed on an annual basis and those who broke it would be fined 1,000 pounds; an enormous sum which must have forced a high level of compliance. The ban was imposed in retaliation for abuses Venetian merchants had suffered in Ilkhanate lands, which had damaged trade as well as the honour

---

[41] *Diplomatarium Veneto-Levantinum*, vol. I, no. 105 (1327); *Le deliberazioni (Senato)*, vol. I, pp. 361–71, docs 31, 98, 127, 137, 138 (Jun–Nov 1328); *The Records of the Venetian Senate on Disk, 1335–1400*, ed. B. Kohl (New York, 2001), doc. 179 (30 Nov 1337). See also Ashtor, *Levant Trade*, pp. 46, 65–6.

[42] Zachariadou, *Trade and Crusade*, pp. 41–2.

[43] Zachariadou, *Trade and Crusade*, p. 46, n. 178.

of the city.[44] This was coupled with another Venetian ban in 1341, this time against trade in the principality of Achaia for similar reasons.[45]

An even more serious threat to the economic stability of the whole Mediterranean region arose in the northern Black Sea in the early 1340s. By this time Venetian and Genoese merchants were well established in the Black Sea, whence they exported large amounts of grain to European markets from their colonies in Caffa and Tana. Relations had been good, but in 1343 a fight broke out in Tana which led to a mob attack on the Venetian residents there. During the clash considerable blood was shed which prompted the khan of the Golden Horde to expel all Latin merchants from Tana, after which he also laid siege to Genoese Caffa and prohibited all grain exports from the region. To make matters worse, Latin communities in Trebizond were also attacked by the local population and forced to submit to harsh restrictions.[46] In response the Venetians and the Genoese made an agreement to ban all trade with the Golden Horde. Even though some individual merchants still traded in Crimea after this point, it was not until 1347 that the two republics made peace with the khan and officially reopened commercial links.[47]

As relations with the Tartar khan began to break down, the Venetians and the other Latin powers stepped up their crusade plans against the Turks by dispatching galleys to the Aegean. It may even be that the Crusade of Smyrna was launched because of Venetian fears over trade. This is intimated by a contemporary from Rimini who suggested that the Turks had broken trade agreements relating to grain with the Venetians, and also by the less reliable Anonimo Romano who reported that Umur had provoked the crusade by raising taxes on Venetian merchants without just cause.[48] However, it seems unlikely that these commercial factors motivated the

---

[44] *Venezia-senato: deliberazioni miste*, vol. 4 (*Registre XVII, 1335–1339*), pp. 459–62, docs 1204–8 (17 Dec 1335); Stantchev, 'The medieval origins of embargo', 392. The Genoese may have implemented a similar ban a few years later: S. Karpov, 'Black Sea and the crisis of the mid XIVth century: an underestimated turning point', *Thesaurismata* 27 (1997), 65–78, at 69.

[45] *Venezia-senato: deliberazioni miste*, vol. 6 (*Registre XIX, 1340–1341*), pp. 195–7, docs 380, 386 (13 and 15 Jan 1341).

[46] For the Black Sea crisis, see Karpov, 'Black Sea and the crisis of the mid XIVth century', 65–78; Zachariadou, *Trade and Crusade*, pp. 45–9. For Latin possessions in Caffa and Tana, see E.Č. Skržinskaja, 'Storia della Tana', *Studi Veneziani* 10 (1968), 3–45 and Balard, *La Romanie génoise*, pp. 114–18, 199–215.

[47] Karpov, 'Black Sea and the crisis of the mid XIVth century', 70; Stantchev, 'The medieval origins of embargo', 393–4.

[48] Marco Battagli of Rimini, *Marcha (1212–1354)*, ed. A.F. Massèra, *RISNS* 16.3 (Città di Castello, 1913), pp. 50–1, his exact words are '[the crusade] happened on account of agreements of grain, which had existed between the Venetians and the Turks, and because of other depredations of the Turks carried out by them tyrannically'; Anonimo Romano, *Cronica*, p. 103. See also Zachariadou, *Trade and Crusade*, p. 44; Fleet, *European and Islamic Trade*, pp. 59, 70.

Venetian contribution to the crusade: the conflict with the Turks actually exacerbated the economic situation in the Aegean, which is something the *Serenissima* surely would have been aware of. The damage done to trade is demonstrated in a letter written from Crete in October 1344, where a group of merchants complained that it was not possible for anyone to come or go from Turkey.[49] By September 1345 things had got so bad that the Cretan administration reported that there was famine on the island.[50] The grain shortage resulted in a general rise in prices, the effects of which were felt most severely in Romania, but also as far afield as Italy. In the face of these problems it comes as no surprise that Latin merchants increasingly turned to the Mamluk sultanate for the shipment of grain to supply Aegean markets as well as those of western Europe. Evidence of this is given by a letter of a merchant in Candia of December 1344, which showed that the Aegean region had become dependent on food supplies from Alexandria.[51]

Trade Wars and Rivalries

The closure of so many markets in the eastern Mediterranean further accentuated the rivalries between the Latins of the East, whose concerns over the security of their colonies prompted them to engage in policies of economic protectionism and opportunism which proved to be detrimental to crusading operations.[52] This can be seen clearly in the activities of the Genoese in regard to the naval leagues. Considering the history of animosity between the maritime republics, it comes as no surprise that Genoa refused to contribute 'officially' to the leagues, which were considered to be Venetian-dominated campaigns designed to further the interests of the Republic. As a consequence some Genoese in the Aegean pursued their own agenda in order to consolidate or recover the possessions of their countrymen overseas. This occurred as early as the first naval league when Domenico Cattaneo, the Genoese ruler of Phokaia, declined to contribute to the fleet but instead launched a failed campaign to conquer Byzantine Lesbos with the assistance of the Hospitallers at the beginning of 1335.[53] A similar situation arose during the Smyrna campaign in 1346 when the Genoese fleet commanded

---

[49] *Lettere di Mercanti a Pignol Zucchello*, pp. 23–6, doc. 9 (5 Oct 1344).

[50] *Duca di Candia: Quaternus consiliorum*, pp. 33–6, doc. 67 (24 Sep 1345).

[51] *Lettere di Mercanti a Pignol Zucchello*, pp. 29–30, doc. 12 (28 Dec 1344).

[52] On economic protectionism, see Stantchev, 'The medieval origins of embargo', 386–90.

[53] Cattaneo had been compelled by the emperor to recognize his suzerainty after the conquest of Chios in 1329. After this his position at Phokaia was weakened considerably and he was forced to pay tribute to the neighbouring Turks, see Zachariadou, *Trade and Crusade*, pp. 37–8. The chronology of the Lesbos attack is obscured by the conflicting Byzantine accounts: John Kantakouzenos, *Ioannis Cantacuzeni eximperatoris Historiarum libri IV*, vol. I, bk. 2, ch. 29–32, pp. 476–95; Nikephoros Gregoras, *Byzantina Historia*, vol. I, bk. II, ch. 1–2, pp. 523–31; P. Schreiner, *Die byzantinischen Kleinchroniken*, 3 vols (Vienna, 1975–9), vol. I, p. 76, vol. 2, pp. 246–7, vol. 3, p. 30.

by Simone Vignoso actively refused to assist Humbert of Viennois in his planned capture of Chios as a base of operations. Instead, Vignoso attacked Humbert's fleet off Negroponte and seized Chios for himself, followed by the Phokaias.[54] The ship owners led by Vignoso set up a cooperative, known as the Mahona, which would rule the island until 1566.[55] In the years immediately after the conquest of Chios, they offered no support to the crusade and instead proceeded to raid Venetian possessions after the outbreak of war between the two sides in 1350. Obviously not all Genoese hindered crusading operations: the Zaccaria, for example, were main players in the Turkish conflicts up to 1329. However, even the appointment of the illustrious Martino Zaccaria as captain of the papal galleys of the league in 1343 appears to have been ill-thought out by the pope, who had to introduce measures to prevent Martino from diverting the crusade to Chios. Even though this was not done, Clement still felt it necessary to permit the papal legate to replace Martino as captain if he failed to carry out papal orders.[56]

The Venetians for their part were equally concerned with commercial rivalries during the Smyrna Crusade. They were already suspicious of the motives of Martino Zaccaria, and even though he was killed by the Turks in January 1345, their commitment to the crusade began to cool. This can be seen in the conduct of the Venetians towards Humbert of Viennois. His force arrived at Negroponte in late 1345, but the Venetian authorities were unwilling to supply him with the vessels he needed to sail to Smyrna. In the following May they eventually agreed to his demands, but six months later the Republic was reprimanded by the pope for preventing crusaders who wished to travel to Smyrna from departing from Venice.[57] By this time the Hospitallers had entered the fray on the side of their old allies the Genoese, who had just captured Chios under Vignoso. In the autumn of 1346 the Hospitallers imposed a new customs duty on Venetian merchants trading in their territories, and although the Cretan government sent an ambassador to protest, the Hospitallers refused to back down. In response, the Cretan administration decreed in March 1347 that all Cretan trade with Hospitaller territories be prohibited, under threat of heavy punishment.[58] A few months later, a merchant wrote from Crete that the trade routes to Rhodes had been

[54] Giorgio Stella, *Annales Genuenses*, ed. G. Petti Balbi, *RISNS* 17.2 (Bologna, 1975), pp. 145–7; Carr, 'Humbert of Viennois and the Crusade of Smyrna', 243; Leonhard, *Genua und die päpstliche Kurie in Avignon*, pp. 176–83.

[55] On the Mahona see P.P. Argenti, 'The Mahona of the Giustiniani: Genoese colonialism and the Genoese relationship with Chios', *Byzantinische Forschungen* 6 (1979), 1–35; Epstein, *Genoa and the Genoese*, pp. 210–11, 219–24, 237, 243, 308.

[56] Clement VI, *Lettres à la France*, vol. 1, docs 405 (16 Sep. 1343), 1113–14 (18 Sep 1344), 1464 (1 Feb 1345); Carr, 'Humbert of Viennois and the Crusade of Smyrna', 244–5.

[57] Clement VI, *Lettres à la France*, vol. 2, doc. 2956 (28 Nov 1346); Clement VI, *Lettres autres que la France*, doc. 1273.

[58] Thiriet, *Assemblées*, vol. 1, docs 532, 533, 539; *Duca di Candia: Quaternus consiliorum*, docs

closed.[59] Given these difficulties is possible that the Venetians sent ambassadors to Umur to agree a truce at this time, as is claimed by the Anonimo Romano. His account – admittedly of an anti-Venetian stance – even went as far as to say that the Venetians prevented supplies from reaching Smyrna by blockading the port and that they fleeced the crusaders in the city of all their money.[60] At this time the Republic also sought to re-open trade in the Black Sea by making a treaty with the Tartars. But once again, this measure seems to have resulted in conflict with the Genoese who captured a Venetian vessel there, in an attempt to exclude their rivals from the Black Sea. The Venetians duly retaliated by seizing Genoese ships. These actions were the prelude to the Venetian-Genoese war which would break out in 1350.[61]

By now the Hospitallers were also suffering from the consequences of the economic collapse in the region and decided to agree a one-year truce with Hizir of Aydin.[62] According to the Anonimo Romano, the Knights were preventing Venetian ships from coming to Smyrna and were even supplying weapons to the Turks.[63] In reality, by this time operations against the Turks were starting to wind down; the papal galleys had already ended their service and the Black Death was beginning to take its toll in the Aegean. Consequently truce negotiations were opened with the Aydin, first with Umur, but then with Hizir, after the death of his brother in the early summer of 1348.[64] Even though every party was in need of peace by this stage, once again old rivalries acted to derail negotiations. The representatives of the Latins in the negotiations with Hizir were Bartolommeo of Tomari, the canon of Negroponte, and Octavian Zaccaria, the son of Martino. The Venetians were suspicious that Octavian Zaccaria would push for Genoese interests and wrote letters of protest to the pope over this.[65] By 1349 Turkish raids resumed once again and the truce negotiations were cancelled. Even though the naval league was temporarily renewed, the rising tensions between

124, 126, 128, 132, 138, 147, 149; Luttrell, 'Crete and Rhodes', pp. 171–2; Zachariadou, *Trade and Crusade*, pp. 48–9.

[59] *Lettere di Mercanti a Pignol Zucchello*, doc. 36, p. 73 (16 May 1347).

[60] Anonimo Romano, *Cronica*, pp. 115–16; Zachariadou, *Trade and Crusade*, pp. 51–2; Carr, 'Humbert of Viennois and the Crusade of Smyrna', 248.

[61] See Zachariadou, *Trade and Crusade*, pp. 48–9.

[62] Full text in Zachariadou, *Trade and Crusade*, pp. 201–4, doc. 1346A.

[63] Anonimo Romano, *Cronica*, p. 116.

[64] For the negotiations with Umur, see Clement VI, *Lettres autres que la France*, docs 1563–4 (20–1 Jan 1348); Clement VI, *Lettres à la France*, vol. 2, doc. 3728 (5 Feb 1348). The full text of the draft treaty with Hizir is in *DVL*, vol. 1, doc. 168; Zachariadou, *Trade and Crusade*, doc. 1348A, pp. 205–10; discussion in Zachariadou, *Trade and Crusade*, pp. 55–6; Lemerle, *L'émirat d'Aydin*, pp. 226–31; Setton, *Papacy and the Levant*, vol. 1. pp. 214–17.

[65] M. Brunetti, 'Contributo alla Storia delle relazioni veneto–genovesi dal 1348 al 1350', *Miscellanea di Storia Veneta* 9 (Venice, 1916), pp. 1–160, at pp. 33–4; Zachariadou, *Trade and Crusade*, pp. 56–7.

Venice and Genoa prevented it from taking any concerted action against the Turks. The escalation of the skirmishes in the Black Sea led the Venetians to dispatch a fleet of around thirty-five galleys to the Aegean in 1350 under the command of Marco Ruzzini, the newly appointed Captain General of the Sea. Ruzzini's fleet attacked fourteen Genoese galleys in the harbour of Castro near Negroponte, capturing ten of them. The Genoese response was to send a fleet of sixty-four galleys to the Aegean in the following year. In order to boost their strength, the Venetians allied themselves with the Greeks of John Kantakouzenos and the Aragonese. Subsequent sea battles were fought in the waters of the Aegean, the Bosphorus, off Modon in the Peloponnese and in the western Mediterranean. A truce was made in 1355, by which time concerted action against the Turks had well and truly taken a back seat.[66]

Trade Licences Granted by Clement VI

Considering the rivalries between the Latins in the Aegean and the detrimental effect this had on the already poor economic situation in the region, it is unsurprising that trade licences, similar to those granted to the Zaccaria in the 1320s, were sought by the Venetians and the other Latins operating in the eastern Mediterranean. These licences represent an important evolution in papal crusading strategy as economic mechanisms began to be employed by the popes in order to facilitate the participation of merchant crusaders in campaigns in the Mediterranean, especially against the Turks. The trade licences fall into three different categories: the first consists of licences which were used strictly *contra Turchos*, i.e. those that permitted trade with Mamluk Egypt in order to subsidize directly expenses incurred in fighting the Turks (as was the case with the Zaccaria licences of the 1320s); the second category is made up by those licences that have an indirect reference to the conflict with the Turks, usually ones in which the recipients cited a connection with the crusade in their supplication in order to improve their chances of success; the third and final category contains 'general' or 'standard' licences which have no connection to the Turks, and consequently will not be discussed here.[67]

There are a total of eight licences granted by Clement VI which fit into the first category (see Appendix 2).[68] One of the first of these – and certainly the most well known – was granted to the Venetians in 1344. The decision to make a petition for this licence was taken by the Senate in December 1343,

---

[66] For more on the Venetian-Genoese war of 1350–5, see Lane, *Venice*, pp. 174–9; Rose, *Medieval Naval Warfare*, pp. 104–7.

[67] The third category of licences is studied in Carr, 'Crossing boundaries', 12–14.

[68] Some of these licences are also discussed by Stantchev, *Spiritual Rationality*, pp. 145–52.

after the closure of the eastern markets had begun to restrict severely the activities of Venetian traders. The Senate supported the idea of re-opening trade with Egypt and decided that two ambassadors should be sent to the curia 'as soon as possible' to implore the pope about this, the argument being that the Venetians were suffering significant economic hardship after the 'loss or obstruction' of the trade routes running to Tana and the Black Sea.[69] Unfortunately the original Venetian petition has been lost, but in the papal response of April 1344, Clement VI recalled the words used by the Venetian ambassadors in their supplication. From this we can reconstruct the tenor of the request and interestingly here the first specific link is made between the Venetians' petition and their participation in the naval league: the pope wrote that the Republic had been incurring 'very great and intolerable labours against the Turks', and that he wished them to continue to 'proceed favourably' in their military activities. Clement ended his letter by granting the *Serenissima* permission to send six galleys and four cargo ships to Mamluk lands for a five-year period, in acknowledgement of their 'sincere zeal and firm purpose [...] for the work of the holy faith and also for the exaltation and increase of God's Church'.[70] Two months later the Senate instructed its ambassadors at the papal curia to pay up to 5,000 florins for this privilege. This was a considerable sum of money, but far less than the total amount the Venetians would be able to recoup from this trade.[71] A year after that, the licence was amended on petition from the Venetians so that seven galleys could be sent for each cargo ship, because of the continued danger from piracy and the relative security of oared vessels.[72] The immediate economic results of the 1344 concession are fairly clear. Only four months after the papal licence had been dispatched from the curia, the Senate agreed to send ambassadors to the Mamluk sultan with orders to

---

[69] ASVen, *Misti del Senato*, reg. 21, fol. 83v (30 Dec. 1343); *Venezia-senato: deliberazioni miste*, vol. 8 (*Registre XXI, 1342–1344*), pp. 341–2, doc. 657. A full translation of the deliberation is given by Lane, 'The Venetian galleys to Alexandria', p. 433.

[70] *DVL*, vol. 1, doc. 144 (27 Apr 1344); summary in Carr, 'Crossing boundaries', doc. 3.

[71] *I libri commemoriali*, vol. 2, pp. 140–1, doc. 134 (30 Jul 1344). It is difficult to calculate the monetary value of the Venetian licence, but it must have been extremely high. To give it some context there is an example of two merchants being granted a licence for one cog, as they were unable to use their old licence to trade in merchandise worth up to 10,000 florins. This suggests that a licence for one cog was equivalent in value to a licence permitting 10,000 florins of trade: ASVat, *RS* 22, fol. 45r; summary in Carr, 'Crossing boundaries', doc. 56. King Peter of Aragon also complained to the pope that his licence for one cog only yielded him 400 florins of profit, suggesting that the licence would usually expected to generate far more money: *RV* 168, fol. 348r–v, ep. 382; *RS* 12, fol. 81r; summaries in Carr, 'Crossing boundaries', docs 14–19. The value of licences is also discussed by Stantchev, *Spiritual Rationality*, pp. 149–50.

[72] The licence was now for thirty-four galleys only: Appendix 4, doc. 6, p. 162; ASVat, *RS* 9, fol. 139v (15 Aug 1345); outgoing papal letter in *Diplomatarium Veneto-Levantinum*, vol. 1, doc. 162; summaries in Clement VI, *Lettres autres que la France*, doc. 756; Carr, 'Crossing boundaries', doc. 12.

obtain a commercial treaty so that galleys could sail directly to Egypt the following year.[73] This facilitated direct trade with Egypt on a grand scale, the level of which had not been seen since the early fourteenth century. For example, in 1346 around nine tons of Egyptian alum were shipped from Crete to Venice by a Siennese trader.[74] At the end of 1347 a merchant wrote from Alexandria to Venice that a cog sailing from Messina with a rich cargo of merchandise was being awaited every day. The author emphasized that the shipment had a licence from the pope.[75] Hereafter, other bulky goods were also shipped to and from Alexandria without the risk of papal sanction.

To return to the rhetoric used by the pope, it is clear that although the Venetian Senate did not originally instruct its ambassadors to make mention of the conflict against the Turks, the supplicants were still able to recognize the value of including such information when they stated their case at the curia.[76] The 1344 licence marks a turning point in papal relations with Venice vis-à-vis trade in Mamluk Egypt and is therefore of great importance. For the first time, the papacy agreed to Venetian appeals to relax trade with Egypt, as long as Venice was a willing participant in its crusading projects. In doing so it also directly mirrored the rhetoric and justification of the Zaccaria licences granted twenty years previously.

As well as the Venetian licence, Clement VI also issued many more concessions to those who were engaged in the crusade against the Turks. Two were issued to the Hospitaller prior of Navarre, Garin of Châteauneuf, in 1344 and again in 1345. He was awarded a permit to send a total of three galleys to Alexandria so that the proceeds could be used to help maintain Hospitaller forces in the Aegean for the 'defence of the faithful in overseas lands who are cruelly molested by the Turks and other infidels'.[77] Considering the greater capacity of cargo ships, this licence was not hugely generous – and nowhere near as valuable as that granted to the Venetians – but it was presumably sufficient to subsidize the upkeep of the Hospitaller

---

[73] *Venezia-senato: deliberazioni miste*, vol. 9 (*Registre XXII, 1344–1345*), pp. 170–7, docs 344–59 (19 and 23 Aug 1344); Lane, 'The Venetian galleys to Alexandria', p. 435; Ashtor, *Levant Trade*, pp. 67–9.

[74] *Lettere di Mercanti a Pignol Zucchello*, pp. 56–8, docs 25–6 (10 Apr and 12 May 1346); Jacoby, 'Production et commerce de l'alun', p. 242; Ashtor, *Levant Trade*, p. 69.

[75] *Lettere di Mercanti a Pignol Zucchello*, pp. 110–12, doc. 58; Ashtor, *Levant Trade*, pp. 69–70.

[76] The link between the licence and the naval league is also discussed by: M. Carr, 'Papal trade licences, Italian merchants and the changing perceptions of the Mamluks and Turkish beyliks in the fourteenth century', in *Diasporic Groups and Identities in the Eastern Mediterranean (1100–1800)*, ed. G. Christ *et al.* (Rome, 2015), pp. 489–97; Ashtor, *Levantine Trade*, pp. 66–7; Lane, *Venice: A Maritime Republic*, p. 131.

[77] ASVat, *RV* 138, fols. 124v–125r, doc. 442 (21 Oct 1344), 268v–269r, doc. 524 (3 May 1345); summaries in Clement VI, *Lettres à la France*, vol. 1, docs 1176, 1677; Carr, 'Crossing boundaries', docs 8, 10.

galleys and the garrison of the recently conquered fortress at Smyrna. The records of the papal camera show that the Hospitallers made a payment of 200 florins for the hire (*locagio*) of one of these galleys; but this must have been a small amount compared with what the Hospitallers hoped to generate from the licence.[78]

A similar licence was issued in 1347 to Barnabò Gerardi, who had been appointed as the papal captain of Smyrna for the following year. He was granted permission to send two cogs to Mamluk lands in order to subsidise the expenditure he would incur when travelling to the East with 'three hundred horsemen and four hundred armed infantry for the whole year'.[79] This licence is unusually detailed in the information it provides and gives an insight into the numbers of crusaders fighting in the papal contingent in the year immediately after the withdrawal of the army of Humbert of Viennois. Gerardi's force was a considerable size and would have cost around 31,680 florins per year to maintain if relatively modest estimates for salary figures are used.[80] Although it is unclear how much of this the licence was intended to cover, it nevertheless suggests that a permit for two cogs would generate a substantial sum of money. Once the crusade was underway, the pope was also willing to issue licences to recompense individuals for past expenditure in fighting the Turks. This was the case in April 1347, when a concession was awarded to Petro of Lucingio, the husband of the illegitimate daughter of the dauphin of Viennois, for permission to send one galley to Mamluk lands 'to relieve some of the expenses he has incurred against the Turks'. This was not as generous as the other examples, but Petro, who accompanied his father-in-law on crusade, had presumably incurred less expense during this campaign.[81]

In the second category are those licences that were not granted strictly *contra Turchos*, but were probably connected to the conflict in the Aegean in some way (see Appendix 3).[82] An example of this can be found in the supplications made by King Hugh IV of Cyprus for permission to trade in Egypt in 1349. Here the petitioners mentioned that their king was maintaining four galleys in the Aegean 'for the defence of the Christian faith against the Turks'. The king was subsequently granted a licence to send two galleys

---

[78] *Die Einnahmen der Apostolischen Kammer unter Klemens VI*, ed. L. Mohler (Paderborn, 1931), p. 357 (6 May 1345).

[79] ASVat, *RS* 13, fol. 167r (4 May 1347); summary in Carr, 'Crossing boundaries', doc. 32.

[80] This is based on salary figures of 2.4 florins a month for each infantryman and 5.6 florins a month for each cavalryman, taken from Housley, 'Costing the crusade', p. 47. For Gerardi's force, this would equate to a total of 2,640 florins per month (960 florins for infantry and 1,680 florins for cavalry).

[81] ASVat, *RS* 13, fol. 145r (23 Apr 1347); summary in Carr, 'Crossing boundaries', doc. 30. Outgoing papal letter in ASVat, *RV* 140, f. 313v, no. 1401 (22 Apr 1347). For more on Petro, see Carr, 'Crossing boundaries', 116.

[82] This link is also made by Stantchev, *Spiritual Rationality*, pp. 147–8.

to Mamluk lands for three years.[83] Unlike the examples discussed above, there is no specific evidence to show that this licence was awarded *because* of the conflict with the Turks, but the fact that the petitioners mentioned the Cypriot contribution to the league, and that this was recorded by the papal scribes, suggests that this factor was important. Similarly, Humbert of Viemois was granted an incredibly generous licence to send twelve galleys and two cargo ships to prohibited lands, possibly because of his prior commitment to the crusade.[84] Other prominent crusaders also made numerous successful petitions for licences, such as Martino Zaccaria and his sons Octavian and Manfred, who received three separate licences permitting trade for one cargo ship, one galley and 25,000 florins worth of merchandise during the period of the Smyrna campaign.[85] In addition to this, the pope granted a licence to one merchant because of the disruption to trade caused by the war against the Turks, and on another occasion he granted a licence to subsidize the war in Granada, but specifically banned trade with the Turks.[86] Finally, a curious supplication was made in 1344, where Peter of Arborea in Sardinia promised to send four galleys to serve against the Turks for six months, as part of a pilgrimage to the Holy Land. This decision was made because the threat from the Turks had prevented him from travelling on one galley as he had originally intended.[87] It may be because of this pious act that three years later Peter was allowed to send one cargo ship to Mamluk lands.[88] In total around 30 per cent of the trade licences issued by Clement VI had some connection to the conflict with the Turks; a figure which confirms the importance of the licensing system to crusades in the Aegean.[89]

Clement VI's policy of granting licences *contra Turchos* should not, however, be seen in isolation. It formed part of a wider policy of facilitating crusading action in the Mediterranean through the temporary alleviation of particular economic difficulties. For example, he continued John XXII's policy of granting licences to facilitate the war against Muslims in

---

[83] ASVat, *RS* 19, fol. 251r (19 Apr 1349); *RS* 20, fol. 147r (1 Sep 1349); summaries in Carr, 'Crossing boundaries', docs 40, 46. Hugh was granted another licence in 1350 for another two galleys for five years: *RS* 21, f. 246r (10 May 1350); summary in Carr, 'Crossing boundaries', doc. 53.

[84] *RS* 21, f. 10r (24 Sep 1349); summary in Carr, 'Crossing boundaries', doc. 48.

[85] ASVat, *RS* 4, fol. 225r (17 Oct 1343), *RS* 20, fols. 44r, 45v (18 Jun 1349), 82r (3 Jul 1349); summaries in Carr, 'Crossing boundaries', docs 1, 43–5.

[86] ASVat, *RS* 9, fol. 122r (4 Aug 1345); *RS* 12, fol. 81r (28 Oct 1346); summaries in Carr, 'Crossing boundaries', docs 11, 19.

[87] ASVat, *RS* 7, fol. 79v (30 Nov 1344).

[88] ASVat, *RV* 140, fol. 300v–301r, doc. 832 (27 Mar 1347); summary in Carr, 'Crossing boundaries', doc. 29.

[89] See Appendices 2 and 3, and the summaries of Clement VI's licences in Carr, 'Crossing boundaries', 120–8.

the western Mediterranean, such as to James II of Majorca who was twice granted licences to help support eight galleys against the enemies of the faith in the Straits of Gibraltar.[90] More importantly, the pope also granted a licence to the Genoese in Caffa in order to help finance their war against the Mongols.[91] This was a particularly generous concession of two round ships and five galleys, valid for the duration of the war. This licence cannot be linked to the crusade against the Turks *per se*, but it suggests that the officials at the papal curia had an intimate knowledge of the dire economic situation in the Aegean and the wider Mediterranean at that time and were concerned about the consequences of this for the Latins in the East.

Further evidence of this attitude is given by two licences which – rather surprisingly – permitted trade in *Turchia*. The first of these was issued in 1345 to an Anconitan merchant resident in Constantinople, who was allowed to import 1,000 *modii* of victuals and other things specifically 'from the lands of the Turks [...] for the aid and need of Christians'.[92] The second more generous exemption was granted two years later to one Greek and two Genoese merchants resident in Constantinople, Pera and Genoa, to import 20,000 *modii* of grain 'from any region and beyond any region of Turkey to Constantinople and the lands of the faithful'. In this case the petitioners stressed that the licence would be used to aid the faithful affected by the 'grave famine' in the region.[93] These examples demonstrate the seriousness of the economic difficulties affecting the Aegean region at the time and show that the pope was willing to grant trade privileges to alleviate famine, even if it meant permitting temporary trade with the Turks on two occasions.

Trade Licences and Papal Finances

If the above licences mostly concern the recompensing of individuals who participated in the naval leagues, then it is also worth discussing the impact of the licensing system on papal finances. The Crusade of Smyrna, and to a lesser extent the 1333–4 naval league, were expensive undertakings which were beset by financial difficulties. Marino Sanudo estimated that the price of vessels, crews and supplies for his proposed flotilla of ten galleys to blockade Mamluk lands would cost 102,000 florins per annum. This figure of 850 florins per galley per month is a useful comparison with the leagues:

---

[90] ASVat, *RV* 168, fol. 348r–v, doc. 382 (8 Feb 1346); *RS* 12, fol. 81r (28 Oct 1346). James was later granted two other licences, but which make no mention of the defence of the faith: *RS* 13, fol. 189r (13 May 1347); *RV* 180, fol. 278r, doc. 867 (17 Mar 1348); summaries in Carr, 'Crossing boundaries', docs 14, 19, 33, 35, and also Trenchs-Odena, '"De Alexandrinis"', 270–1, but with some inaccurate resumes and references.

[91] ASVat, *RS* 11, fol. 117r (4 Aug 1346); summary in Carr, 'Crossing boundaries', doc. 18.

[92] ASVat, *RS* 9, fol. 168r (3 Sep 1345); summary in Carr, 'Crossing boundaries', doc. 13.

[93] ASVat, *RS* 13, fol. 50v (30 Jan 1347); summary in Carr, 'Crossing boundaries', doc. 21.

John XXII paid the slightly lesser sum of 600 florins a month for the maintenance of his four papal galleys in 1334, but these were initially expected
to generate additional funds to cover provisions through the shipment of
goods on their outward journey.[94] The cost of these galleys for the initial
five-month period of service was therefore an affordable, but not inconsid-
erable, sum of 12,000 florins. Clement VI paid the higher amount of 800
florins a month per galley in 1343, as well as a stipend of 150 florins for
the galley captains.[95] The second league was active for a far greater length
of time and Housley has calculated that the pope spent between 112,846
and 144,346 florins on his galleys from 1344 to 1347.[96] This was already a
considerable amount, but it did not include the costs of supplies and the
hire of extra soldiers which were incurred when the nature of the expedition
changed from a flotilla to an army for defending land, as was the case when
the harbour fortress of Smyrna was taken.

Funding the papal contribution to the crusade was therefore a difficult
undertaking and it appears that licences were used to try and complement
more traditional fundraising mechanisms such as clerical taxation and the
sale of indulgences. Evidence for this can be found in a licence granted to
Mathieu Gayta of Clermont-Ferrand in November 1343, before the second
naval league had assembled in the Aegean. Unlike the examples discussed
above, Mathieu did not participate in the crusade against the Turks, but
instead petitioned for a licence to send one cargo ship to trade in Mamluk
Egypt to help fund a pilgrimage to the Holy Sepulchre. This was granted
by the pope, but on condition that one-quarter of the proceeds be paid for
the subsidy against the Turks levied in that same year.[97]

Considering the problems in financing the crusade it is of little surprise
that the payment of wages became a significant issue.[98] Initially the funds
were to be handed to the *patroni* of the galleys and the papal captain
Martino Zaccaria, who would distribute the wages amongst their crews.

---

[94] See *Documents on the Later Crusades*, p. 73, doc. 20.

[95] Marino Sanudo, 'Liber Secretorum', pp. 30–1; Lock trans., pp. 60–2; Housley, 'Costing
the crusade', p. 47.

[96] Housley, *Avignon Papacy*, pp. 301–2; Housley, 'Costing the crusade', p. 48.

[97] ASVat, *RS* 5, fol. 49r (16 Nov 1343); summary in Carr, 'Crossing boundaries', doc. 2.
Outgoing papal letter in: ASVat, *RV* 137, fol. 145r, no. 502–3; summaries in Clement VI,
Lettres à la France, vol. 1, docs 528–9. Interestingly, in September 1344 a merchant named
Johannes Fererius acting as the agent of Mathieu Gayta, was loading goods onto a vessel
in Beirut, captained by a Genoese, Franciscus Ultramarinus. In the documents tracing the
journey of Ultramarinus, it is repeatedly stated that he was travelling with a papal licence
for his vessel (*absoluti cum dicta chocha per dominum sacrum papam*), which may have been a
reference to the licence granted to Gayta the previous year: *Gênes et l'outre-mer: Actes notaries
de Famagouste et d'autres localités du Proche-Orient (XIVe–XVe s.)*, ed. M. Balard, L. Balletto
and C. Schabel (Nicosia, 2013), section I.II, p. 34 and docs 2, 3, 5, 6, 7, 8, 11, 12, 13, 15.

[98] See Housley, *Avignon Papacy*, pp. 195–8.

However, soon after Martino's death it emerged that these funds had not been distributed properly.[99] Centurione Zaccaria, one of the captains of the galleys and the son of Martino, appealed successfully to the pope for the payment of 1,200 florins which he claimed was due to his father.[100] But four years later it emerged that Conrad Piccamiglio, the captain of one of the other papal galleys, along with his brother Manuel, were still awaiting the payment of 2,700 florins for their services, which equates to eighteen months' wages. On this occasion the pope used a trade licence to address the problem, granting the Piccamiglio brothers permission to send four galleys to Mamluk lands over a five-year period. This was presumably deemed sufficient to compensate them for their outstanding wages, although it was less than the licence the brothers had originally requested (for merchandise worth up to 25,000 florins).[101]

To add to this, there is the example discussed earlier of the papal captain of Smyrna, Bernabò Gerardi, who was granted a licence to help pay for the army he was to hold in the city for one year, the salaries for which would have amounted to over 30,000 florins. How much of this amount was covered by the licence is impossible to say, but it presumably subsidized payments which would otherwise have been taken from the papal coffers.[102] The licences granted to the Hospitallers can also be linked to the wages of crusaders. By 1345 the Knights were acting as papal creditors for the league by subsidizing wages until papal funds had been shipped to the Aegean.[103] In fact, in 1344–6, Garin of Châteauneuf, the prior of Navarre and procurator-general of the Hospitallers at the papal curia, received several payments from the papal treasury for the wages of the crews. As was seen earlier, in 1344 and again in 1345 he was awarded licences to send three galleys to Alexandria for the 'defence of the faithful in overseas lands'.[104] Were these licences designed to mitigate some of the wages owed by the pope? Unfortunately papal records of the licences do not provide that level of information, but it is tempting to connect them to papal expenditure on the crusade, and even if the licences were not used in lieu of papal payments, then the awarding of them would have at least sweetened the deal for the Hospitallers, who had been forced to subsidize papal payments at this time.

There is also evidence to suggest that trade licences were sold in order to generate income for the papacy. Calculating the amount with any degree

[99]   Clement VI, *Lettres à la France*, vol. 1, doc. 1713, vol. 2, docs 1834, 2281. This is discussed in detail by Housley, *Avignon Papacy*, pp. 196–7; Setton, *Papacy and the Levant*, vol. 1, pp. 202–3.

[100]   Setton, *Papacy and the Levant*, vol. 1, p. 203.

[101]   ASVat, *RS* 22, fol. 98r (11 Jul 1350); summary in Carr, 'Crossing boundaries', doc. 59.

[102]   See above, note 80.

[103]   See Housley, *Avignon Papacy*, pp. 196–7.

[104]   See above, note 77.

of accuracy is, however, extremely difficult. Stefan Stantchev has illustrated the problems by highlighting the vast differences in the amounts received for licences over a period of time: in 1361, for example, a licence for six galleys was sold to the Venetians for 9,000 florins, meaning that each galley was worth 1,500 florins, whilst sixteen years earlier, in the time of Clement VI, the Hospitallers paid only 200 florins to the pope for one galley. These discrepancies mean that very different amounts of revenue can be calculated: using the price of a cog at 900 florins, and the highest price for a galley (1,500 florins), Stantchev has calculated that Clement VI could have received just over 200,000 florins in total during his ten-year pontificate, or 20,000 florins per year. That is an impressive 11 per cent of his annual revenue of 187,000 florins; but compare this with the lower calculation for galleys (200 florins) and the total revenue is 68,100 florins, or 6,810 florins per year, so only 3.6 per cent of annual revenue.[105]

To further complicate things, Stantchev has not used the data from the payment for another licence made during Clement VI's pontificate: the 5,000 florins paid by Venice for four cogs and six galleys in 1344. This licence was amended in 1345, when each cog was exchanged for seven galleys, turning it into a licence for thirty-four galleys. From this we can calculate the relative price of each vessel type: each cog was valued at 1,029 florins and each galley at 147 florins, making a cog the same value of seven galleys and the total of both licences 5,000 florins. If this is then multiplied by a rough estimate of the known vessels for which Clement issued licences,[106] then the total revenue for his pontificate comes to 65,562 florins, or 6,556 florins per year. That is just under 3.5 per cent of Clement VI's annual revenue; a very similar number to Stantchev's lowest estimate, albeit using very different data.

However, one should question whether the amount paid by the Venetians can be considered as representative of licences more generally. The Venetians were, after all, a special case who were paying for an exceptionally large privilege which was also issued in connection to their crusading commitments overseas. The evidence for other payments for licences is also far from reliable in this manner. Take, for example, the Hospitaller licence for two galleys used by Stantchev in his calculations. The only record of payment for this licence is found in the papal camera, where it is stated that the Hospitallers paid 200 florins to the pope for the hire of one galley

[105] Stantchev's calculations are based on 900 florins per cog, multiplied by the licences issued for fifty-three cogs and 102 galleys: Stantchev, *Spiritual Rationality*, pp. 152–3. Clement's annual revenue is calculated by W.E. Lunt, *Papal Revenues in the Middle Ages* (New York, 1934), p. 14.

[106] This is fifty-two cogs and eighty-two galleys before the amendment of the Venetian licence and forty-eight cogs and 110 galleys after. My numbers are slightly different to those given by Stantchev and are based on the licences analysed in: Carr, 'Crossing boundaries', 120–8.

(*pro locagio unius galee*).[107] Was this then the payment for the whole licence, or was another payment made at a later date? It is tempting to argue that the Hospitallers paid a further 200 florins at another time, but there is no evidence in the papal accounts to suggest that this was the case. Therefore this record should not be considered as a payment for a licence in its own right.[108]

The unreliability of the data demonstrates the pitfalls of attempting to calculate the precise amounts that licence sales generated. However, having said that, it is probable that Clement VI's income was at the lower end of the scale and possibly even lower than the more conservative estimates given above. This is on account of the fact that presumably some licences were not sold for cash at all: in particular those granted *contra Turchos*, and those which were designed to mitigate expenditure on the crusade. In these instances it would have been counter-productive if the recipients were compelled to pay large sums of money in exchange for their privileges. It should also be remembered that Clement granted licences to papal favourites as well as to help facilitate pious deeds. Presumably these too would have been offered either free, or at a discounted rate. That is not to say that payments were not made for licences – the Venetians are proof that they were – but it seems logical that the costs would have been minimal compared with the benefits they would bring to the recipient. But still, if it is accepted that licences unconnected to crusading generated more revenue, then it is plausible that the money from licences could have covered a reasonable portion of the papal crusading budget if it was intended for that purpose.

If the practice of issuing licences *contra Turchos* was begun by John XXII in the 1320s, then it reached its apogee during the pontificate of Clement VI. In fact, his ten-year reign marks the high point of licensing for the entire Avignon period, where at least forty-eight cogs and 110 galleys were permitted to trade in Mamluk lands (including the galleys detailed in the amendment made to the Venetian licence in 1345).[109] In terms of vessels, this number is almost four times that for entire the period between 1291 and 1342, and around half of the total from 1352 to 1378.[110] On the one hand, this can be

---

[107] *Die Einnahmen der Apostolischen Kammer unter Klemens VI*, p. 357.

[108] Evidence also exists of lay rulers selling licences to their subjects, such as in 1344 when King Peter IV of Aragon received a payment from Pedro de Mediavilla and Arnaldo Llorens of 6,000 Barcelonan *solidos* for a licence to send one cog to Mamluk lands: L. de Meneses, 'Florilegio documental del Reinado de Pedro IV de Aragón', *Cuadernos de historia de España* 13 (1950), 181–90, at 188–90, doc. 11 (1 Jun 1344); Carr, 'Crossing boundaries', doc. 5; Ashtor, *Levant Trade*, p. 69.

[109] See Carr, 'Crossing boundaries', 120–8, and Stantchev, *Spiritual Rationality*, p. 153, who gives the slightly different number of fifty-three cogs and 102 galleys.

[110] These figures are taken from Stantchev, *Spiritual Rationality*, p. 152, who points out that the *Registra Supplicationum* – the main source for licences – is not extant for all of this period. On the licences issued after 1352, see Stantchev, *Spiritual Rationality*, pp. 150–1.

seen as an example of the greater shift of merchant influence over crusade policy in the fourteenth century – as the licences were more often than not granted on petition from those operating in the East. But on the other hand, they can be viewed as the emergence of a pragmatic papal economic policy which was ideally suited to the situation in the Aegean, where crusading against the Turks often coincided with a breakdown of trade in the eastern Mediterranean.[111] In fact, the licences should be regarded as the product of the attempts of both merchants and the papacy to reconcile the otherwise opposing notions of crusade and economic embargo with trade in Muslim lands. In this sense the licences were an evolutionary step away from crusade theory at the turn of the fourteenth century – which placed so much importance on the blockade of Egypt – to one which focussed instead on the defence of Christian territories from the Turks and the relaxing of trade with the Mamluks.[112]

[111] Cf. the comments of Stantchev who argues that the embargo was above all a pastoral tactic rather than an object of foreign policy: Stantchev, 'The medieval origins of embargo', 398–9.

[112] In some senses this was a step closer to the views of Emmanuele Piloti, who, seventy years later, argued that the embargo could not be enforced because Levant trade was too important to Christians, see: Christ, *Trading Conflicts*, pp. 116–18.

Conclusion

> Even if the Greeks deserve to pay for their stubborn persistence in rebellious sinfulness, the Turks are nevertheless crossing over from there towards us and true Catholicism. Already Cyprus, Crete, Rhodes, Euboea, and, closer to us, Achaia and Epiros, are being attacked.
>
> Francesco Petrarch, letter to Pope Urban V, 29 June 1366 x 1368.[1]

The words of Francesco Petrarch, echoing those of Marino Sanudo some thirty years earlier, aptly sum up the shift in the perceptions of the Turks and in the focus of crusading which came about during the first half of the fourteenth century. This was a time in which the religious and political makeup of the eastern Mediterranean was fundamentally altered. By the end of the period, the Turks and not the Byzantines were the undisputed masters of Asia Minor and were considered the greatest threat to Latin Christendom in the region. After this point the Ottomans were able to secure a foothold in Europe and overcome any Latin and Greek attempts to halt their advance. They expanded their empire at breakneck speed – only checked by Timur in 1402 – before conquering Constantinople itself in 1453. The Ottoman sieges of Vienna in the sixteenth and seventeenth centuries were the ultimate manifestation of Turkish military might born on the plains of Anatolia in the early years of the fourteenth century.

The merchant crusaders of the Aegean played a fundamental role in helping shape the image of the Turks in western Europe, which would prevail into the early modern period. The reports of several significant naval victories against the beyliks, most notably the defeat of Masud the Menteshe-oglu by the Hospitallers in 1312 and the joint victory of the Hospitallers and Zaccaria over a fleet from Aydin in 1319, combined with the reports of Turkish raids on Venetian territories, began the first step in this shift in the perception of the beyliks in the West.[2] This was from one of general ambivalence to one where crusading could be considered as a feasible means

---

[1]   Francesco Petrarch, *Letters of Old Age*, vol. 1, p. 255 (VII.1).

[2]   Finke, *Papsttum und Untergang des Templerordens*, vol. 2, pp. 298–302, doc. 146; *Chroniques d'Amadi et de Strambaldi*, vol. 1, p. 391; Mas Latrie, *Histoire de l'île de Chypre*, vol. 2, pp. 118–25; Gatto, 'Martino Zaccaria', 337–9, doc. 1; Delaville le Roulx, *Les Hospitaliers à Rhodes*, pp. 365–7, doc. 2.

with which to oppose them, reflected by the reports of these victories in the writings of the crusade theorists, as well as by authors from the Italian peninsula.[3] The western perception of the Byzantines, on the other hand, gradually changed to one of reconciliation as it became apparent that a united Christian front would be the best means of holding back the Turks.

As the century progressed and the Turks became the target of crusading, their depiction took on another form which was also very much influenced by the mercantile context in which western authors operated. These were predominantly Italian and had close connections to the merchant classes and consequently to eastern trade and the operations of the Genoese and Venetians overseas. Against the backdrop of the Crusade of Smyrna and the economic difficulties affecting the Mediterranean world in the 1340s, Umur Pasha, in particular, emerged as a significant figure in the writings of the Anonimo Romano and the apocryphal *Epistola Morbasiani*, as well as featuring in the works of Giovanni Villani and Giovanni Boccaccio.[4] However, by now the menace of the Turks was well known in the West, and *Morbasanus* was instead used as a mouthpiece by which these authors could criticize the policies of the Venetians overseas, as well as the factional strife which both hindered the Crusade of Smyrna and also caused turmoil within Italy. This mechanism became widespread in the fifteenth century and beyond as western writers continued to use Turkish rulers as a mouthpiece for voicing criticisms within Christendom.

Merchant crusaders also played a fundamental role in attempting to halt the Turkish advances. In the early years this took the form of mutual naval assistance from the eastern Aegean powers on Chios and Rhodes who utilized their shared intelligence networks to keep the nearby beyliks in check. Gradually this concept was blended with the idea of a united Christian fleet, at times including the Byzantines, initially envisaged as a means to enforce the economic embargo on trade with Muslims. Marino Sanudo first proposed this idea and by 1333–4 it had become a reality in the form of a naval league. The leagues, although limited in scope to temporarily halting Turkish raids in the Aegean, both enjoyed remarkable success. They were great feats of logistics and cooperation, consisting of large numbers of well-equipped galleys, commanded by skilled captains and crews from five separate Christian powers. At their peak they probably numbered up to 15,000 men for each league. In terms of their military success, both of the leagues went undefeated during the time in which they patrolled the Aegean

[3] Giovanni Villani, *Nuova cronica*, vol. 2, bk. 10, ch. 120, p. 323; *Chroniques d'Amadi et de Strambaldi*, vol. 1, p. 400; William of Adam, *How To Defeat the Saracens*, pp. 53–5, 65–7, 81; Marino Sanudo, 'Epistolae', pp. 297–8 (letter 5); Roddy trans., pp. 156–60 (letter 15); 'Directorium ad Passagium Faciendum', pp. 457–8.

[4] Anonimo Romano, *Cronica*, pp. 84–5; Giovanni Villani, *Nuova cronica*, vol. 3, bk. 13, ch. 39, pp. 388–91; Giovanni Boccaccio, *The Decameron*, pp. 124–5 (II.7).

and each managed to inflict significant damage on the maritime beyliks. They were able to achieve this through a combination of detailed local geographical knowledge and effective communication. This often resulted in a surprise attack followed by the successful pursuit of the Turks onto land.

But what level of support did these leagues enjoy from the papacy, and can we really consider them as crusades? Until the 1330s papal crusading initiatives planned for the Aegean were dictated more by the priorities of the Capetians, Angevins and Valois than by those of the local powers in the eastern Mediterranean. In the first two decades of the century Popes Benedict XI and Clement V partially justified their crusade plans on the basis that an expedition to recover Constantinople would help drive the Turks from western Anatolia, but the rhetoric they contained undoubtedly suggested that the primary 'target' of the crusade was still the schismatic Greeks.[5] The planned crusades of Charles of Valois and Philip of Taranto are prime examples of this. In the 1320s, at a time when crusade strategy was beginning to shift slowly away from the Greeks and towards the Turks, John XXII still harboured hopes of launching a general passage to the Holy Land with the kings of France. As negotiations with the French became increasingly hindered by financial constraints and the escalating conflicts with England, an Aegean campaign led first and foremost by the resident Latin states became a more likely alternative to the grand projects of the French Crown. However, John XXII did not see eye-to-eye with the Venetians in the run-up to the first naval league; he was wary of their conciliatory attitude towards the Catalans and the Byzantines, both of whom were considered as a threat to papal-Angevin interests in Greece. He also considered the union of the Greek and Latin Churches as being an important component of any crusade against the Turks which included Greek participation. Nevertheless, the skilful linking by the Venetians of the naval league to the Holy Land crusade of Philip IV was enough to garner papal support. The eventual contribution of the papacy towards the league was an important development in crusade strategy. It was the first campaign in which the pope had actively committed papal resources (four galleys), and consequently marked an acceptance that a primarily maritime expedition, organized by the Aegean powers, was the most effective method of defending the region.

Despite John XXII's eventual commitment to the first naval league, its status alongside other crusading projects of the time suggests that it was conceived as a lesser campaign, especially if the privileges granted are compared with those issued to participants in other operations. John XXII was the first to grant mechanisms in support of an Aegean campaign against the Turks. He decreed indulgences *in articulo mortis* to the Latins in Achaia

---

[5]   *Le registre de Benoit XI*, doc. 1006; Clement V, *Regestum*, vol. 1, doc. 243.

in 1322 and to Martino Zaccaria in 1323 and 1325.[6] He awarded the same *in articulo mortis* indulgences to John of Cepoy and his contingent for the league in 1334, which were still less generous than those granted for the Holy Land crusade being planned by Philip VI at the same time.[7] Preaching was also not decreed for the league and although papal funds were used to pay for the galleys, clerical tithes were not levied. These privileges were significantly less than those decreed for the Crusade of Smyrna, which can rightly be seen as the first expedition against the Turks to receive all of the mechanisms traditionally allocated to a crusade to the Holy Land. It was the high point of crusading against the Turks in this period – both in terms of papal support and the achievement of the mission. Housley was correct to suggest that the pope's role in the Crusade of Smyrna had been decisive: he secured Venetian participation in the league in early 1343 and published crusade bulls for the expedition in that summer.[8] These bulls announced a level of papal support greater than any previously received for a crusade solely aimed at the Turks: preaching of the crusade was ordered, clerical tithes were used to fund it and the full crusade indulgence was issued for participation on the campaign alone, or to those who could make financial contributions. That the Crusade of Smyrna was allocated such a high level of involvement by the Church was both a reflection on Clement's commitment to the crusade and of the change of perception of the Turks, who were now regarded as representing the most serious threat to Christendom. This was mirrored in the enthusiastic response to the expedition which came from those, especially from northern Italy, who had no commercial interests in the Aegean.

Papal support for a campaign against the Turks and the eventual formation of a fleet to be used in the Aegean did, however, pose its own problems. Secure commerce in the Aegean was of paramount importance to the Latin states of the region, both in order to sustain their maritime empires, as was the case with Genoa and Venice, but also to provision the Aegean islands and hinterland. Because of this, promoting and participating in military action against the beyliks created a vicious circle of sorts: both of the naval leagues, for example, were designed to bring security and stability to the Latins of Romania, but they also had the adverse effect of limiting trade with Asia Minor. This cut off a potential source of trade, which consequently threatened the livelihood of some participants and also restricted

---

[6]   ASVat, *RA* 18, fol. 152v, ep. 209; *RV* 74, fol. 93v, ep. 209 (20 Dec 1322); summary in JXXII *Lettres communes*, vol. 4, doc. 16672; Gatto, 'Martino Zaccaria', 344–5, doc. 5 (20 Feb 1323); ASVat, *RA* 22, fol. 450v; *RV* 78, ep. 882 (28 Apr 1325); summaries in John XXII, *Lettres communes*, vol. 4, doc. 16977, vol. 5, doc. 22117.

[7]   ASVat, *RA* 46, fol. 560v; *RV* 107, fol. 243r, ep. 729–30 (19 May 1334); summaries in John XXII, *Lettres communes*, vol. 13, docs 63170–1.

[8]   Housley, *Avignon Papacy*, pp. 121–2.

the provisions needed to supply both the combatants and the Aegean colonies. A solution to this conundrum was found in the widespread issuing of trade licences, which harmonized the contrasting ideals of cross-cultural exchange and holy war, and adequately served the purposes of both the papacy and the merchant crusaders.

The first example of this is given by the Zaccaria, whose rulership over the rich island of Chios and dominance of the alum trade bought them much wealth. However, without the resources of a maritime empire – as the Venetians enjoyed – they required papal support in order to maintain a hostile policy against the Turks. In their petitions for trade licences made at Avignon (in 1320 and 1325), they specifically linked the maintenance of secure trade with the protection of the Christians in the Aegean.[9] Thus for both the Zaccaria and the papacy, trade and crusade had begun to be perceived and projected as two complementary facets in the defence of the faith. In the following years Martino Zaccaria, probably aided by the close support of the papacy, managed to form a small empire in Romania. He enjoyed the acclaim of the crusade theorists and intermarried with the nobility of Frankish Greece. However, by furthering his own personal interests, Martino antagonized his overlord Emperor Andronikos III and his own brother Benedetto II, eventually losing Chios to the Byzantines in 1329.[10] Martino reappeared as the papal captain during the Crusade of Smyrna, but his participation was viewed with suspicion by the pope. He died outside the city walls along with the other crusade leaders in 1345. The involvement of other Genoese in the Crusade of Smyrna was similarly undistinguished: Simone Vignoso's capture of Chios caused problems for Humbert of Viennois and Genoese conflicts with Venice in the early 1350s eventually ended any hope of re-forming the naval league. Although the crusade had reached a stalemate by this point, it is clear that the rivalries between the two great maritime republics still remained a potentially devastating obstacle to any crusade.

Like John XXII, Clement VI also recognised the concerns and interests of the maritime republics in the crusade. He was aware of the difficult economic situation in the Aegean after the closing of the Black Sea markets and the problems this caused for trade in the eastern Mediterranean. He granted the Venetians and others extensive licenses to trade with Egypt in order to facilitate continued participation in the naval league. These licences reveal the complex attitude of the papacy in regard to trade with the infidel. They show that limited trade with certain Muslim groups was acceptable, so long as it was conducted with papal permission and ideally in order to aid the defence of the faith in other regions. Given this, it can also

[9] Delaville le Roulx, *Les Hospitaliers à Rhodes*, pp. 367–8, doc. 3 (5 Mar 1320); summary in John XXII *Lettres communes*, vol. 3, doc. 11081.
[10] Carr, 'Trade or crusade?', pp. 127–34.

be said that the licences and the merchant crusaders who petitioned for and received them helped to break down black and white conceptions of Islam which usually characterized papal policy towards Islam in the Middle Ages and the attitudes of crusaders. In fact, it could even be argued that through the widespread use of licences, the Crusade of Smyrna actually led to greater exchange between European merchants and Egypt, even if it aimed to restrict contact with the Turks.[11] In many senses the licences prove that holy war and trade between different religious groups were not mutually exclusive.[12]

Bearing these things in mind, it may be necessary for a reappraisal to be made of the role of the maritime republics in the crusades. It is hoped that this study has shown that the motivations of the papacy, the Genoese and the Venetians towards the crusade were multi-faceted and inseparable. In the fourteenth-century Aegean, as the maritime states became the primary participants in a crusade against the Turks, motivating factors of religion and commerce became blended together. The Zaccaria and the Venetians were no doubt fighting for the preservation of their trade routes, but they were also fighting for the defence of the faith. This was understood by the papacy and the merchants alike. As has been explained in another context, the idea of "religious ideology" positing consistent fanaticism and zealotry, such as Gibbon's myth of the possessed Muslim riding out of the desert offering the cowering infidel the Quran or the sword, seldom reflects the complexity of human religious and material motivations.[13] It must be remembered that religion can play a variety of roles in situations which involve confrontation, as can commerce, and that motives can rarely be separated. In the second half of the century, as the Turks increased their expansion into the Aegean and the Ottomans emerged as the dominant power in the eastern Mediterranean, the maritime republics would begin to play an even greater role in the defence of the faith. The strategies and attitudes developed in the first half of the fourteenth century would henceforth come to dominate western contact with the Turks in the following years.

[11] Lane, 'The Venetian galleys to Alexandria', pp. 435–6.
[12] See similar observations by Chrissis, 'New frontiers', p. 19.
[13] See for example, the comments of B. Braude, 'Review of *Nomads and Ottomans in Medieval Anatolia* by Rudi Paul Lindner', *Speculum* 62 (1987), 701–3, at 702.

Appendix 1

Indulgences for Crusades in the Aegean

Date	Addressee	Recipient, purpose and target of indulgence	Conditions of indulgence
20 Jun 1304 (reissued 14 Jan 1306)[1]	All of the faithful of Christ	'to those who go to recover the said empire [of Constantinople]' against the schismatic Greeks	Plenary indulgence 'as for the Holy Land'
11 Aug 1308[2]	All the clergy of Europe and the Levant	'to those who go with the said passage in aid of the same [Holy] Land' against the Saracens (this became the Hospitaller *passagium*)	Plenary indulgence For one year's service
7 May 1312[3]	Philip of Taranto	'to the 2,000 cavalry and 4,000 infantry [who will accompany Philip of Taranto] across the sea to the lands of Romania in support of the Holy Land against the [Greek] schismatics'	Plenary indulgence 'as for the Holy Land' Valid for three years
29 Nov 1322[4]	All of the faithful of Christ in the principality of Achaia	'to those in the principality of Achaia and the surrounding lands [who will fight] against the schismatic Greeks, Bulgars, Alans and Turks and other diverse nations of Infidels'	Plenary indulgence For death on campaign or thereafter from wounds received Valid for three years

[1] Benedict XI, *Le registre de Benoit XI*, BEFAR, ed. C. Grandjean (Paris, 1903), doc. 1006–7; reissue: Clement V, *Regestum*, vol. 1, docs. 246–7.

[2] Clement V, *Regestum*, vol. 3, docs. 2988–90.

[3] Clement V, *Regestum*, vol. 7, doc. 7893.

[4] ASVat, *RA* 18, fol. 152v; *RV* 74, fol. 93v, ep. 209; Appendix 4, doc. 2.

20 Dec 1322[5]	The archbishops of Reims, Toulouse and Paris	'to those who go in aid and succour of the kingdoms of Armenia and Cyprus against the Sultan and other infidels [i.e. the Tartars and Karaman Turks (*Haramanus Turcomanorum*)]'	Plenary indulgence 'as for the Holy Land' For one year's service
20 Feb 1323 (renewed 28 April 1325)[6]	Martino Zaccaria	'to all those faithful to Christ from the island of Crete to the state of Caffa [who go] against the Turks and infidels' on Chios and the lands nearby	Full forgiveness of sins (*omnium veniam peccatorum*) For death on campaign or thereafter from wounds received Valid for three years
14 Mar 1326[7]	Philip VI of France	'to those who go in aid of the Christians and for the expulsion of the Saracens [from Granada]'	Plenary indulgence 'as for the Holy Land'
14 Jun 1330[8]	Walter of Brienne	'to those who go to Romania with the said Duke [of Athens] against the schismatic [Catalan] invaders and occupiers of the same Duchy [of Athens]'	Plenary indulgence 'as for the Holy Land' For one year's service

[5] John XXII, *Lettres secrètes*, vol. 2, docs. 1571–3.
[6] Gatto, 'Martino Zaccaria', 344–5; reissue: *RA* 22, fol. 450v; *RV* 78, doc. 882; Appendix 4, doc. 3.
[7] John XXII, *Lettres secrètes*, vol. 3, doc. 2739.
[8] *DOC*, doc. 150.

5 Dec 1331[9] (reissued 26 Jul 1333)[10]	Philip VI of France, various prelates in the kingdom of France and the archbishops of Genoa and Riga	'to those who go in aid of the Holy Land'	Plenary indulgence
19 May 1334[11]	John of Cepoy	To John of Cepoy and those who will accompany him 'for the defence and protection of the Christians of the said lands [of Romania]' against the Turks	Plenary indulgence *in mortis articulo* For death on campaign or thereafter from wounds received
19 April 1335[12]	Hugh Quiéret	To Hugh Quiéret and those who will accompany him 'for the defence and protection of the Christians of the said lands [of Romania]' against the Turks	As above
1 May 1336[13]	All the faithful on the islands of Sicily, Cyprus, Rhodes, Negroponte and further east	'to those who go in aid of the Armenians against the aforesaid enemies of the faith [i.e. the Saracens]'	Plenary indulgence For one year's service

---

9   *AE*, vol. 24, pp. 478–80 (ch. 30); John XXII, *Lettres communes*, vol. 13, doc. 58207.
10   John XXII, *Lettres secrètes*, vol. 4, docs 5210, 5226–7.
11   ASVat, *RA* 46, fol. 560v; *RV* 107, fol. 243r, ep. 729–30; Appendix 4, doc. 4.
12   ASVat, *RA* 48, fols. 194r–v; *RV* 119, fol. 132v–3r, ep. 343–7.
13   Benedict XII, *Lettres à la France*, doc. 175.

30 Sep 1343[14]	The kingdoms of Italy, Germany, Central and Eastern Europe and Romania	'to those of the faithful who proceed with the flotilla, or in another fashion, in support of the Christians of the regions of Romania against the unbelievers [i.e. the Turks]'	Plenary indulgence 'as for the Holy Land' For one year's service
18 Dec 1345[15]	The citizens and people of Genoa	'to those who go in aid and defence of the said city [of Caffa] against the infidels [i.e. the Tartars and Saracens]'	Plenary indulgence 'as for the Holy Land' For one year's service

[14] *Documents on the Later Crusades*, pp. 78–80, doc. 22.
[15] Clement VI, *Lettres autres que la France*, doc. 847.

Appendix 2

Trade Licences Granted *contra Turchos*

Date	Recipient	Conditions [all licences permit trade with Mamluk lands in non-prohibited merchandise]
5 March 1320[1]	Martino and Benedetto II Zaccaria	Licence to ship mastic Valid for two years Proceeds to be used to maintain army against the Turks
25 Jun 1322[2]	Martino Zaccaria	Renewal of above Valid for four years
29 Jan 1325[3]	Martino Zaccaria	Renewal of above Valid for three years
16 Nov 1343[4]	Mathieu Gayta of Clermont-Ferrand	Licence to send one cog to the Holy Land One quarter of proceeds to be used for subsidy against the Turks
27 Apr 1344[5]	Venice	Licence for four cogs and six galleys Valid for five years Proceeds to facilitate crusade against the Turks
21 Oct 1344[6]	Garin of Châteauneuf, Hospitaller Prior of Navarre	Licence for one galley Proceeds to be used to maintain forces against the Turks
3 May 1345[7]	Garin of Châteauneuf, Hospitaller Prior of Navarre	Licence for two galleys Proceeds to be used to maintain forces against the Turks

[1] Delaville le Roulx, *Les Hospitaliers à Rhodes*, pp. 367–8; Appendix 4, doc. 1.
[2] ASVat, *RA* 17, fols. 242–242v; *RV* 73, ep. 1071.
[3] ASVat, *RA* 23, fol. 143; *RV* 79, ep. 1449.
[4] ASVat, *RS* 5, fol. 49r.
[5] *DVL*, vol. 1, doc. 144.
[6] ASVat, *RV* 138, fols. 124v–125r, ep. 442.
[7] ASVat, *RV* 138, fols. 268v–269r, ep. 524.

15 Aug 1345[8]	Venice	Amendment of licence issued on 27 April 1344, each cog exchanged for seven galleys (= licence for thirty-four galleys)
23 Apr 1347[9]	Petro de Lucingio	Licence for one galley To relieve expenses incurred in fighting the Turks
4 May 1347[10]	Barnabò Gerardi, papal captain of Smyrna	Licence for two cogs To relieve expenses that will be incurred in maintaining 300 cavalry and 400 infantry for a year against the Turks
11 Jul 1350[11]	Manuel and Conrad Piccamiglio	Licence for four galleys Valid for five years To compensate for late payment of wages for fighting against the Turks

[8] ASVat, *RS* 9, fol. 139v; Appendix 4, doc. 6.
[9] ASVat, *RS* 13, fol. 145r.
[10] ASVat, *RS* 13, fol. 167r.
[11] ASVat, *RS* 22, fol. 98r.

Appendix 3

Trade Licences Related to Crusades against the Turks

Date	Recipient	Conditions and possible links to crusades against the Turks [all licences permit trade with Mamluk lands in non-prohibited merchandise]
17 Oct 1343[1]	Martino Zaccaria	Licence for one cargo ship Recipient had been appointed as captain of the papal galleys against the Turks in the previous month
4 Aug 1345[2]	Guy de Chauliac	Licence valid for merchandise up to 3,000 gold florins Valid for three years Licence granted because of disruption to trade caused by war with the Turks
28 Oct 1346[3]	James II of Majorca	Licence for one cog Trade with the Turks specifically forbidden
27 Mar 1347[4]	Peter of Arborea	Licence for one cog Recipient had sent galleys against the Turks in 1344
18 Jun 1349[5]	Octavian and Manfred Zaccaria	Licence for one galley Recipients were prominent figures in the crusade against the Turks
3 Jul 1349[6]	Octavian Zaccaria	Licence valid for merchandise up to 25,000 gold florins Valid for three years Recipient was a representative during peace negotiations with the Turks in 1347–9

[1] ASVat, *RS* 4, fol. 225r.
[2] ASVat, *RS* 9, fol. 122r; outgoing papal letter in: *RV* 139, fol. 66v, ep. 211; Clement VI, *Lettres à la France*, vol. 2, doc. 1863.
[3] ASVat, *RS* 12, fol. 81r.
[4] ASVat, *RV* 140, fol. 300v–301r, ep. 832.
[5] ASVat, *RS* 20, fol. 44r.
[6] ASVat, *RS* 20, fols. 45v, 82r.

1 Sep 1349[7]	Hugh IV of Cyprus	Licence for two galleys Valid for three years Petitioners cite his contribution to the naval league against the Turks
24 Sep 1349[8]	Humbert of Viennois	Licence for ten galleys and two cogs Replacement of a lost licence Recipient was captain-general of the crusade against the Turks in 1345–7
10 May 1350[9]	Hugh IV of Cyprus	Licence for two galleys Valid for five years Recipient was a contributor of galleys to the league against the Turks
2 May 1352[10]	William de Montague, marshal of the Hospitallers	Licence for two galleys Recipient was responsible for payment of wages to the captains of the papal galleys in 1345–6

---

[7]   ASVat, *RS* 19, fol. 251r; *RS* 20, fol. 147r.
[8]   ASVat, *RS* 21, fol. 10r.
[9]   ASVat, *RS* 21, fol. 246r.
[10]   ASVat, *RS* 23, fol. 266v.

Appendix 4
Documents

I.

Pope John XXII authorizes Benedetto II and Martino Zaccaria to export mastic from Chios to Alexandria and Egypt.
5 March 1320.
Vatican, Archivio Segreto, *Registra Avenionensia*, reg. 13, fol. 717r; *Registra Vaticana*, reg. 70, fol. 589v, ep. 1529; also printed in Delaville le Roulx, *Les Hospitaliers à Rhodes*, pp. 367–8, doc. 3; summary in John XXII, *Lettres communes*, vol. 3, doc. 11081.[1]

Dilectis filiis Benedicto et Martino de Zachariis, fratribus, civibus Januensibus. Habet quamplurimum religiosorum et aliorum fidelium fidedigna relatio quod vos, zelo fidei et pie devotionis accensi, in insula Chii cunctis fidelibus, per partes illas habentibus transitum, magne humanitatis solatia exhibetis, dirigentes ipsos et eos ab incursibus hostium fidei defendentes; ex quibus, preter premium retributionis eterne, apud Sedem Apostolicam et fideles laudabilis fame preconio vos plurimum commendabiles exhibetis. Cum itaque, sicut accepimus, propter defensionem insule supradicte, ad cuius occupationem Turchi, eiusdem insule vicini, fidei catholice ferventer aspirant, armatam militiam contra Turchos eosdem jugiter oporteat vos tenere, ac proventus eiusdum insule, de quibus huiusmodi militiam sustinetis, de mastice, que in dicta insula nascitur, provenire noscantur, dictaque mastix ad presens, ut hactenus consuevit, propter instantem Januensium guerram a christianis mercatoribus non ematur, ac propterea vos, sufficientes redditus non habentes, necessitate urgente cogamini remittere stipendiarios de insula memorata, sicque dicta insula, necessaria et oportuna fidelium militia destituta, timeatur ad manus dictorum hostium devenire, ex eo maxime quod dicti Turchi, per vos pluries temporibus proximis debellati, ad occupationem eiusdem insule amaro et concitato animo sunt amplius solito provocati, et eiusdem insule occupatione, quod Deus avertat, cunctis fidelibus, in aliis insulis convicinis morantibus, magna destructionis pericula imminerent, dictaque mastix quasi pro majori parte non nisi a Sarracenis

---

[1] Documents 1 and 3 have been copied verbatim from the published transcriptions. For the other documents, transcriptions largely follow the manuscripts with a few amendments for clarity, such as the capitalization of sentences and proper nouns, and the addition of punctuation marks.

portatur, vos huiusmodi non solum vestra sed aliorum fidelium utilitate et necessitate diligenter attentis, vestris supplicationibus inclinati, vobis, de fratrum nostrorum consilio, quod usque ad biennium predictam masticem dumtaxat, cum nostro (*sic*)[2] navigio tamen deferre in personis propriis vel per alios vestros familiares seu servitores mittere ad partes Alexandrie et Egipti, nulla illuc alia mercimonia deferendo, vel etiam transmittendo, dictamque masticem vendere et precium vel merces alias inde recipere et reportare possitis, nec propter ea excommunicationis sententias et penas alias, per Lateranense concilium et constitutiones quascunque seu processus a prede-cessoribus nostris Romanis pontificibus et a nobis editas, factas, habitas et quomodolibet promulgatas adversus euntes vel mittentes seu cum Sarra-cenis contrahentes aut mercimonia seu res quascunque deferentes ad dictas partes Alexandrie et Egipti, vos et illos, quos ad id mittetis, contingat incur-rere quoquo modo, constitutionibus et processibus supradictis nequaquam obstantibus, auctoritate presentium, de speciali gratia, liberam concedimus facultatem.

Datum Avinione, iii nonas Marcii, anno quarto.

2.

Pope John XXII issues indulgences for three years to those fighting against the Greeks, Bulgars, Alans, Turks and other infidels in the principality of Achaia.
29 November 1322.
Vatican, Archivio Segreto, *Registra Avenionensia*, reg. 18, fol. 152v; *Registra Vaticana*, reg. 74, fol. 93v, ep. 209; summary in John XXII, *Lettres communes*, vol. 4, doc. 16672.

Universalis Christiani fidelibus per principatu Achaye constitutis.
Inter alia que salutem fidelium operant ad illa libenter dirigimus mentem nostram per que fides catholica roboretur et gentes que Deum ignorant et in sua confidunt potencia consternantur. Cum itaque sicut ex parte vestra fuit nobis expositum vos et Ecclesiae Romanie fideles [et] aliarum partium adja-cencium Romanie a scismaticis Grecis, Bulgaris, Alanis et Turchis aliisque permixtis infidelium nationibus, impugnatores, depopulatores, captivitatores, servitores, et carceretores et alias diversorum generum penas et cruciatus multiplices patiamini, quibus nec obviare potestis nec resistere per vos ipsos. Nos huiusmodi vestris tantis calamitatibus, miseriis et pressuris, affectu paterno compatientes ab intimis, libenter vobis illo quo possumus spirituali subsidio quod cuilibet temporali prevalet misericorditer subvenimus. Ut

---

[2] Presumably this is meant to refer to a Zaccaria, and not a papal vessel, as is stated in the renewal of the licence issued to Martino Zaccaria in 1322 (*tuos navigio*): ASVat, RA 17, fols. 242–242v; RV 73, ep. 1071.

igitur vos aliique Christi fideles ad defensionem catholice fidei contra scismaticos, et infideles eosdem, eo amplius animemini, quo temporale in hoc
vitam sperabitis in perpetuam commutare, nos de omnipotentis Dei misericordia et beatorum Petri et Pauli apostolorum eius auctoritate confisi, vobis
omnibus, ceterisque Christi fidelibus, quos pro defensione catholice fidei in
bello, seu pugna in principatu Achaye, aliisque fidelium terris et partibus
eidem principatu adjacentibus supradictis, aut vicinis eisdem habitis, contra
scismaticos Grecos, Bulgaros, Alanos et Turchos aliasque permixtas nationes
infidelium supradictas, aut ex vulneribus in eisdem bello, vel pugna receptis
postmodum mori contigerit vestrorum omnium de quibus vere contriti
fuistis et confessi, plenam concedimus veniam peccatorum. Presentibus post
triennium minime valituris.
Datum Avinione, iii kalendas Decembris, anno septimo.

3.

*Pope John XXII grants Martino Zaccaria and his followers plenary
indulgences if they die in battle, or thereafter of wounds received
in war against the Turks.*
20 February 1323.
Vatican, Archivio Segreto, *Registra Avenionensia*, reg. 18, fol. 380r-v;
Registra Vaticana, reg. 74, fol. 168r-v; also printed in Gatto, 'Martino
Zaccaria', 344-5, doc. 5; summary in John XXII, *Lettres communes*,
vol. 4, doc. 16977.

Dilecto filio nobili viro Martino Zacharie civi Januensi, salutem.
Quanto catholice fidei ardentius cupimus incrementum tanto acrius pertur-
bamur in intimis et duriores sentimus in animo punctiones cum illud per
emulorum insolentium crucis Christi Sathane filiorum audaciam pertur-
batur, ideoque libenter officii nostri partes apponimus, efficax impendimus
studium et favoris oportuni suffragium impartimur, ut tam nefando quam
horrendo iniquo eorum represso conamine vigor eiusdem fidei habundan-
tius invalescat. Exhibita siquidem nobis tua petitio continebat quod tu et
insula de Chio cui prees, positi estis in medio Turchorum et aliarum infidelium nationum a quibus hostiles insultus et impugnationes multiplices pati
sepius vos contingit, in quibus dextera Domini tecum faciente virtutem,
cui propterea humiles gratiarum actiones exolvimus, successus quamplures
prosperos habuisti. Cum itaque nonnumquam aliquos ex Christi fidelibus
et stipendiariis quos expensis propriis ad eorumdem Turchorum et infidelium audaciam conatusque nepharios reprimendos retines, in congressibus
et preliis cum eisdem Turchis et infidelibus vulnerari et mori contingat,
nobis humiliter supplicasti ut providere super hoc tam tibi quam eis misericorditer dignaremur. Nos itaque tuam et ipsorum salutem ingenti desiderio

affectantes et ut tu ac omnes huiusmodi stipendiarii dicte catholice fidei
professores ac omnes Christi fideles qui ab insula Cretense usque ad civi-
tatem Capha inclusive inveniri potuerunt quique zelo devotionis accensi te
iuvare voluerunt huiusmodi negotium prosequentem, de felici retributione
securi contra Turchos et infideles eosdem eo amplius animemini quo temporale in hoc vitam sperabitis in perpetuam commutare, de omnipotentis Dei
misericordia et beatorum Petri et Pauli apostolorum eius auctoritate confisi,
tibi et stipendiariis ac fidelibus memoratis quos pro defensione fidei sepe
dicte in bello seu pugna in Chio aliisque insulis seu terris eidem insule
Chio adiacentibus aut vicinis habitis contra Turchos et alias nationes infidelium supradictas aut ex vulneribus in eisdem bello seu pugna receptis
postmodum mori contigerit, vestrorum omnium de quibus corde contriti et
ore confessi fueritis concedimus veniam peccatorum. Ceterum volumus et
presentium auctoritate decernimus quod omnes et singuli qui cum eisdem
Turchis et infidelibus te, aut cum ipsis in dictis Chio vel aliis insulis seu terris
eidem insule Chio adiacentibus aut vicinis stipendiarios et fideles eosdem
vel cum eisdem eandem insulam Chio invadere hostiliter aut impugnare
presumpserint, si cum ipsis Turchis et infidelibus colligationem, societatem
aut confederationem ad huiusmodi hostilem invasionem et impugna-
tionem contra te dictosque stipendiarios et fideles, ut predicitur, fecerint
sive scienter eis dederint in hoc auxilium, consilium vel favorem, ipso facto
sententiam excomunicationis incurrant, non obstante si aliquibus ab eadem
Sede indultum existat, quod interdici, suspendi, vel excommunicari non
possint per litteras apostolicas non facientes plenam et expressa ac de verbo
ad verbum de indulto huiusmodi mentionem, presentibus post triennium
minime valituris.

Datum Avinione, x kalendas Marcii, anno septimo.

4.

Pope John XXII grants John of Cepoy plenary indulgences in articulo mortis.[3]
19 May 1334.
Vatican, Archivio Segreto, *Registra Avenionensia*, reg. 46, fol. 560v;
Registra Vaticana, reg. 107, fol. 243r, ep. 729; summary in
John XXII, *Lettres communes*, vol. 13, doc. 63170.

Dilecto filio nobili viro Johanni domino de Cepeyo militi Belvacensis diocesis
salutem, etc.
Provenit ex tue devotionis affectu quo nos et Romanam Ecclesiam rever-
eris, ut petitiones tuas illas presertim que anime tue salutem respiciunt, ad

---

[3] This is the standard form of a grant of indulgence *in articulo mortis*. It was repeated to
Hugh of Quiéret in 1335: ASVat *RV*, 119, fol. 133, ep. 348.

exauditionis gratiam admittamus. Nos itaque tuis supplicationibus inclinati, ut confessor tuus quem duxeris eligendum, omnium peccatorum tuorum de quibus corde contritus, et ore confessus fueris, semel tantum in mortis articulo, eam plenam remissionem quam Romani pontifices consueverunt interdum per speciale privilegium personis aliquibus impertiri, tibi in sinceritate fidei, et devotione sancte matris ecclesie persistenti, quatinus claves ecclesie se extendunt, et gratum in occulis divine majestatis extiterit, auctoritate apostolica concedere valeat, devotioni tue tenore presentium indulgemus, sic tamen quod idem confessor de hiis de quibus fuerit alteri satisfactio impendenda, eam tibi per te si supervixeris, vel per heredes tuos si tunc forte transieris faciendi iniungat, quam tu vel illi facere teneamini ut prefertur. Et ne, quod absit, propter huiusmodi gratiam reddaris proclivior ad illicita imposterum commitenda, volumus quod si ex confidentia remissionis huiusmodi aliqua forte committeres, quo ad illa predicta remissio tibi nullatenus suffragentur. Nulli ergo etc. Nostre concessionis et voluntatis infringere etc.

Datum Avinione, xiiii kalendas Junii, anno xviii.

5.

Pope Clement VI makes Martino Zaccaria captain of the papal galleys for the naval league against the Turks.
16 September 1343.
Vatican, Archivio Segreto, *Registra Vaticana*, reg. 137, fols 102v-103r, ep. 323; summary in Clement VI, *Lettres à la France*, vol. 1, doc. 404.

Dilecto filio nobili viro Martino Zacharie militi Januensi.
Commotis paterne pietatis visceribus erga fideles, in Romanie, et aliis partibus et insulis adjacentibus commorantes, quos diris afflictionibus et persecutionibus Turchorum infidelium molestari et lacerari non sine mentis amaritudine audivimus et audimus pro ipsorum defensione ac tuitione fidelium et repressione infidelium eorundem, certum galerarum armatarum et munitiarum subsidium ordinavimus in eisdem partibus, per nos, et quosdam fideles alios usque ad certi temporis spacium exhibendum. Cum autem pro eodem subsidio quatuor galeas armatas et munitas decenter, nostris et ecclesie Romane sumptibus et expensis tenendas illuc per unum annum continuum, faciamus transmitti. Nos cupientes galeas ipsas una cum aliis que per fideles alios ut premittitur destinantur sic prudenter et utiliter gubernari, quod ad dei laudem et gloriam, fidei exaltationem catholice, ac predictorum consolationem fidelium, fructus exinde proveniant uberes et votum, ac de tue fidelitatis et pericie probate in talibus industria plenius in domino confidentes, te predictarum quatuor galearum generalem capitaneum usque ad nostrum beneplacitum constituimus tenore presencium

ac eciam deputamus faciendi gerendi et exercendi omnia et singula que spectant ad officium capitaneatus huiusmodi potestatem tibi plenariam concedentes. Volumus cum quod venerabili fratri nostro Henrico, Patriarche Constantinopolitano, apostolice sedis legato eiusque mandatis et beneplacitis, super hiis pareas et intendas. Quocirca nobilitati tue per apostolica scripta mandamus quatenus super predictis sic te gerere studeas fideliter et prudenter, quod exinde preter mercedis perenius premium nostrum et apostolice sedis gratiam uberius merearis.

Datum apud Villamnovam Avinionensis diocesis, xvi kalendas Octobris, anno secundo.

6.

Amendment to a trade licence granted to the Doge and Commune of Venice, allowing them to exchange seven galleys for every one navis.

15 August, 1345.

Vatican, Archivio Segreto, *Registra Supplicationum*, reg. 9, f. 139v.

Significant s. v. devoti filii vestri .. Dux & Commune Veneciarum quod s. v. in restaurationem et alienationem dampnorum que in partibus exinde passi fuerint volens de solita benignitate sua eisdem gratiam facere spiritualem navigandi in Alexandriam et ad partes quaslibus Soldano Babilonie subjectas cum sex galeis et quatuor navibus et cum mercibus tum non expresse prohibis licentiam concedere dignata fuit, voluit tam s. v. quod ipsi dux et commune possent uti gratiam huiusmodi usque ad quinquennium a tempore dati litterarum ipsius gratie conputandum. Verum cum predictis duci et communi periculosum existat ad dictas partes cum navibus navigare, tum propter piratharum discrimina, tum etiam ob multa alia pericula evidentia que navibus potius quam galeis accidere possunt. Ideo supplicant s. v. prefati dux et commune quatenus eisdem quibus precluse sunt vie quelibus navigandi specialem gratiam faciens predictas quatuor naves eis ut premittitur sic concessas in galeis convertere et mutare, reservato tamen numero galearum in arbitrio s. v. cum unaquaque navis communiter portet pondus et caritum decem vel octo galearum. Et cum omnibus non obstantibus et clausulis oportunis. Commutetur quelibet navis in septem galeis, sed non vadatur illuc simul ultra sex. R.

Datum Avinione, xviii kalendas Septembris, anno quarto.

Appendix 5

List of Rulers

Menteshe[1]

Karmanos, founder of Menteshe?, d. c.1313
Masud, emir of Menteshe, c.1311–c.1319
Orkhan, c.1319–c.1337
Ibrahim, c.1337–c.1355

Aydin

Mehmed, founder of Aydin, c.1313–1334
Hizir, lord of Ephesos and emir of Aydin, 1334–c.1360
Umur Pasha, younger brother of Hizir, lord of Smyrna, d.1348
Ibrahim, younger brother of Hizir, lord of Bodemya (Potamia) from 1330s
Suleymanshah, younger brother of Hizir, ruler of Tire from 1330s
Isa, younger brother of Hizir, not allocated land because of young age

Ottomans

Osman, founder of Ottomans, d. c.1324
Orkhan, emir of Ottomans, c.1324–1360

Karasi

Timurkhan, d. after 1329?
Yakhshi, c.1334–?
Ottoman annexation, 1346

Chios

Under Byzantine control until c.1305
Manuel and Benedetto I Zaccaria, c.1305–1307
Manuel and Palaeologo Zaccaria, 1307–1309/10
Palaeologo and Benedetto II Zaccaria, 1309/10–1314
Benedetto II and Martino Zaccaria, 1314–1320/22
Martino Zaccaria, 1320/22–1329
Under Byzantine control, 1329–1346
Under control of the Genoese Mahona of the Giustiniani, 1346–1566

---

[1] A great deal of ambiguity surrounds the rulers of the Turkish beyliks and I have only included the most relevant here. For more information, see Zachariadou, *Trade and Crusade*, pp. 106–16; Bosworth, *The New Islamic Dynasties*, pp. 213–42. For the Latins in Romania, see Lock, *Franks in the Aegean*, pp. 330–7.

Rhodes
Under Byzantine control until c.1306–10
Fulk of Villaret, Master of the Hospitallers, 1305–1317
Gerard of Pins (temporary papal *vicarius*), 1317–1319
Hélion of Villeneuve, Master of the Hospitallers, 1319–1346
Dieudonné of Gozon, Master of the Hospitallers, 1346–1353

Dukes of the Archipelago / Naxos
Marco II Sanudo, 1262–1303
Guglielmo I Sanudo, 1303–1323
Niccolò I Sanudo, 1323–1341
Giovanni I Sanudo, 1341–1362

Princes of Achaia
Charles I of Naples, 1278–1285
Charles II of Naples, 1285–1289
Isabelle of Villehardouin, 1289–1307
Florent of Hainault, 1289–1297
Phillip of Savoy, 1301–1306
Phillip of Taranto, 1307–1313
Matilda of Hainault, 1313–1318
Louis of Burgundy, 1313–1316
John of Gravina, 1318–1332
Catherine of Valois, 1332–1346
Robert of Taranto, 1346–1364

Dukes of Athens
William I de la Roche, 1280–1287
Guy II de la Roche, 1287–1308
Walter I of Brienne, 1308–1311
Walter II of Brienne, 1311–1356 (titular)

Catalan rulers of Athens
Roger Deslaur, vicar-general, 1311–1312
Berenguer Estañol, 1312–1316
Alfonso Fadrique, 1317–1330
Nicholas Lancia, vicar-general, c.1331–c.1335
Odo de Novelles, marshal, 1331?–1354?
James Fadrique, 1356–1359

Emperors of Byzantium
Michael VIII Palaiologos, 1259–1282
Andronikos II Palaiologos, 1282–1328
Andronikos III Palaiologos, 1328–1341

John V Palaiologos, 1341–1391
John VI Kantakouzenos, 1347–1354

Titular Latin Emperors of Constantinople
Philip of Courtenay, 1273–1301
Catherine of Courtenay, 1301–1308 (married to Charles of Valois, 1301–1308)
Catherine of Valois, 1308–1346 (married to Philip of Taranto, 1313–1331)
Robert of Taranto, 1346–1364

Popes
Nicholas IV, 1288–1292
Celestine V, 1294
Boniface VIII, 1294–1303
Benedict XI, 1303–1304
Clement V, 1305–1314
John XXII, 1316–1334
Benedict XII, 1334–1342
Clement VI, 1342–1352

Doges of Venice
Giovanni Dandolo, 1280–1289
Pietro Gradenigo, 1289–1311
Marino Zorzi, 1311–1312
Giovanni Soranzo, 1312–1328
Francesco Dandolo, 1328–1339
Bartolommeo Gradenigo, 1339–1342
Andrea Dandolo, 1342–1354

Kings of France
Philip III, 1270–1285
Philip IV, 1285–1314
Louis X, 1314–1316
John I, 1316
Philip V 1316–1322
Charles IV, 1322–1328
Philip VI of Valois, 1328–1350
John II, 1350–1364

Bibliography

Manuscript Sources

Genoa, Archivio di Stato di Genoa
    Notai Antichi, Not. Andreolus de Laneris
Munich, Bayerische Staatsbibliothek
    Ital. 90; Cgm 216; Cgm 317; Cgm 4692; Clm 9503 [Ob. Alt. 3]
Paris, Archives nationales
    J509, docs 16, 16bis
Vatican City, Archivio Segreto Vaticano (ASVat)
    Registra Avenionensia (*RA*), reg. 17, 18, 22, 23, 44, 46, 48, 54
    Registra Supplicationum (*RS*), reg. 4, 5, 7, 9, 18, 11, 12, 13, 19, 20, 21, 22, 23
    Registra Vaticana (*RV*), reg. 62, 73, 74, 78, 79, 98, 104, 107, 115, 116, 119, 137, 138, 140, 157, 168, 169, 180
Vatican City, Biblioteca Apostolica Vaticana
    Vat. lat. 2915
Venice, Archivio di Stato di Venezia (ASVen)
    Deliberazioni Misti del Senato, reg. 15, 16, 17, 21
Weimar, Herzogin Anna Amalia Bibliothek
    Q 108; Q 109/9

Printed Primary Sources

Acta Pontificum Suecica, ed. L.M. Baath, 2 vols (Stockholm, 1936–57).
Amalric Auger, 'Actus Romanorum Pontificum (Sexta Vita)', in *Vita Paparum Avenionensium*, ed. S. Baluze and G. Mollat, 4 vols (Paris, 1914), vol. 1, pp. 89–106.
Annales Ecclesiastici, ed. C. Baronio, O. Raynaldi and J. Laderchi, 37 vols (Paris, 1608–1883).
Anonimo Romano, *Cronica*, ed. G. Porta, 2nd edition (Milan, 1981).
Athanasios I, *The Correspondence of Athanasius I Patriarch of Constantinople: Letters to the Emperor Andronicus II, Members of the Imperial Family and Officials*, ed. and trans. A.-M.M. Talbot (Washington, 1975).
Benoît XII (1334–1342): Lettres closes et patentes intéressant les pays autres que la France, ed. G. Mollat and J.-M. Vidal, BEFAR (Paris, 1913–50).
Benoît XII (1334–1342): Lettres closes, patents et curiales se rapportant à la France, ed. G. Daumet, BEFAR (Paris, 1920).
Bernard Gui, 'E Floribus Chronicorum (Quarta Vita)', in *Vita Paparum Avenionensium*, ed. S. Baluze and G. Mollat, 4 vols (Paris, 1914), vol. 1, pp. 59–80.
Calendar of Entries in the Papal Registers Relating to Great Britain and Ireland: Petitions to the Pope (1342–1419), ed. W.H. Bliss *et al.*, 20 vols (Dublin, 1896–, in progress).

Cartulaire général des hospitaliers de S. Jean de Jérusalem, 1100–1310, ed. J. Delaville le Roulx, 4 vols (Paris, 1894–1905).

Chroniques d'Amadi et de Strambaldi, ed. R. de Mas Latrie, 2 vols (Paris, 1891–3).

Cronaca del Templare di Tiro: 1243–1314, ed. L. Minervini (Naples, 2000).

'Cronica di Bologna', in *RIS* 18 (Milan, 1731), cols. 242–792.

Délibérations des assemblées Vénitiennes concernant la Romanie: 1160–1463, ed. F. Thiriet, 2 vols (Paris, 1966–71).

Die Einnahmen der Apostolischen Kammer unter Klemens VI, ed. L. Mohler (Paderborn, 1931).

'Die Protokollbücher der päpstlichen Kammerkleriker: 1329–1347', ed. H. Schröder, *Archiv für Kulturgeschichte* 27 (1937), 121–286.

'Directorium ad Passagium Faciendum', in *Recueil des historiens des croisades: documents arméniens*, 2 vols (Paris, 1869–1906).

Diplomatari de l'Orient català, 1301–1409: colleció de documents per a la història de l'expedició catalana a Orient i dels ducats d'Atenes i Neopàtria, ed. A. Rubió i Lluch (Barcelona, 1947).

Diplomatarium Veneto-Levantinum: sive Acta et Diplomata res Venetas Graecas atque Levantis Illustrantia a. 1300–1454, ed. G.M. Thomas, 2 vols (Venice, 1880–99).

Documents on the Later Crusades, 1274–1580, ed. and trans. N. Housley (London, 1996).

Duca di Candia: Bandi (1313–1329), ed. P. Ratti Vidulich (Venice, 1965).

Duca di Candia: Quaternus consiliorum (1340–1350), ed. P. Ratti-Vidulich (Venice, 1976).

Enveri, *Le destān d'Umūr Pacha (Düstūrnāme-i Enverī)*, trans. I. Mélikoff-Sayar (Paris, 1954).

Francesco Balducci Pegolotti, *La Pratica Della Mercatura*, ed. A. Evans (New York, 1936).

Francesco Petrarch, *Letters of Old Age: Rerum Senilium Libri I–XVIII*, ed. and trans. A.S. Bernardo et al., 2 vols (Baltimore, 1992).

George Pachymeres, *Relations historiques*, ed. A. Failler, trans. V. Laurent, 5 vols (Paris, 1984–1999).

Gênes et l'outre-mer: Actes notaries de Famagouste et d'autres localités du Proche-Orient (XIVe–XVe s.), ed. M. Balard, L. Balletto and C. Schabel (Nicosia, 2013).

Gesta Francorum et Aliorum Hierosolimitanorum, ed. and trans. R. Hill (London, 1962).

Giorgio Stella, *Annales Genuenses*, ed. G. Petti Balbi, *RISNS* 17.2 (Bologna, 1975).

Giovanni Boccaccio, *The Decameron*, trans. G. Waldman, ed. J. Usher (Oxford, 1993).

Giovanni Villani, *Nuova cronica*, ed. G. Porta, 3 vols (Parma, 1990–1).

Guglielmo Cortusi, *Chronica de novitatibus Padue et Lombardie*, ed. B. Pagnin, *RISNS* 12.5 (Bologna, 1941–9).

'Historia Gulielmi et Albrigeti Cortusiorum de novitatibus Paduae, et Lombardiae', *RIS* 12 (Milan, 1728), cols. 767–954.

I libri commemoriali della Republica di Venezia regesti, ed. R. Predelli, 4 vols (Venice, 1876–83).

Ibn Battuta, *The Travels*, trans. H.A.R. Gibb et al., 5 vols (Cambridge, 1958–2000).

John Kantakouzenos, *Ioannis Cantacuzeni eximperatoris Historiarum libri IV*, ed. L. Schopen and B.G. Niebuhr, 3 vols (Bonn, 1828–32).

John of Winterthur, *Chronica*, ed. C. Brun, *MGHSS*, n.s. 3 (Berlin, 1955).

Le deliberazioni (Senato): Serie 'mixtorum', ed. R. Cessi and P. Sambin, 2 vols (Venice, 1960).

Le registre de Benoît XI, ed. C. Grandjean, Bibliothèque des Écoles françaises d'Athènes et de Rome (Paris, 1903).

Les registres du Benoît XII, lettres communes, ed. J.M. Vidal, *BEFAR*, 3 vols (Paris, 1903–11).

Les relations commerciales entre Gênes, la Belgique et l'Outremont d'après les archives notariales génoises aux XIII et XIV siècles, ed. R. Doehaerd, 3 vols (Brussels, 1941).

Les relations commerciales entre Gênes, la Belgique et l'Outremont: d'après les archives notariales génoises (1320–1400), ed. L. Liagre-de Sturler, 2 vols (Brussels, 1969).

Lettere di Mercanti a Pignol Zucchello (1336–1350), ed. R. Morozzo della Rocca (Venice, 1957).

Lettres communes de Jean XXII (1316–1334): analyses d'après les registres dits d'Avignon et du Vatican, ed. G. Mollat, BEFAR, 16 vols (Paris, 1904–47).

Lettres secrètes et curiales du pape Jean XXII (1316–1334), relatives à la France, ed. A. Coulon and S. Clémencet, BEFAR, 4 vols (Paris, 1900–72).

Lettres closes, patentes et curiales du pape Clément VI se rapportant à la France, ed. E. Depréz et al., BEFAR, 3 vols (Paris, 1901–61).

Lettres closes, patentes et curiales du pape Clément VI intéressant les pays autres que la France, ed. E. Depréz and G. Mollat, BEFAR (Paris, 1960–1).

Ludolph of Sudheim, 'De itinere Terre Sancte', ed. G.A. Neumann, in *Archives de l'Orient Latin*, 2 vols (Paris, 1881–4), vol. 2, part 2, pp. 305–77.

English translation in: *Description of the Holy Land, and of the Way Thither*, trans. A. Stewart (London, 1895).

Ludovico Bonconte Monaldesco, 'Fragmenta Annalium Romanorum', *RIS* 12 (Milan, 1728), cols. 527–42.

Marco Battagli of Rimini, *Marcha (1212–1354)*, ed. A.F. Massèra, *RISNS* 16.3 (Città di Castello, 1913).

Matthew, Archbishop of Ephesus, *Die Briefe des Matthaios von Ephesos im Codex Vindobonensis Theol. Gr. 174*, ed. D. Reinsch (Berlin, 1974).

Marino Sanudo Torsello, *Istoria di Romania*, ed. and Greek trans. E. Papadopoulou (Athens, 2000).

—— 'Liber Secretorum Fidelium Crucis', in *Gesta Dei per Francos*, ed. J. Bongars, 2 vols (Hannover, 1611; repr. Jerusalem, 1972), vol. 2, pp. 1–287.

English translation in: *Book of the Secrets of the Faithful of the Cross*, trans. P. Lock (Farnham, 2011).

—— 'Letters', printed in:
Gesta Dei per Francos, ed. J. Bongars, 2 vols (Hannover, 1611; repr. Jerusalem, 1972), vol. 2, pp. 289–316.

Kunstmann, F., 'Studien über Marino Sanudo Torsello den Aelteren', *Abhandlungen der Historischen Classe der Königlich Bayerischen Akademie der Wissenschaften* 7 (Munich, 1855), 695–819.

Roncière, C.B. de la and L. Dorez, 'Lettres inédites et mémoires de Marino Sanudo l'ancien (1334–1337)', *Bibliothèque de l'École des chartes* 56 (1895) 21–44.

A. Cerlini, 'Nuovo lettere di Marino Sanudo il vecchio', *La bibliofilia* 42 (1940), 321–59.

English translations in: S. Roddy, 'The Correspondence of Marino Sanudo Torsello' (unpublished doctoral thesis, University of Pennsylvania, 1971).

Medieval Trade in the Mediterranean World: Illustrative Documents, ed. and trans. R. Lopez and I.W. Raymond (New York, 1967).

Necrologio di S. Maria Novella: testo integrale dall'inizio (MCCXXXV) al MDIV, ed. S. Orlandi, 2 vols (Florence, 1955).

Nicholas IV, *Les registres de Nicolas IV: Recueil des bulles de ce pape*, ed. M.E. Langlois, 2 vols (Paris, 1905).

Nikephoros Gregoras, *Byzantina Historia*, ed. L. Schopen and I. Bekker, 3 vols (Bonn, 1829–55).

Odo of Deuil, *De Profectione Ludovici VII in Orientem*, ed. and trans. V.G. Berry (New York, 1948).

Philippe de Mézières, *Le songe du Vieil Pelerin*, ed. G.W. Coopland, 2 vols (Cambridge, 1969).

Philippe de Mézières, *Une epistre lamentable et consolatoire, adressée en 1397 à Philippe le Hardi, duc de Bourgogne, sur la défaite de Nicopolis, 1396*, ed. P. Contamine and J. Paviot (Paris, 2008).

Pietro Pizolo, notaio in Candia, ed. S. Carbone, 2 vols (Venice, 1978–85).

Projets de croisade (v. 1290 – v. 1330), ed. J. Paviot (Paris, 2008).

Ramon Muntaner, *The Catalan Expedition to the East: from the Chronicle of Ramon Muntaner*, trans. R. Hughes (Barcelona, 2006).

Régestes des délibérations du sénat de Venise concernant la Romanie: 1329–1463, ed. F. Thiriet, 3 vols (Paris, 1958–61).

Regestum Clementis Papae V, editum cura et studio monachorum Ordinis S. Benedicti, 10 vols (Rome, 1885–92).

Riccold of Monte Croce, *Pérégrination en Terre Sainte et au Proche Orient: Lettres sur la chute de Saint-Jean d'Acre*, ed. R. Kappler (Paris, 1997).

Shams al-Din Ahmad-e Aflaki, *The Feats of the Knowers of God (Manaqeb al-'arefin)*, trans. J. O'Kane (Leiden, 2002).

Simon of Saint-Quentin, *Histoire des Tartares*, ed. J. Richard (Paris, 1965).

Sources for Turkish History in the Hospitallers' Rhodian Archive: 1389–1422, ed. A.T. Luttrell and E.A. Zachariadou (Athens, 2008).

Storie pistoresi (1300–1348), ed. S.A. Barbi, *RISNS* 11.5 (Città di Castello, 1927).

The Crusades: Idea and Reality, 1095–1274, ed. and trans. L. Riley-Smith and J.S.C. Riley-Smith (London, 1981).

The Records of the Venetian Senate on Disk, 1335–1400, ed. B. Kohl (New York, 2001).

'Thespismata tês Benetikês gerousias: 1281–1385', *Istorika krêtika eggrafa ekdidomena ek tou arheiou tês Benetias*, ed. S.M. Theotokes, 2 vols (Athens, 1933–7).

Venezia-senato: deliberazioni miste, ed. F.-X. Leduc *et al.*, 20 vols (Venice, 2004–, ongoing).

William of Adam, *How To Defeat the Saracens*, ed. and trans. G. Constable (Washington, 2012).

William of Boldensele, 'Des Edelherrn Wilhelm von Boldensele Reise nach dem gelobten Lande', in *Die Edelherren von Boldensele oder Boldensen*, K.L. Grotefend (Hannover, 1855), pp. 18–78.

William of Nangis and Continuator, *Chronique latine de Guillaume de Nangis de 1113 à 1300, avec les continuations de cette chronique de 1300 à 1368*, ed. H. Géraud, 2 vols (Paris, 1843).

William of Tyre, *Chronicon*, ed. R.B.C. Huygens, 2 vols (Turnhout, 1986).

Secondary Works

Abulafia, D., 'Venice and the kingdom of Naples in the last years of Robert the Wise: 1332–43', *Papers of the British School at Rome* 48 (1980), 186–204.

Agosto, A. and A.M. Salone, *Mostra Documentaria Genova e Venezia tra i secoli XII e XIV* (Genoa, 1984).

Akbari, S.C., *Idols in the East: European Representations of Islam and the Orient, 1100–1450* (Ithaca, 2009).

Akin, H., *Aydın Oğulları tarihi hakkında bir araştırma* (Istanbul, 1946).

Airaldi, G., 'Roger of Lauria's expedition to the Peloponnese', *Mediterranean Historical Review* 10 (1995), 14–23.

Andrea, A.J., *Contemporary Sources for the Fourth Crusade: Revised Edition* (Leiden, 2008).

Angold, M., *A Byzantine Government in Exile: Government and Society Under the Laskarids of Nicaea, 1204–1261* (London, 1974).

—— *The Fourth Crusade: Event and Context* (Harlow, 2003).

—— 'Michael VIII Palaiologos and the Aegean', in *Liquid and Multiple: Individuals and Identities in the Thirteenth-Century Aegean*, ed. G. Saint-Guillain and D. Stathakopoulos (Paris, 2012), pp. 27–44.

Arbel, B., 'Slave trade and slave labour in Frankish and Venetian Cyprus (1191–1571)', in Idem, *Cyprus, the Franks and Venice, 13th–16th Centuries*, Variorum Reprints (Aldershot, 2000), IX, 151–90.

Argenti, P.P., *The Occupation of Chios by the Genoese and their Administration of the Island: 1346–1566*, 3 vols (Cambridge, 1958).

—— 'The Mahona of the Giustiniani: Genoese colonialism and the Genoese relationship with Chios', *Byzantinische Forschungen* 6 (1979), 1–35.

Asbridge, T.S., *The First Crusade: A New History* (London, 2004).

Ashtor, E., *Levant Trade in the Later Middle Ages* (Princeton, 1983).

Atiya, A.S., *The Crusade in the Later Middle Ages* (London, 1938).

Backman, C.R., 'Piracy', in *A Companion to Mediterranean History*, ed. P. Horden and S. Kinoshita (Chichester, 2014), pp. 172–83.

Balard, M., *La Romanie génoise, XIIe – début du XVe siècle*, 2 vols (Rome, 1978).

—— 'Latins in the Aegean and the Balkans in the fourteenth century', *The New Cambridge Medieval History*, ed. M. Jones, 7 vols (Cambridge, 1995–2005), vol. 6, pp. 825–38.

Balletto, L., 'Les Génois à Phocée et à Chio du XIIIe au XIVe siècle', in *Byzance et le monde extérieur. Contacts, relations, échanges*, ed. M. Balard, E. Malamut and J.-M. Spieser (Paris, 2005), pp. 45–57.

Barber, M., *The Trial of the Templars*, 2nd edition (Cambridge, 2006).

—— 'The pastoureaux of 1320', *Journal of Ecclesiastical History* 32 (1981), 143–66.

Barker, H., 'Egyptian and Italian Merchants in the Black Sea Slave Trade, 1260–1500' (Unpublished PhD thesis, Columbia University, 2014).

Barry S. and N. Gualde, 'La Peste noire dans l'Occident chrétien et musulman, 1347–1353', *Canadian Bulletin of Medical History* 25.2 (2008), 461–98.

Benedictow, O.J., *The Black Death, 1346–1353: The Complete History* (Woodbridge, 2004).

Belles, C., *Mastiha Island*, trans. C. Sachtouri (Athens, 2005).

Berg, B., 'The Moreote expedition of Ferrando of Majorca in the Aragonese Chronicle of Morea', *Byzantion* 55 (1985), 69–90.

Binbaş, E., 'A Damascene eyewitness to the battle of Nicopolis: Shams al-Dīn Ibn al-Jazarī (d. 833/1429)', in *Contact and Conflict in Frankish Greece and the Aegean*, ed. M. Carr and N.G. Chrissis (Farnham, 2014), pp. 153–75.

Bintliff, J.L., *The Complete Archaeology of Greece: From Hunter-Gatherers to the 20th Century AD* (Chichester, 2012).

Bisaha, N., *Creating East and West: Renaissance Humanists and the Ottoman Turks* (Philadelphia, 2004).

—— 'Petrarch's vision of the Muslim and Byzantine East', *Speculum* 76 (2001), 284–314.

Blumenfeld-Kosinski, R. and K. Petkov, 'Introduction', in *Philippe de Mézières and His Age: Piety and Politics in the Fourteenth Century*, ed. R. Blumenfeld-Kosinski and K. Petkov (Leiden, 2011), pp. 1–16.

Boase, T.S.R., 'The history of the kingdom', in *The Cilician Kingdom of Armenia*, ed. T.S.R. Boase (Edinburgh, 1978), pp. 1–33.

Boojamra, J.L., 'Athanasios of Constantinople: a study of Byzantine reactions to Latin religious infiltration', *Church History* 48.1 (1979), 27–48.

Bosworth, C.E., *The New Islamic Dynasties: A Chronological and Genealogical Manual* (Edinburgh, 1996).

Boyle, L.E., *A Survey of the Vatican Archives and of its Medieval Holdings* (Toronto, 1972).

Brundage, J.A., *Medieval Canon Law and the Crusader* (Madison, 1969).

Brunetti, M., 'Contributo alla Storia delle relazioni veneto-genovesi dal 1348 al 1350', *Miscellanea di Storia Veneta* 9 (Venice, 1916).

Bryer, A.A.M., *The Empire of Trebizond and the Pontos* (London, 1980).

Burns, R.I., 'The Catalan Company and the European powers, 1305–1311', *Speculum* 29 (1954), 751–71.

Cagesse, A., *Roberto d'Angiò e i suoi tempi*, 2 vols (Florence, 1922–30).

Cahen, C., *Pre-Ottoman Turkey: A General Survey of the Material and Spiritual Culture and History c.1071–1330*, trans. J. Jones-Williams (London, 1968).

—— 'Les principautés turcomanes au debut du XIVe siècle d'aprés Pachymere et Gregoras', *İstanbul Üniversitesi Edebiyat Fakültesi Tarih Dergisi* 32 (1979), 111–16.

Carr, M., 'The Hospitallers of Rhodes and their alliances against the Turks', in *Islands and Military Orders, c.1291–c.1798*, ed. S. Phillips and E. Buttigieg (Farnham, 2013), pp. 167–76.

—— 'Between Byzantium, Egypt and the Holy Land: The Italian maritime republics and the First Crusade', in *Jerusalem the Golden: The Origins and Impact of the First Crusade*, ed. S.B. Edgington and L. García-Guijarro (Turnhout, 2014), pp. 75–87.

—— 'Humbert of Viennois and the Crusade of Smyrna: A reconsideration', *Crusades* 13 (2014), 237–51.

—— 'Trade or Crusade? The Zaccaria of Chios and crusades against the Turks', in *Contact and Conflict in Frankish Greece and the Aegean*, ed. M. Carr and N.G. Chrissis (Farnham, 2014), pp. 115–34.

—— 'Crossing boundaries in the Mediterranean: Papal trade licences from the *Registra Supplicationum* of Pope Clement VI (1342–1352)', *Journal of Medieval History* 41 (2015), 107–29.

—— 'Papal trade licences, Italian merchants and the changing perceptions of the Mamluks and Turkish beyliks in the fourteenth century', in *Diasporic Groups and Identities in the Eastern Mediterranean (1100–1800)*, ed. G. Christ *et al.* (Rome, 2015), pp. 489–97.

Carr, M. and N.G. Chrissis (eds), *Contact and Conflict in Frankish Greece and the Aegean, 1204–1453* (Farnham, 2014).

Chaplais, P., *The War of Saint-Sardos (1323–1325): Gascon Correspondence and Diplomatic Documents* (London, 1954).

Charanis, P., 'Piracy in the Aegean during the reign of Michael VIII Palaeologus', *Annuaire de l'Institut de Philologie et d'Histoire Orientales et Slaves* 10 (1950), 127–36.

Chevalier, M.-A., *Les ordres religieux-militaires en Arménie cilicienne: templiers, hospitaliers, teutoniques and Arméniens à l'époque des croisades* (Paris, 2009).

Chrissis, N.G., *Crusading in Frankish Greece: A Study of Byzantine-Western Relations and Attitudes, 1204–1282* (Turnhout, 2012).

—— 'New frontiers: Frankish Greece and the development of crusading in the early thirteenth century', in *Contact and Conflict in Frankish Greece and the Aegean, 1204–1453*, ed. M. Carr and N.G. Chrissis (Farnham, 2014), pp. 17–41.

Christ, G., *Trading Conflicts: Venetian Merchants and Mamluk Officials in Late Medieval Alexandria* (Leiden, 2012).

—— 'Sliding legalities: Venetian slave trade in Alexandria and the Aegean', in *Slavery and the Slave Trade in the Mediterranean Region during the Medieval Period (1000–1500)*, ed. C. Cluse and R. Amitai (Turnhout, 2015), pp. 210–29.

—— 'Kreuzzug und Seeherrschaft. Clemens V., Venedig und das Handelsembargo von 1308', in *Maritimes Mittelalter*, ed. N. Jaspert and M. Borgolte, Vorträge und Forschungen / Konstanzer Arbeitskreis für mittelalterliche Geschichte (Ostfildern, 2015), pp. 261–82.

—— 'Materials, products and services of exchange 300–1550', in *Mapping the Medieval Mediterranean, c. 300–1550*, ed. A. Nichols Law (Leiden, 2015), forthcoming.

Ciciliot, F., 'Sources for medieval nautical archaeology: Genoese notarial records', *International Journal of Nautical Archaeology* 25/3–4 (1996), 239–242.

Cocci, A., 'Le projet de blocus naval des côtes égyptiennes dans le *Liber secretorum fidelium Crusis* (1321c) de Marino Sanudo il Vecchio (1279c.–1343)', in *La Méditerranée médiévale: Perceptions et représentations*, ed. H. Akkari (Paris, 2002), pp. 171–88.

Coureas, N., *The Latin Church in Cyprus: 1313–1378* (Nicosia, 2010).

Curtin, P.D., *Cross-Cultural Trade in World History* (Cambridge, 1984).

Delaville le Roulx, J., *La France en Orient au XIVe siècle*, 2 vols (Paris, 1886).

—— *Les Hospitaliers en Terre Sainte et à Chypre: 1100–1310* (Paris, 1904).

—— *Les Hospitaliers à Rhodes, 1310–1421* (Paris, 1913; repr. London, 1974).

Demurger, A., 'Le pape Clément VI et l'Orient: ligue ou croisade?', in *Guerre, pouvoir et noblesse au Moyen Âge, Mélanges en l'honneur de Philippe Contamine*, ed. J. Paviot and J. Verger (Paris, 2000), pp. 207–14.

Depping, G.-B., *Histoire du commerce entre le Levant et l'Europe depuis les croisades jusqu'à la fondation des colonies en Amérique*, 2 vols (Paris, 1830).

Depréz, E., *Les préliminaires de la guerre de cent ans: La papauté, la France et l'Angleterre (1328–1342)* (Paris, 1902).

Dols, M.W., *The Black Death in the Middle East* (Princeton, 1977).

Dotson, J.E., 'Merchant and naval influences on galley design at Venice and Genoa in the fourteenth century', in *New Aspects of Naval History: Selected Papers Presented at the Fourth Naval History Symposium, United States Naval Academy*, ed. C.L. Symonds (Annapolis, 1981), pp. 20–32.

—— 'Venice, Genoa and control of the seas in the thirteenth and fourteenth centuries', in *War at Sea in the Middle Ages and Renaissance*, ed. J.B. Hattendorf and R.W. Unger (Woodbridge, 2003), pp. 119–36.

—— 'Ship types and fleet composition at Genoa and Venice in the early thirteenth century', in *Logistics of Warfare in the Age of the Crusades*, ed. John H. Pryor (Farnham, 2006), pp. 63–75.

—— 'Everything is a compromise: Mediterranean ship design, thirteenth to sixteenth centuries', in *The Art, Science, and Technology of Medieval Travel*, ed. R.O. Bork and A. Kann (Farnham, 2008), pp. 31–40.

Du Cange, C. du F., *Histoire de l'Empire de Constantinople sous les empereurs français jusqu'a la conquête des turcs*, ed. J.A. Buchon, 2 vols (Paris, 1826).

Dunbabin, J., *Charles I of Anjou: Power, Kingship and State-Making in Thirteenth Century Europe* (London, 1998).

Dunn, R.E., *The Adventures of Ibn Battuta: A Muslim Traveler of the 14th Century* (Berkeley, 1986).

Durrholder, G., *Die Kreuzzugspolitik unter Papst Johann XXII* (Strasbourg, 1913).

Dursteler, E.R., 'On bazaars and battlefields: Recent scholarship on Mediterranean cultural contacts', *Journal of Early Modern History* 15 (2011), 413–34.

Edbury, P.W., *The Kingdom of Cyprus and the Crusades: 1191–1374* (Cambridge, 1991).

Epstein, S.A., *Genoa and the Genoese, 958–1528* (Chapel Hill, 1996).

—— *Purity Lost: Transgressing Boundaries in the Eastern Mediterranean, 1000–1400* (Baltimore, 2007).

Esch, A., 'Der Handel zwischen Christen und Muslimen im Mittelmeer-Raum. Verstöße gegen das päpstliche Embargo geschildert in den Gesuchen an die Apostolische Pönitentiarie (1439–1483)', *Quellen und Forschungen aus italienischen Archiven und Bibliotheken* 92 (2012), 85–140.

Failler, A., 'Éphèse fut-elle prise en 1304 par les Turcs de Sasan?', *Revue des études byzantines* 54 (1996), 245–8.

Faure, M.C., 'Le dauphin Humbert II à Venise et en Orient (1345–1347)', *Mélanges d'archéologie et d'histoire* 27 (1907), 509–562.

Fedalto, G., *La chiesa latina in Oriente*, 3 vols (Verona, 1973–8).

Finke, H., *Papsttum und Untergang des Templerordens*, 2 vols (Münster, 1907).

Fleet, K., *European and Islamic Trade in the Early Ottoman State: The Merchants of Genoa and Turkey* (Cambridge, 1999).

Foss, C., *Ephesus after Antiquity: A Late Antique, Byzantine and Turkish City* (Cambridge, 1979).

France, J., 'Philippe de Mézières and the military history of the fourteenth century', in *Philippe de Mézières and His Age: Piety and Politics in the Fourteenth Century*, ed. R. Blumenfeld-Kosinski and K. Petkov (Leiden, 2012), pp. 283–93.

Frankopan, P., *The First Crusade: The Call from the East* (London, 2012).

Freedman, P., 'Mastic: A Mediterranean luxury product', *Mediterranean Historical Review* 26 (2011), 99–113.

Gatto, L., 'Per la storia di Martino Zaccaria, signore di Chio', *Bullettino dell'Archivio Paleografico Italiano*, n.s., 2–3, part 1 (1956–7), 325–45.

Gay, J., *Le Pape Clément VI et les affaires d'Orient (1342–1352)* (Paris, 1904).

Geanakoplos, D.J., *Emperor Michael Palaeologus and the West, 1258–1282: A Study into Byzantine-Latin Relations* (Cambridge, MA, 1959).

—— 'Byzantium and the Crusades: 1261–1354', in *A History of the Crusades*, ed. K.M. Setton, 6 vols (Madison, 1969–1989), vol. 3, pp. 27–68.

Georgiou, C., 'Propagating the Hospitallers' *passagium*: Crusade preaching and liturgy in 1308–9', in *Islands and Military Orders, c.1291–c.1798*, ed. S. Phillips and E. Buttigieg (Farnham, 2013), pp. 53–63.

Gertwagen, R., 'Nautical technology', in *A Companion to Mediterranean History*, ed. P. Horden and S. Kinoshita (Chichester, 2014), pp. 154–69.

Gill, J., *Byzantium and the Papacy, 1198–1400* (New Brunswick, 1979).

Giunta, F., 'Benedetto XII e la crociata', *Anuario de estudios medievales* 3 (1966), 215–34.

Gluzman, R., 'Between Venice and the Levant: Re-evaluating maritime routes from the fourteenth to the sixteenth century', *The Mariner's Mirror* 96 (2010), 264–94.

Goitein, S.D., *A Mediterranean Society: The Jewish Communities of the Arab World as Portrayed in the Documents of the Cairo Geniza*, 6 vols (Berkeley, 1967–93).

—— *Letters of Medieval Jewish Traders* (Princeton, 1979).

Guard, T., *Chivalry, Kingship and Crusade: The English Experience in the Fourteenth Century* (Woodbridge, 2013).

Guilmartin Jr., J.F., *Gunpowder and Galleys: Changing Technology and Mediterranean Warfare at Sea in the Sixteenth Century* (London, 1974).

Goodwin, G., *A History of Ottoman Architecture* (London, 1971).

Guzman, G.G., 'Simon of Saint Quentin as historian of the Mongols and the Seljuk Turks', *Medievalia et Humanistica* 3 (1972), 155–78.

Hankins, J., 'Renaissance crusaders: humanist crusade literature in the age of Mehmed II', *Dumbarton Oaks Papers* 49 (1995), 111–207.

Harris, J., 'Collusion with the infidel as a pretext for western military action against Byzantium (1180–1204)', in *Languages of Love and Hate: Conflict, Communication and Identity in the Medieval Mediterranean*, ed. S. Lambert and H. Nicholson (Turnhout, 2012).

Heath, M.J., 'Renaissance scholars and the origins of the Turks', *Bibliothèque d'Humanisme et Renaissance* 41 (1979), 453–71.

Hellenkemper, H. and F. Hild, *Lykien und Pamphylien* (Vienna, 2004).

Henneman, J.B., *Royal Taxation in Fourteenth-Century France: The Development of War Financing, 1322–1356* (Princeton, 1971).

Heyd, W., *Histoire du commerce du Levant au moyen-âge*, 2 vols (Leipzig, 1885–6).

Hill, G., *A History of Cyprus*, 4 vols (Cambridge, 1940–52).

Hillenbrand, C., *Turkish Myth and Muslim Symbol: The Battle of Manzikert* (Edinburgh, 2007).

Herrin, J. and G. Saint-Guillan (eds), *Identities and Allegiances in the Eastern Mediterranean after 1204* (Farnham, 2011).

Holmes, C., J. Harris and E. Russell (eds), *Byzantines, Latins, and Turks in the Eastern Mediterranean World after 1150* (Oxford, 2012).

Housley, N., 'The Franco-papal crusade negotiations in 1322–3', *Papers of the British School at Rome* 48 (1980), 166–85 (repr. in Idem, *Crusading and Warfare in Medieval and Renaissance Europe*, Variorum Reprints (Aldershot, 2001), XII).

—— 'Angevin Naples and the defence of the Latin East: Robert the Wise and the naval league of 1334', *Byzantion* 51 (1981), 548–56 (repr. in Idem, *Crusading and Warfare in Medieval and Renaissance Europe*, Variorum Reprints (Aldershot, 2001), XIII).

—— *The Italian Crusades: The Papal-Angevin Alliance and the Crusades against Christian Lay Powers, 1254–1343* (Oxford, 1982).

—— 'The mercenary companies, the papacy and the crusades, 1356–1378', *Traditio* 38 (1982), 253–80 (repr. in Idem, *Crusading and Warfare in Medieval and Renaissance Europe*, Variorum Reprints (Aldershot, 2001), XV).

—— 'Pope Clement V and the crusades of 1309–10', *Journal of Medieval History* 8 (1982), 29–43 (repr. in Idem, *Crusading and Warfare in Medieval and Renaissance Europe*, Variorum Reprints (Aldershot, 2001), XI).

—— *The Avignon Papacy and the Crusades, 1305–1378* (Oxford, 1986).

—— 'France, England and the "national crusade", 1302–86', in *France and the British Isles in the Middle Ages and Renaissance*, ed. G. Jondorf and D.N. Dumville (Woodbridge, 1991), pp. 183–201 (repr. in Idem, *Crusading and Warfare in Medieval and Renaissance Europe*, Variorum Reprints (Aldershot, 2001), VII).

—— *The Later Crusades, 1274–1580. From Lyons to Alcazar* (Oxford, 1992).

—— 'Costing the crusade: budgeting for crusading activity in the fourteenth century', in *The Experience of Crusading*, ed. M. Bull and N. Housley, 2 vols (Cambridge, 2003), pp. 45–58.

—— *Contesting the Crusades* (Oxford, 2006).

—— *Crusading and the Ottoman Threat: 1453–1505* (Oxford, 2012).

Hunt, E.S., *The Medieval Super Companies: A Study of the Peruzzi Company of Florence* (Cambridge, 1994).

Jackson, P., *The Mongols and the West, 1221–1410* (Harlow, 2005).

Jacoby, D., 'Catalans, Turcs et Vénitiens en Romanie (1305–1332): Un nouveau témoignage de Marino Sanudo Torsello', *Studia Medievali* 15.1 (1974), 217–61 (repr. in Idem, *Recherches sur la Méditerranée orientale du XIIe au XVe siècle: peuples, sociétés, économies*, Variorum Reprints (London, 1979), V).

—— *Société et démographie à Byzance et en Romanie latine*, Variorum Reprints (London, 1975).

—— 'Social evolution in Latin Greece', *A History of the Crusades*, ed. K.M. Setton, 6 vols (Madison, 1969–1989), vol. 6, pp. 175–221.

—— *Studies on the Crusader States and on Venetian Expansion*, Variorum Reprints (Northampton, 1989).

—— *Trade, Commodities and Shipping in the Medieval Mediterranean*, Variorum Reprints (Aldershot, 1997).

—— *Byzantium, Latin Romania and the Mediterranean*, Variorum Reprints (Aldershot, 2001).

—— *Commercial Exchange across the Mediterranean: Byzantium, the Crusader Levant, Egypt and Italy*, Variorum Reprints (Aldershot, 2005).

—— 'Production et commerce de l'alun oriental en Méditerranée, XIᵉ–XVᵉ siècles', in *L'alun de Méditerranée*, ed. P. Borgard, J.-P. Brun and M. Picon (Naples, 2005), pp. 219–67.

—— 'La consolidation de la domination de Venise dans la ville de Négrepont (1205–1390): un aspect de sa politique coloniale', in *Bisanzio, Venezia e il mondo franco-greco (XIII-XV secolo)*, ed. C.A. Maltezou and P. Schreiner (Venice, 2002), pp. 151–89 (repr. in Idem, *Latins, Greeks and Muslims: Encounters in the Eastern Mediterranean, Tenth–Fifteenth Centuries*, Variorum Reprints (Farnham, 2009), IX).

—— 'The eastern Mediterranean in the later Middle Ages: An island world?', in *Byzantines, Latins, and Turks in the Eastern Mediterranean World after 1150*, ed. C. Holmes, J. Harris and E. Russell (Oxford, 2012), pp. 93–117.

—— 'The economy of Latin Greece', in *A Companion to Latin Greece*, ed. N.I. Tsougarakis and P. Lock (Leiden, 2014), pp. 185–216.

Jenkins, H., 'Papal Efforts for Peace under Benedict XII: 1334–1342' (Unpublished PhD thesis, University of Pennsylvania, 1933).

Jordan, W.C., *The Great Famine: Northern Europe in the Early Fourteenth Century* (Princeton, 1996).

Jorga, N., 'Une lettre apocryphe sur la bataille de Smyrne', *Revue d'orient Latin* 3 (1895), 27–31.

—— *Philippe de Mézières, 1327–1405, et la croisade au XIVe siècle* (Paris, 1896).

Inalcik, H., 'The rise of the Turkish maritime principalities in Anatolia, Byzantium and the Crusades', *Byzantinische Forschungen* 9 (1985), 179–217.

Ivanov, V., '*Sancta Unio* or the Holy League 1332–36/7 as a political factor in the eastern Mediterranean and the Aegean', *Études Balkaniques* 48 (2012), 142–76.

Kafadar, C., *Between the Two Worlds: The Construction of the Ottoman State* (Berkeley, 1995).

Karpov, S., 'Black Sea and the crisis of the mid XIVth century: an underestimated turning point', *Thesaurismata* 27 (1997), 65–78.

Kedar, B.Z., *Merchants in Crisis: Genoese and Venetian Men of Affairs and the Four-teenth-Century Depression* (London, 1976).

Kedar, B.Z. and S. Schein, 'Un projet de "passage particuliare" proposé par l'ordre de l'Hôpital, 1306–7', *Bibliothèque de l'École des chartes* 137.2 (1979), 211–26.

Keightley, R.G., 'Muntaner and the Catalan Grand Company', *Revista Canadiense de Estudios Hispánicos* 4 (1979), 37–58.

Kinoshita, S., 'Re-viewing the eastern Mediterranean', *Postmedieval: A Journal of Medieval Cultural Studies* 2 (2011), 369–85.

—— 'Locating the eastern Mediterranean', in *Locating the Middle Ages: The Spaces and Places of Medieval Culture*, ed. J. Weiss and S. Salih (London, 2012), pp. 39–52.

Kinoshita S. and J. Jacobs, 'Ports of call: Boccaccio's Alatiel in the medieval Medi-terranean', *Journal of Medieval and Early Modern Studies* 37.1 (2007), 163–95.

Kunstmann, F., 'Studien über Marino Sanudo Torsello den Aelteren', *Abhandlungen der Historischen Classe der Königlich Bayerischen Akademie der Wissenschaften* 7 (Munich, 1855), 695–819.

Kyriakidis, S., 'The employment of large groups of mercenaries in Byzantium in the period ca. 1290–1305 as viewed by the sources', *Byzantion* 79 (2009), 208–30.

Laiou, A.E., 'Marino Sanudo Torsello, Byzantium and the Turks: the background to the anti-Turkish league of 1332–1334', *Speculum* 45 (1970), 374–92.

—— *Constantinople and the Latins: The Foreign Policy of Andronicus II, 1282–1328* (Cambridge, MA, 1972).

—— 'Italy and the Italians in the political geography of the Byzantines (14th century)', *Dumbarton Oaks Papers* 49 (1995), 73–98.

Lane, F.C., 'Venetian merchant galleys, 1300–1334: Private and communal opera-tion', *Speculum* 38.2 (1963), 179–205.

—— *Venice: A Maritime Republic* (London, 1973).

—— 'The Venetian galleys to Alexandria, 1344', in Idem, *Studies in Venetian Social and Economic History*, Variorum Reprints (London, 1987), XIII, pp. 431–3.

Langer, W.L. and R.P. Blake, 'The rise of the Ottoman Turks and its historical background', *American Historical Review* 37 (1932), 477–80.

Laurent, V., 'Action de grâces pour la victoire navale remportée sur les Turcs à Atramyttion au cours de l'automne 1334', *Eis Mnemen K.I. Amantou* (Athens, 1960), pp. 25–41

Lemerle, P., *L'émirat d'Aydin, Byzance et l'occident: Recherches sur 'La geste d'Umur pacha'* (Paris, 1957).

Leonhard, J., *Genua und die päpstliche Kurie in Avignon (1305 – 1378): politische und diplomatische Beziehungen im 14. Jahrhundert* (Frankfurt am Main, 2013).

Leopold, A., *How To Recover the Holy Land: The Crusade Proposals of the Late Thir-teenth and Early Fourteenth Centuries* (Aldershot, 2000).

Lindner, R.P., *Explorations in Ottoman Prehistory* (Ann Arbor, 2007).

Lock, P., *The Franks in the Aegean, 1204–1500* (London, 1995).

—— 'Sanudo, Turks, Greeks, and Latins in the early fourteenth century', in *Contact and Conflict in Frankish Greece and the Aegean, 1204–1453*, ed. M. Carr and N.G. Chrissis (Farnham, 2014), pp. 135–49.

Lock P. and G.D.R. Sanders (eds), *The Archaeology of Medieval Greece* (Oxford, 1996)

Loenertz, R.-J., 'Athènes et Néopatras: Régestes et documents pour servir à l'histoire ecclésiastique des Duchés catalans (1311–1395)', *Archivum Fratrum Praedicatorum* 28 (1958), 5–91.

—— *Les Ghisi: Dynastes vénitiens dans l'Archipel, 1207–1390* (Florence, 1975).

Lopez, R., *Benedetto Zaccaria: ammiraglio e mercante* (Milan, 1933; repr. with intro-duction by Michel Balard, Genoa, 1996).

—— 'Venice and Genoa: two styles, one success', *Diogenes* 71 (1970), 39–47.

Lowry, H.W., *The Nature of the Early Ottoman State* (Albany, 2003).

Lunardi, G., *Le monete delle colonie Genovesi* (Genoa, 1980).

Lunt, W.E., *Financial Relations of the Papacy with England to 1327–1534*, 2 vols (Cambridge, MA, 1939).

Luttrell, A.T., 'Venice and the Knights Hospitallers of Rhodes in the fourteenth century', *Papers of the British School at Rome* 13 (1958), 195–212 (repr. in Idem, *The Hospitallers in Cyprus, Rhodes, Greece, and the West, 1291–1440: Collected Studies*, Variorum Reprints (Aldershot, 1978), V).

—— 'Feudal tenure and Latin colonization at Rhodes', *The English Historical Review* 85 (1970), 755–75 (repr. in Idem, *The Hospitallers in Cyprus, Rhodes, Greece, and the West, 1291–1440: Collected Studies*, Variorum Reprints (Aldershot, 1978), III).

—— 'Crete and Rhodes: 1340–1360', in *Acts of the International Congress of Cretan Studies II* (Athens, 1974), pp. 167–75.

—— 'The Hospitallers' interventions in Cilician Armenia: 1271–1375', in *The Cilician Kingdom of Armenia*, ed. T.S.R. Boase (Edinburgh, 1978), pp. 118–44.

—— 'The Hospitallers of Rhodes: Prospectives, problems, possibilities', in *Die geistlichen Ritterorden Europas*, ed. J. Fleckenstein and M. Hellmann (Thorbecke, 1980), pp. 243–66 (repr. in Idem, *Latin Greece, the Hospitallers and the Crusades, 1291–1440*, Variorum Reprints (Aldershot, 1982), I).

—— 'Notes on Foulques de Villaret, Master of the Hospital 1305–1319', in *Guillaume de Villaret, 1er recteur du Comtat-Venaissin 1274, Grand Maitre de l'Ordre des hospitaliers de Saint-Jean de Jerusalem, Chypre 1296* (Paris, 1985), pp. 73–90 (repr. in Idem, *The Hospitallers of Rhodes and their Mediterranean World*, Variorum Reprints (Aldershot, 1992), IV).

—— 'The Hospitallers of Rhodes confront the Turks: 1306–1421', in *Christians, Jews and Other Worlds: Patterns of Conflict and Accommodation: the Avery Lectures in History*, ed. P.F. Gallagher (Lanham, 1988), pp. 80–116 (repr. in Idem, *The Hospitallers of Rhodes and Their Mediterranean World*, Variorum Reprints (Aldershot, 1992), I).

—— 'The Genoese at Rhodes: 1306–1312', in *Oriente e Occidente tra Medioevo ed età moderna: studi in onore di Geo Pistarino*, ed. L. Balletto, 2 vols (Genoa, 1997), vol. 1, pp. 743–61 (repr. in Idem, *The Hospitaller State on Rhodes and its Western Provinces, 1306–1462*, Variorum Reprints (Aldershot, 1999), I).

—— 'The Hospitallers and the papacy, 1305–1314', in *Forschungen zur Reichs-, Papst-, und Landesgeschichte: Peter Herde zum 65. Geburstag*, ed K. Borchardt and E. Bunz, 2 vols (Stuttgart, 1998), vol. 2, pp. 595–622 (repr. in Idem, *Studies on the Hospitallers after 1306*, Variorum Reprints (Aldershot, 2007), V).

—— *The Town of Rhodes: 1306–1356* (Rhodes, 2003).

—— 'The Hospitallers and their Florentine bankers: 1306–1346', in *Karrissime Gotifride: Historical Essays Presented to Professor Godfrey Wettinger on his Seventieth Birthday*, ed. P. Xuereb (Msida, 1999), pp. 17–24 (repr. in Idem, *Studies on the Hospitallers after 1306*, Variorum Reprints (Aldershot, 2007), VI).

—— 'The island of Rhodes and the Hospitallers of Catalunya in the fourteenth century', in *Els Catalans a la Mediterrània Oriental a l'Edat Mitjana*, ed. M.T. Ferrer i Mallol (Barcelona, 2003), pp. 155–65 (repr. in Idem, *Studies on the Hospitallers after 1306*, Variorum Reprints (Aldershot, 2007), XVIII).

Magnocavallo, A., *Marin Sanudo il Vecchio e il suo progetto di Crociata* (Bergamo, 1901).

Martin, L.R., 'Horse and cargo handling on medieval Mediterranean ships', *The International Journal of Nautical Archaeology* 31 (2002), 237–47.

Mas Latrie, M.L. de, *Histoire de l'île de Chypre sous le regne des princes de la maison de Lusignan*, 3 vols (Paris, 1852–61).

—— *Commerce et expéditions militaires de la France et de Venise au moyen âge*, ed. L. de Mas Latrie (Paris, 1880) = vol. 3 of *Mélanges historiques: Choix de documents*, 5 vols (Paris, 1873–86).

Mastnak, T., *Crusading Peace: Christendom, the Muslim World and Western Political Order* (London, 2002).

Mazarakis, A., 'The Chios mint during the rule of the Zaccaria family (1304–1329)', *Nomismatika Chronika* 2 (1992), 43–52.

—— 'A martinello of Manuele and Paleologo Zaccaria (1307–1310)', trans. M.J. Tzamali, *Nomismatika Chronika* 18 (1999), 111–18.

Menache, S., *Clement V* (Cambridge, 1998).

Meneses, L. de, 'Florilegio documental del Reinado de Pedro IV de Aragón', *Cuadernos de historia de España* 13 (1950), 181–90

Meserve, M., *Empires of Islam in Renaissance Historical Thought* (Cambridge, MA, 2008).

Metcalf, D.M., *Coinage of the Crusades and the Latin East in the Ashmolean Museum, Oxford*, 2nd edition (London, 1995).

Miller, W., 'The Zaccaria of Phocaea and Chios, 1275–1329', *The Journal of Hellenic Studies* 31 (1911), 44–55.

Mollat, G., *The Popes at Avignon: 1305–1378*, trans. J. Love (London, 1963).

Moore, R.I., *The Formation of a Persecuting Society: Power and Deviance in Western Europe, 950–1250* (Oxford, 2007).

Moranvillé, H., 'Les projets de Charles de Valois sur l'Empire de Constantinople', *Bibliothèque de l'École des chartes* 51 (1890), 63–86.

Mott, L.V., 'Serving in the fleet: crews and recruitment issues in the Catalan-Aragonese fleets during the war of the Sicilian Vespers (1282–1302)', *Cross-cultural Encounters on the High Seas (Tenth–Sixteenth Centuries)*, ed. K.L. Reyerson = *Journal of Medieval Encounters* 13 (2006), 56–77.

Muldoon, J., 'The Avignon Papacy and the frontiers of Christendom: The evidence of Vatican Register 62', *Archivium Historiae Pontificiae* 17 (1979), 125–95.

Murray, A.V., 'William of Tyre and the origin of the Turks: On the sources of the *Gesta Orientalium Principum*', in *Dei Gesta per Francos: Etudes sur les croisades dédiés à Jean Richard*, ed. M. Balard, B.Z. Kedar and J.S.C. Riley-Smith (Aldershot, 2001).

Nicol, D.M., *The Despotate of Epiros 1267–1479: A Contribution to the History of Greece in the Middle Ages* (Cambridge, 1984).

—— *The Last Centuries of Byzantium, 1261–1453*, 2nd edition (Cambridge, 1993).

—— *The Reluctant Emperor: A Biography of John Cantacuzene, Byzantine Emperor and Monk, c.1295–1383* (Cambridge, 1996).

Nicholas, D., *Medieval Flanders* (London, 1992).

O'Connell, M., 'The Italian Renaissance in the Mediterranean, or, between East and West: A review article', *California Italian Studies Journal* 1 (2010), 1–30.

Ortalli, G., 'Venice and papal bans on trade with the Levant: The role of the jurist', *Mediterranean Historical Review* 10 (1995), 242–58.

Orth, P., 'Papst Urbans II. Kreuzzugsrede in Clermont bei lateinischen Schriftstellern des 15. und 16. Jahrhunderts', in *Jerusalem im Hoch- und Spätmittelalter*.

Konflikte und Konfliktbewältigung - Vorstellungen und Vergegenwärtigungen, ed. D. Bauer, K. Herbers and N. Jaspert (Frankfurt a. Main, 2001), pp. 367–405.

Page, G., *Being Byzantine: Greek Identity before the Ottomans* (Cambridge, 2008).

Papi, M.D., 'Santa Maria Novella di Firenze e l'*Outremer* domenicano', *Toscana e Terrasanta nel Medioevo*, ed. F. Cardini (Florence, 1982), pp. 87–101.

Partner, P., *The Lands of St Peter: The Papal States in the Middle Ages and Early Renaissance* (London, 1972).

Philips, J.P., *The Second Crusade: Extending the Frontiers of Christendom* (London, 2007).

Perikos, J., *The Chios Gum Mastic* (Athens, 1993).

Po-chia Hsia, R., 'Religion and race: Protestant and Catholic discourses on Jewish conversions of the sixteenth and seventeenth centuries', in *The Origins of Racism in the West*, ed. M. Eliav-Feldon, B. Isaac and J. Ziegler (Cambridge, 2009), pp. 265–75.

Preiser-Kapeller, J., 'Liquid frontiers: A relational analysis of maritime Asia Minor as a religious contact zone in the thirteenth–fifteenth centuries', in *Islam and Christianity in Mediaeval Anatolia*, ed. A.C.S. Peacock, B. de Nicola and S.N. Yıldız (Ashgate, 2015), pp. 117–45.

Pryor, J.H., 'The naval architecture of crusader transport ships: A reconstruction of some archetypes for round-hulled sailing ships', in Idem, *Commerce, Shipping and Naval Warfare in the Medieval Mediterranean*, Variorum Reprints (London, 1987), VII, pp. 171–219, 275–92, 363–86.

—— 'The naval battles of Roger of Lauria', in Idem, *Commerce, Shipping and Naval Warfare in the Medieval Mediterranean*, Variorum Reprints (London, 1987), VI, pp. 179–216.

—— *Geography, Technology and War: Studies in the Maritime History of the Mediterranean, 649–1571* (Cambridge, 1988).

—— 'The naval architecture of crusader transport ships, revisited', *The Mariner's Mirror* 76 (1990), 255–73.

—— 'The geographical conditions of galley navigation in the Mediterranean', in *The Age of the Galley: Mediterranean Oared Vessels Since Pre-Classical Times*, ed. R. Gardiner (London, 1995), pp. 206–16.

Purcell, M., *Papal Crusading Policy: The Chief Instruments of Papal Crusading Policy and Crusade to the Holy Land from the Final Loss of Jerusalem to the Fall of Acre: 1244–1291* (Leiden, 1975).

Queller, D.E. and T.F. Madden, *The Fourth Crusade: The Conquest of Constantinople*, 2nd edition (Philadelphia, 1997).

Richard, J., 'Le royaume de Chypre et l'embargo sur le commerce avec l'Egypte (fin XIIIe–début XIVe siècle)', *Académie des Inscriptions et Belles-Lettres* (1984), pp. 120–34.

Riefstahl, R.M., *Turkish Architecture in Southwestern Anatolia* (Cambridge, MA, 1931).

Riley-Smith, J.S.C., *The Knights of St. John in Jerusalem and Cyprus, c.1050–1310* (London, 1967).

—— *What Were the Crusades?*, 4th edition (Basingstoke, 2009).

Roncière, C.B. de la, *Histoire de la Marine Française*, 5 vols (Paris, 1889–1920).

—— 'Une escadre Franco-papale (1318–1320)', *Mélanges d'archéologie et d'histoire publiés par l'École française de Rome* 13 (1893), 5–26.

Rose, E., *Medieval Naval Warfare: 1000–1500* (London, 2002).

Runciman, S., *The Sicilian Vespers: A History of the Mediterranean World in the Later Thirteenth Century* (Cambridge, 1958).

Ryder, J., 'Demetrius Kydones' "History of the Crusades": Reality or rhetoric?', in *Contact and Conflict in Frankish Greece and the Aegean*, ed. M. Carr and N.G. Chrissis (Farnham, 2014), pp. 92–112.

Sarnowsky, J., 'Die Johanniter und Smyrna 1344–1402 (Teil 2: Quellen)', *Römische Quartalschrift* 87 (1992), 47–98.

Schein, S., 'Philip IV and the crusade: a reconsideration', in *Crusade and Settlement: Papers Read at the First Conference of the Society for the Study of the Crusades and the Latin East and Presented to R.C. Smail*, ed. P.W. Edbury (Cardiff, 1985), pp. 121–6.

—— *Fideles Crucis: The Papacy, the West, and the Recovery of the Holy Land 1274–1314* (Oxford, 1991).

Schevill, F., *A History of Florence: From the Founding of the City through the Renaissance* (New York, 1936).

Schlumberger, G., *Numismatique de l'orient Latin*, 2 vols (Paris, 1878).

Schreiner, P., *Die byzantinischen Kleinchroniken*, 3 vols (Vienna, 1975–9).

Schwoebel, R., *The Shadow of the Crescent: The Renaissance Image of the Turk (1453–1517)* (Nieuwkoop, 1967).

Seibt, G., *Anonimo romano: scrivere la storia alle soglie del Rinascimento* (Rome, 2000).

Setton, K.M., *The Catalan Domination of Athens: 1311–1388* (Cambridge, MA, 1948).

—— *The Papacy and the Levant: 1204–1571*, 4 vols (Philadelphia, 1976–84).

Skinner, P., *Medieval Amalfi and its Diaspora, 800–1250* (Oxford, 2013).

Singer, C., *The Earliest Chemical Industry: An Essay in the Historical Relations of Economics and Technology Illustrated from the Alum Trade* (London, 1948).

Skržinskaja, E.Č., 'Storia della Tana', *Studi Veneziani* 10 (1968), 3–45.

Stantchev, S., '*Devedo*: The Venetian response to Sultan Mehmed II in the Venetian-Ottoman conflict of 1462–79', *Mediterranean Studies (The Journal of the Mediterranean Studies Association)* 19 (2010), 43–66.

—— 'The medieval origins of embargo as a policy tool', *History of Political Thought* 33.3 (2012), 373–99.

—— *Spiritual Rationality: Papal Embargo as Cultural Practice* (Oxford, 2014).

Strayer, J.R., 'France: The Holy Land, the Chosen People, and the Most Christian King', in Idem, *Medieval Statecraft and the Perspectives of History: Essays by Joseph R. Strayer* (Princeton, 1971), pp. 300–14.

—— *The Reign of Philip the Fair* (Princeton, 1980).

Tabacco, G., *La casa di Francia nell'azione politica di Papa Giovanni XXII* (Rome, 1953).

Tanner, N.P., *Decrees of the Ecumenical Councils: Nicaea I to Vatican II*, 2 vols (London, 1990).

Taylor, C.H., 'French assemblies and subsidy in 1321', *Speculum* 43 (1968), 217–44.

Theotokes, S.M., 'E prôte summachia tôn kuriarchôn kratôn tou aigaiou chata tês kathodou tôn tourkôn archomenou tou 14 aiônos', *Epeteris Etaireias Byzantinon Spoudon* 7 (1930), 283–98.

Theunissen, H., 'Ottoman-Venetian diplomatics: the Ahd-names. The historical background and the development of a category of political-commercial instruments together with an annotated edition of a corpus of relevant documents', *Electronic Journal of Oriental Studies* 1.2 (1998), 1–698.

Thiriet, F., 'Les chroniques vénitiennes de la Marcienne et leur importance pour l'histoire de la Romanie Gréco-vénitienne', *Mélanges d'archéologie et d'histoire* 66 (1954), 241–292.

—— 'Sui dissidi sorti tra il Comune di Venezia e i suoi feudatari di Creta nel Trecento', *Archivio Storico Italiano* 114 (1956), 699–712.

—— *La Romanie vénitienne au moyen âge: le développement et l'exploitation du domaine colonial vénitien, XIIe–XVe siècles* (Paris, 1959).

Toffanin, G., *Lettera a Maometto II: (Epistola ad Mahumetem)* (Napoli, 1953).

Tolan, J.V., *Saracens: Islam in the Medieval European Imagination* (New York, 2002).

Topping, P., 'The Morea, 1311–1364', in *A History of the Crusades*, ed. K.M. Setton, 6 vols (Madison, 1969–1989), vol. 3, pp. 104–40.

Trenchs-Odena, J., '"De Alexandrinis" (El comercio prohibido con los Musulmanes y el papado de Avinon durante la primera mitad del siglo XIV)', *Anuario de estudios medievales* 10 (1980), 237–320.

Trim, D.J.B. and M.C. Fissel, 'Amphibious warfare, 1000–1700: Concepts and contexts', in *Amphibious Warfare 1000–1700: Commerce, State Formation and European Expansion*, ed. D.J.B. Trim and M.C. Fissel (Leiden, 2011), pp. 1–50.

Trivellato, F., *The Familiarity of Strangers: The Sephardic Diaspora, Livorno, and Cross-Cultural Trade in the Early Modern Period* (New Haven, 2009).

—— 'Renaissance Italy and the Muslim Mediterranean in recent historical works', *Journal of Modern History* 82 (2010), 127–55.

Tyerman, C.J., 'Marino Sanudo Torsello and the lost crusade: lobbying in the fourteenth century: the Alexander Prize essay', *Transactions of the Royal Historical Society* 32 (1982), 57–73 (repr. in Idem, *The Practices of Crusading: Image and Action from the Eleventh to the Sixteenth Centuries*, Variorum Reprints (Farnham, 2013), I).

—— 'Philip V of France, the assemblies of 1319–20 and the crusade', *Bulletin of the Institute of Historical Research* 57 (1984), 15–34 (repr. in Idem, *The Practices of Crusading: Image and Action from the Eleventh to the Sixteenth Centuries*, Variorum Reprints (Farnham, 2013), II).

—— 'Sed nihil fecit? The last Capetians and the recovery of the Holy Land', in *War and Government in the Middle Ages*, ed. J. Gillingham and J.C. Holt (Woodbridge, 1984), pp. 170–81 (repr. in Idem, *The Practices of Crusading: Image and Action from the Eleventh to the Sixteenth Centuries*, Variorum Reprints (Farnham, 2013), III).

—— 'Philip VI and the recovery of the Holy Land', *English Historical Review* 100 (1985), 25–52 (repr. in Idem, *The Practices of Crusading: Image and Action from the Eleventh to the Sixteenth Centuries*, Variorum Reprints (Farnham, 2013), V).

—— *God's War: A New History of the Crusades* (London, 2006).

—— 'New wine in old skins? The crusade and the eastern Mediterranean in the later Middle Ages', in *Byzantines, Latins and Turks in the Eastern Mediterranean World after 1150*, ed. C. Holmes and J. Harris (Oxford, 2012), pp. 265–89.

Valbonnais, J.-P., *Histoire du Dauphiné et des princes qui ont porté le nom de dauphins*, 2 vols (Geneva, 1721–2).

Vionis, A.K., *A Crusader, Ottoman and Early Modern Aegean Archaeology: Built Environment and Domestic Material Culture in the Medieval and Post-Medieval Cyclades, Greece (13th–20th Centuries AD)* (Leiden, 2014).

Vryonis Jr., S., *The Decline of Medieval Hellenism in Asia Minor and the Process of Islamization from the Eleventh through the Fifteenth Century* (Berkeley, 1971).

Wagner, B., *Die 'Epistola Presbiteri Johannis': Lateinisch und Deutsch* (Tubingen, 2000).

—— 'Sultansbriefe', *Die deutsche Literatur des Mittelalters. Verfasserlexikon* 11 (2004), 1463–4.

Wittek, P., 'Turkish architecture in southwestern Anatolia. Part II', *Art Studies* (1931), 173–212.

—— *Das Fürstentum Mentesche, Studie zur Geschichte Westkleinasiens im 13.-15. Jahre* (Istanbul, 1934).

—— *The Rise of the Ottoman Empire* (London, 1938).

—— *The Rise of the Ottoman Empire: Studies into the History of Turkey, Thirteenth–Fifteenth Centuries*, ed. C. Heywood (London, 2012).

Wolff, R.L., *Studies in the Latin Empire of Constantinople*, Variorum Reprints (London, 1976).

Wood, D., *Clement VI: The Pontificate and Ideas of an Avignon Pope* (Cambridge, 1989).

Wood, J.T., *Discoveries at Ephesus: Including the Site and Remains of the Great Temple of Diana* (London, 1877).

Wright, C.F., 'Florentine alum mining in the Hospitaller islands: the *appalto* of 1442', *Journal of Medieval History* 32 (2010), 175–91.

—— *The Gattilusio Lordships and the Aegean World, 1355–1462* (Leiden, 2014).

Zachariadou, E.A., *Trade and Crusade: Venetian Crete and the Emirates of Menteshe and Aydin: 1300–1415* (Venice, 1983).

—— 'The Catalans of Athens and the beginning of Turkish expansion in the Aegean area', *Studia Medievali* 21.2 (1980), 821–38 (repr. in Idem, *Romania and the Turks, c.1300–1500* (London, 1985), V).

—— 'Holy war in the Aegean during the fourteenth century', in *Latins and Greeks in the Eastern Mediterranean after 1204*, ed. B. Arbel, B. Hamilton and D. Jacoby (London, 1989), pp. 212–25 (repr. in Idem, *Studies in pre-Ottoman Turkey and the Ottomans* (Aldershot, 2007), XVII).

Zachariadou, E.A., (ed.), *The Ottoman Emirate (1300–1389): Halcyon Days in Crete I: A Symposium Held in Rethymnon, 11–13 January 1991* (Rethymnon, 1993).

Zutshi, P.N.R., 'The letters of the Avignon popes (1305–1378): A source for the study of Anglo-Papal relations and of English ecclesiastical history', in *England and her Neighbours, 1066–1453. Essays in honour of Pierre Chaplais*, ed. M. Jones and M. Vale (London 1989), pp. 259–275.

—— 'The personal role of the pope in the production of papal letters in the thirteenth and fourteenth centuries', in *Vom Nutzen des Schreibens: soziales Gedächtnis,*

Herrschaft und Besitz im Mittelalter, ed. W. Pohl and P. Herold (Vienna, 2002), pp. 225–36.

—— 'The origins of the registration of petitions in the Papal Chancery in the first half of the fourteenth century', in *Suppliques et requêtes: Le gouvernement par la grâce en Occident (XIIe–XVe siècle)*, ed. Hélène Millet (Paris, 2003), pp. 177–91.

Index

John XXII (pope), 57, 59, 68, 79, 83, 104,
    106, 125 n.35, 136, 145, 147
    and the naval league of 1333–4, 72, 83–4,
        94–100
    crusade privileges granted by, 56,
        108–14, 118
    early crusade plans, 30–1
    registers of, 9–10
    trade licences granted by, 121–3, 123 n.21,
        136, 138, 141
John of Gravina, *see under* Anjou/Angevins
John the Baptist, 116

Kantakouzenos, John VI (Byzantine
    emperor and author), 14, 122, 132
Karahissar (Koloneia), 120
    see also alum
Karaman (Anatolian beylik), 34, 41, 45 n.45,
    49, 55, 102, 110, 110 n.72
Karasi (Anatolian beylik), 33, 34, 37, 73
    see also Yakhshi (emir of Karasi)
Karpathos, 21, 47
Koloneia, *see* Karahissar
Komnenos, Alexios I (Byzantine emperor),
    37
Konya, 38
Kos, 48
Köse Dağ, battle of (1243), 33
Kutahya, 126
    see also alum
Kydones, Demetrius, 52 n.81

L'Aquila, 116
Lajazzo (Ayas), 26, 127
Lampsakos, 83, 90 n.48
Latin Empire of Constantinople, 20, 22,
    27–9, 42, 108
    see also individual Latin emperors
Lauria, Roger of, 85, 92–3
Lesbos, 20, 73, 129
Levant, 1, 4, 18, 26, 41, 57, 61, 63, 64, 77,
    142 n.112
    see also Palestine, Syria
Liber Pontificalis, 102
Liber Secretorum Fidelium Crucis, 13, 41, 60
    n.115, 69, 84, 87
lignae, see under ships/shipping
Liguria, 122
Lombardy, 116
Longos, battle of (1344), 75, 87, 88, 89, 93
Louis IX (king of France), 27
Lull, Ramon, 65
Lyons, Second Council of (1274), 20

Macedonia, 20, 25, 50
Madachia, see Masud (emir of Menteshe),
Magnesia, *see* Manisa

Mahmud Pasha, 51
Mahona of the Giustiniani, 130
Makre, 34, 41, 123
Malestroit, Truce of (1343–5), 105
Malta, 85
Mamluks, 1, 6, 7, 22, 26, 40, 56, 63, 110
    crusades against, *see under* crusades, in
        support/for the recovery of the Holy
        Land
    sultans, 63, 110 n.72, 119, 121 n.9, 133
    trade embargo against, 41, 64–5, 98,
        120, 137
    trade with, 8, 18, 23, 57, 64–5, 98, 106,
        120–7, 129, 132–7, 138–9, 141–2,
        147–8
    see also Egypt; trade, trade embargo,
        trade licences
Manaqeb al-'arefin, 122
Manisa (Magnesia), 37
manpower and crews, 83–7
    archers, 83, 90, 91–2
    crossbowmen, 81, 83, 91
    horse archers, 90
    horsemen/cavalry, 29 n.41, 83, 84, 85,
        90, 114, 135
    marines, 81–2, 83, 87, 89, 91–2, 99
    medics, 83
    oarsmen, 80–2, 83–6, 88, 88–9 n.43,
        92, 113
    sailors, 8, 24, 52, 82, 83, 87, 88–9 n.43,
        113, 119
    scribes, 83, 99
    terzaroles, 83
Manuel Zaccaria, *see under* Zaccaria family
Manzikert, battle of (1071), 37
marines, *see under* manpower and crews
Marseille, 99, 100
mastic, 19, 111, 121–3
    see also Chios
Masud (emir of Menteshe), 33–4, 44–8, 55,
    68, 143
Martino Zaccaria, *see under* Zaccaria family
Meander (valley), 33
medics, *see under* manpower and crews
Mehmed (emir of Aydin), 33, 35–6, 49, 51,
    52
Mehmed the Conqueror (Ottoman sultan),
    51, 54
Meltemi winds, 81
Menteshe (Anatolian beylik), 6, 33, 34–5,
    41, 44, 47, 51 n.75, 55, 67
    alliances with Genoese, 44–6, 67–8
    early conflicts with the Hospitallers,
        44–6, 67–8, 89–90, 143
    trade/treaties with Venice, 34, 49, 123–6
    see also Orkhan (emir of Menteshe)
mercenaries, 25, 40

Warfare in History

The Battle of Hastings: Sources and Interpretations, *edited and introduced by Stephen Morillo*

Infantry Warfare in the Early Fourteenth Century: Discipline, Tactics, and Technology, *Kelly DeVries*

The Art of Warfare in Western Europe during the Middle Ages, from the Eighth Century to 1340 (second edition), *J.F. Verbruggen*

Knights and Peasants: The Hundred Years War in the French Countryside, *Nicholas Wright*

Society at War: The Experience of England and France during the Hundred Years War, *edited by Christopher Allmand*

The Circle of War in the Middle Ages: Essays on Medieval Military and Naval History, *edited by Donald J. Kagay and L.J. Andrew Villalon*

The Anglo-Scots Wars, 1513–1550: A Military History, *Gervase Phillips*

The Norwegian Invasion of England in 1066, *Kelly DeVries*

The Wars of Edward III: Sources and Interpretations, *edited by Clifford J. Rogers*

The Battle of Agincourt: Sources and Interpretations, *Anne Curry*

War Cruel and Sharp: English Strategy under Edward III, 1327–1360, *Clifford J. Rogers*

The Normans and their Adversaries at War: Essays in Memory of C. Warren Hollister, *edited by Richard P. Abels and Bernard S. Bachrach*

The Battle of the Golden Spurs (Courtrai, 11 July 1302): A Contribution to the History of Flanders' War of Liberation, 1297–1305, *J.F. Verbruggen*

War at Sea in the Middle Ages and the Renaissance, *edited by John B. Hattendorf and Richard W. Unger*

Swein Forkbeard's Invasions and the Danish Conquest of England, 991–1017, *Ian Howard*

Religion and the conduct of war, c.300–1215, *David S. Bachrach*

Warfare in Medieval Brabant, 1356–1406, *Sergio Boffa*

Renaissance Military Memoirs: War, History and Identity, 1450–1600, *Yuval Harari*

The Place of War in English History, 1066–1214, *J.O. Prestwich, edited by Michael Prestwich*

War and the Soldier in the Fourteenth Century, *Adrian R. Bell*

German War Planning, 1891–1914: Sources and Interpretations, *Terence Zuber*

The Battle of Crécy, 1346, *Andrew Ayton and Sir Philip Preston*